SMALL ANTIQUE
SILVERWARE

1, 2, 3   LONDON-MADE CREAM PAILS: (1 and 3) with hand-pierced decoration and blue glass liners, 1759 and 1786; (2) chased with hoops and staves to represent a pail, 1791

4, 5   HOT-MILK JUG (4) approximately the size and shape of a goose egg.   *In the collection of Mrs. William B. Munro.*   COW MILK JUG (5); maker's mark T.H., London, 1774
Courtesy of Messrs. William Bruford and Son Ltd.

6, 7, 8   SUGAR BASKETS (6 and 8), press-pierced, by William Purse, London, 1775, and Scottish, approximately same date. *Courtesy of Mr. John Bell.* CREAM PAIL (7), hand-pierced, by Charles Aldridge and Henry Green, 1779. *In the collection of Mrs. William B. Munro*

SMALL
ANTIQUE
SILVERWARE

✳ ✳ ✳ ✳ ✳

G. Bernard Hughes

✳ ✳ ✳

BRAMHALL HOUSE : NEW YORK

First Published, 1957

This edition published by Bramhall House,
a division of Clarkson N. Potter, Inc.,
by arrangement with B. T. Batsford Ltd
(A)

CONTENTS

CONTENTS

LIST OF ILLUSTRATIONS

The numerals in parentheses in the text refer to the *figure numbers*
of the illustrations

9

LIST OF ILLUSTRATIONS

Chapter One

I MILK AND CREAM JUGS AND CREAM PAILS

For two and a half centuries the lovely English ritual of tea-time has been enriched by the gracious charm of the tea equipage. In handsomely proportioned silver and colourful porcelain English craftsmen have produced some of their most brilliant imaginative creations in the service of this delicate repast. Tea might be served with bread and butter during the morning and again from about seven in the evening. Dinner began at four and there was no supper, to the consternation of foreign visitors.

When tea-drinking was introduced to London in the 1650s, the leaves were rolled and dried whole. Thomas Worlidge recorded tea-making instructions in 1678: "Let a few of these dry leaves stand in a covered Pot two or three minutes, in which time the leaves will be spread to their original breadth and shape, and yield their bitter yet pleasant taste. You may add, if you please, a little Sugar." Worlidge made no reference to milk or cream and the English epicure who first tempered tea with milk remains unchronicled. There is, however, the evidence of Peter de Goyer and Jacob de Keyser in the late 1650s that hot milk was added to tea served in China. At a dinner given in their honour by the Grand Cham of Tartary, Emperor of China, they observed that "the Chinese added warm milk to the tea, about a fourth part, with a little salt, and then drank it as hot as they can well endure."

Collectors search vainly for a silver milk jug displaying hall-marks struck before the accession of Queen Anne in 1702. Although commonly referred to as "milk potts" the London assay office entered them on their price list as "milk ewers" and charged one penny each for the assay. Cream does not appear to have been served with tea until about 1780. The Hon. John Byng, in *The Torrington Diaries* for 1785 recorded that "tea with cream is a great curiosity," and similarly on several occasions during the late 1780s he expressed surprise at this novelty. Byng owned a spacious London house at the corner of Duke Street and Jermyn Street, St. James's, and may be considered to have been fully informed regarding fashionable tea-drinking. Yet cream ewers were included with the costly tea equipage in Chelsea porcelain sold at Christie's during the 1770s. Diarists between the 1780s and 1834 recorded that the East India Company provided both cream and milk with the breakfast tea given free to members of the staff arriving early at the office. From as early as 1715, however, silver jugs with wide throated lips, decidedly vessels for slow-pouring cream had played their part on the dessert table, and continued in use there until the end of the century (37).

That milk was at first served hot with tea is confirmed not only by writers of the period but by the silver ware, including such notable tea services as one belonging to the Duke of Grafton, made in 1712 by Richard Watts. This octagonal set consists of tea-pot, sugar bowl and milk jug, the jug being fitted with an ivory handle, a highly domed lid hinging from an upper handle attachment, a sharp beaked spout and a moulded foot. Other hot-milk jugs have smoothly round baluster bodies, a form which continued in use until the mid-eighteenth century (26).

Hot-milk jugs with bodies approximating the size and shape of goose eggs were made during the 1720s and 1730s (4). Body and cover, purely ovoid, were raised from the plate and supported on three short, equidistantly placed legs, one beneath the beak spout and two flanking the hard-wood handle. Early examples were entirely plain, apart from a crest that might be engraved on one side of the body. The spout opening was partially covered in an effort to prevent the escape of heat. Such a vessel, hand-raised and lacking the ornament that could disguise imperfections of shape or finish, was a considerable test of craftsmanship. Its association with the period's bullet tea-pots is obvious.

By 1725 such a jug might have scroll legs with hoof feet, two of them flanking the spout and the third immediately below the handle, the lower handle socket being attached to the boss of the leg. Ornate jugs of this type were made in the 1730s. In these the moulded spout was enlarged and extended forward, the opening being covered by an extension attached to the lid. The ebony or hard-wood handle was of the single scroll type and the cover finial was an expansive knop of similar material. The body rim and the upper dome of the cover were encircled with bands of engraving.

The earliest silver jugs for cold milk were tiny baluster-shaped vessels with plain D-handles of silver, sharp beak spouts, and rim feet (14). They measured between $2\frac{1}{2}$ inches and $3\frac{1}{2}$ inches in height and were, of course, lidless. Their small size is understandable when it is remembered that silver tea-cups at this period were tiny too, measuring no more than about $1\frac{3}{4}$ inches in height (see p. 209). Such a jug was assembled from four units:

(a) the body, smoothly pear-shaped in uninterrupted curves. It has been noted hand-raised from a single piece of plate; raised from two halves and joined invisibly with a flat inserted base; cast and turned in high standard silver, although labour costs saved by not raising from the plate were usually offset by the increased cost of silver used. The rim might be plain, encircled with narrow strengthening moulding, or turned over into a narrow exterior strengthening welt. During the early 1720s the bulge of the milk jug tended to become bolder than formerly.

9, 10, 11   MILK JUGS: (9) oval with gadrooned base, by Q. Sibley, 1800; (10) oval with flat base and band of bright-cut engraving, by Peter, Ann, and William Bateman, 1804; (11) octagonal, interior gilded, by David and Robert Hennell, 1796. *In the collection of Mrs. William B. Munro*

12, 13   (*top*) MILK JUGS: helmet-shaped with applied rib, unmarked, 1730s; baluster-shaped with three scroll legs, by Paul de Lamerie, 1738

14, 15   (*bottom*) MILK JUGS: plain baluster with beak spout, by William Fleming, 1720; ogee-shaped with relief ornament, by Charles Hillan, 1740. *In the collection of Mrs. William B. Munro*

16, 17 *(top)* MILK JUGS: fluted ovoid body, chased, by John Pollock, 1736; baluster-shaped with sheared rim, by G.B. of Guernsey, 1738
18, 19 *(bottom)* MILK JUGS by Ayme Videau, 1736; baluster with octagonal body, *c.* 1740. *In the collection of Mrs. William B. Munro*

20, 21, 22 HOT-MILK JUG (20), cast, with hinged cover, maker's mark W.G., 1749; CREAM BOAT (21), cast, by Thomas England, 1750; MILK JUG (22), cast, 1740s
In the collection of Mrs. William B. Munro

23, 24, 25 MILK JUGS: (23) pierced, on pedestal foot and with blue glass liner, by Edward Aldridge, 1772; (24) with oval body, encircled with bright-cut engraving, by Solomon Hougham, 1799; (25) helmet-shaped with spun foot, probably by John West, Dublin, 1799. *In the collection of Mrs. William B. Munro*

(b) a beaked spout shaped from the plate: a touch of ornament was applied to an otherwise plain body by introducing a moulded drop immediately below the spout.

(c) a rim foot, shaped from a flat strip of plate or, more usually, of narrow moulding.

The circular spreading moulded foot with a lathe-turned surface was introduced to the pear-shaped milk jug in the mid-1720s, becoming a fashionable feature in the late 1720s (39).

(d) a plain D-handle attached directly to the body with expanded ends; or the more harmonious S-shape with a boldly round inner profile and a tiny thumbpiece cresting the upper curve, soldered to the body immediately below the rim, and extending downward to the widest spread of the body. The handle was placed diametrically opposite to the spout.

All association with the serving of hot milk in tea was abandoned by the beginning of George II's reign (1727) as silversmiths began to appreciate the possibilities of graceful design, previously restricted to such vessels as rosewater ewers—among the most satisfying pieces of early plate. The beak-spout was rejected in favour of a broad, open-curved lip, rising upward and forward from an undulating rim (39). To balance, a scroll handle was developed, first with a single scroll at one end, then with a small scroll added to each end of an S-shaped unit which was extended away from the body. Early scroll handles were flat-oval in section. The S-shaped handle continued, and in the late 1730s might possess a cast and chased leaf crest so that the thumb could take a firmer grip. The handle joined the jug with circular flanges top and bottom.

Other early pear-shaped milk jugs were hexagonal or octagonal (27): examples are usually found to be either cast or built from strips of plate, invisibly joined. Such a jug stands upon a moulded foot, having the same number of sides.

The three-footed style (27) appears to have had early associations with the octagonal milk jug and examples have been noted bearing hall-marks of the early 1720s. In these, three cast scroll and hoof feet lifted the base of the jug slightly above the table or tray. At first they were attached immediately below the widest diameter of the body, one beneath the centre of the lip, the other two equidistant at the rear. The advantage of a three-footed design was obvious, ensuring a steady stance for the light little vessel even when roughly handled in cleaning. The feature at once proved equally successful on the baluster-shaped jug which now might have an oval body instead of round, an undulating rim, and a forward-reaching lip. By the late 1720s in these, as in the ovoid hot-milk jugs, a change was made in the placing of the legs, one being set beneath the handle, the other two equidistantly flanking the lip (17). From about 1730 the scroll and hoof foot (30) ran concurrently with

23

the mask and paw (*33*), and with an expansive escallop shell scrolling to a hoof or shell foot (*17*).

The graceful helmet-shaped milk jugs (*12*) in a form long associated with rose-water ewers, may be grouped into two classes: those hall-marked from the introduction of this design to milk jugs early in the reign of George I until 1760 (*43*); and the so-called neo-classic form dating from the 1750s until the end of the century (*38*). In this design the broad lip was an integral feature of the body, raised from the plate so that there was no interruption in the flowing curves from rounded base to undulating rim. At first the lip was low and each side of the rim might be curved in a cyma outline (*28*). By the mid-1720s the spout rose high above the rim and extended forward, often to a distance equal to about half the length of the body (*12*). The double scroll handle was outspreading and cast in an elaborate pattern, the upper terminal often clipping the rim. At first the helmet stood upon a round, moulded foot, but this was obviously unsuited to the deeply rounded hemispherical base. It is probable that the helmet jug was the earliest design to include the three scroll and hoof feet.

From the late 1730s the helmet might be made in two sections (*12*), an encircling rib strengthening the joint which was invisible within. The lower half was raised from the plate and the upper part shaped from a strip of silver seamed at the handle. At about the same time appeared the milk jug with a hand-raised ovoid body and a helmet-shaped neck with widely flared lip, attached to the body by soldering (*16*).

Helmet and baluster jugs were usually severely plain with perhaps an engraved coat of arms beneath the lip or on one side. Gilded interiors are noticed from time to time throughout the century. Flat chasing has been noted on work as early as 1728 in designs of rococo scrollwork. The undulating rim strengthened with ornamental moulding might have a twisted shell on each side and an applied scroll volute at the lip extremity (*12*). Beneath the scroll might be a cast and chased motif, the acanthus leaf and shell being frequent and sometimes forming the ground for an expansive mask. Three moulded and chased feet completed the design.

Then came all-over embossed and chased decoration, body and foot forming a ground for associated designs (*29*). Hunting and sporting scenes are found, landscapes, classic themes such as Apollo and Daphne (*22*), flowers and birds (*21*), sprays of flowers and foliage, fruiting vine, fruit and scrollwork. There was a vogue for illustrating farmyard scenes from the 1740s to the 1760s: cows were popular motifs and may be seen grazing, being milked, chewing the cud, even bellowing (*15*). Relief work in the 1740s might be applied to the surface of the jug, hand-pressed motifs from thin sheet silver being soldered upon the smooth surface. Considerable numbers must have been made from each set of tools, but existing examples do not provide many duplicates. It is possible that such ornament was added at a later date.

This was the 1740s' more restrained prelude to the vogue for heavy cast milk jugs smothered beneath high relief ornament in complicated patterns, body, foot, and handle being cast, joined, chased, and burnished (43). Examples have been noted in which the body was cast in two vertical sections soldered together in such a way that seams were invisible. Such milk jugs, no taller than hand-raised examples, may yet weigh twice as much: the labour saved by avoiding hand-raising outweighed the cost of extra metal required for casting, and inordinately high relief work could be produced without the ever-present hazard of splitting the metal by deep embossing. A set of casting patterns might be used to produce innumerable copies, but here again exact duplicates are seldom observed. The body was usually of the ogee or inverted pyriform outline, with a short-stemmed spreading foot of shaped or circular outline. The handle might be an S-scroll or double scroll, and occasionally a free-standing scroll is noted (15).

Pierced decoration is rarely found on silver milk jugs. A helmet-shaped type, known to collectors as à jour, was possibly used for cream on the dessert table in the late 1760s and early 1770s (23). This had a hand-raised body enriched with hand-piercing in all-over patterns, and fitted with a blue-glass liner held in position with clips. The low-stemmed pedestal foot was encircled with a wide band of matching piercing. The rims of body and foot were finished with burnished gadrooning or corded moulding.

The rise of the manufacturing silversmiths at Birmingham during the 1760s is demonstrated with interesting clarity in the development of milk jug production methods. The factors leading to their success are plain enough. One was the increasingly widespread use of the spring flatting mill. This had been invented in 1727 by John Cook but was little used until after the patent had lapsed in 1741. A technical work published in the late 1740s recorded under the section devoted to silversmiths that: "there are now invented Flatting Mills which reduce their Metal to what Thinness they require at very small expense."

A contemporary engraving shows a flatting mill operated manually by a wheelboy. Each skillet of sterling silver, instead of being laboriously hammered into plate, was passed between steel rollers many times with frequent intermissions for annealing at a charcoal fire, expanding in width and length until the required degree of thinness was achieved. Silver sheets produced in this way were not by any means so closely textured as battery silver and in consequence could be raised when required into high relief much more quickly and the hazard of splitting was lessened.

Comparatively inexpensive milk jugs were in production by the 1760s in an inverted pyriform design supported on a hollow pedestal stem. Some of these were hand-raised, but the majority were spun on the lathe from rolled plate. Such units, body and foot, could be bought by master silversmiths from the factory at considerably less than half the cost of a hand-raised production from their own workshops. In London such units were available from stock at Matthew Boulton's warehouse in Salisbury Square.

The pedestal foot remained plain or might be encircled with sparse ornament, its rim being strengthened with moulding, pressed beading or swage-produced ribbon, with matching ornament on the body rim. Most milk jugs of this type were devoid of decoration, but some were embossed in swirling patterns of tapering convex flutes. Others continued the earlier rococo mood, being chased with floral sprays and irregularly shaped cartouches.

The English method of producing thinly rolled sheets of silver became even more valuable to the manufacturing silversmiths from the 1770s. Tools for shaping the silver were sunk in Huntsman's recently invented crucible-cast steel. This was scarce until the 1790s as each crucible produced no more than about twelve pounds. Matthew Boulton overcame scarcity by making his own from about 1768. The use of tools made from this steel gave perfect contours to a profitable run of thinly rolled plate units. Tools of ordinary case-hardened steel produced by the cementation process were inadequate for the purpose. As a result the milk jug body might be stamped in two vertical halves and soldered together in such a way that seams were invisible. The foot was made separately.

Greco-Roman vases and urns had become fashionable forms in silver hollow-ware by the early 1770s and the English tea equipage displayed unencumbered flowing Grecian outlines, thus introducing the second group of helmet-shaped milk jugs (25). Again the finer specimens were hand-raised from the plate, but the majority of these essentially dainty, graceful little vessels bear evidence of spinning in the factory. The body tapered smoothly from rim to base, with one side of the rim extended into a wide, highly everted lip. It joined the slender stem of a circular or oval hollow pedestal foot mounted on a four-sided plinth. The handle displayed a similar simplicity of outline, rising sharply to the rim, recurving and sweeping down to the base. When decoration was present it usually consisted of engraving, typically in encircling bands: bright-cut engraving might be used from the early 1780s (25).

A less easily overturned milk jug was introduced during the mid-1780s, achieving popularity during the following decade (11). Instead of tapering to a stem-foot the whole body of the jug was wide and rested flatly upon the tea-tray, matching teapot and sugar basin. This little jug was made from flat plate shaped into a cylinder, the upper part with the high everted lip adapted from the classic design. The handle rose vertically from the rim, then projected horizontally for perhaps three-quarters of an inch before flowing smoothly down to a point slightly above the base. The rim was strengthened by reeded moulding, quickly produced by means of the swage block, invented in 1768 but little used until the late 1770s. This enabled a silver ribbon to be drawn in which one side followed any desired contour.

The lower part of the body, which might be oval, circular, seven-sided, or barrel-shaped, might be ornamented with wide facets below a band of engraving, sometimes in patterns resembling the relief diamonds cut upon flint-glass jugs of this period. Many of these small pitchers were decorated with wide bands of bright-cut engraving immediately below their rims and narrow bands around their bases. In the first few years of the nineteenth century this style of milk jug, in more graceful lines than formerly, and in harmony with the teapot it accompanied, was raised upon four ball feet and its wavy rim encircled with gadrooned ornament.

Milk jugs of the first twenty years of the nineteenth century were designed in the style of a Roman urn, the lower half of the body encircled with flutes, the body-neck junction concealed beneath gadrooned ribbon. The flutes gradually became wider and more convex, and the jug was made taller by the addition of a vertical neck. The gadrooned ribbon tended to lose its deep relief shaping and to be interrupted with shell or other motifs. A band of mechanically produced embossment might encircle the body immediately below the rim. Such a jug was supported on a low rim foot, which might itself be raised on ball feet, or on the subsequent very squat stemmed feet. The square shouldered or hoop handle remained, often with a foliage attachment at the lower end. In some instances a beak spout replaced the curved lip. Towards 1820 began a series of smooth-surfaced jugs with a patterned fillet in relief encircling the body. By 1820 the lower part of a milk jug might be embossed lavishly in a wide variety of scenic panels or with classical and historical figures: these might be in relief against a matted ground. Some handles were heavily elaborated with such motifs as dragons or flowers and foliage, but the majority were in square-cut ivory. The foot designs already described were now augmented by the use of four scroll and mask feet or a four-footed ring-base.

In conformity with the design of other table silver, the George IV milk jug carried ornateness to the point of florid vulgarity, although most of the plainer designs continued in production. In addition to flamboyant embossed work, rims were decorated with extravagantly heavy moulding, and four short scroll feet might be moulded in a piece with a shallow base rim. Feet and handles might be in the form of figures.

The melon-shaped body with wide convex flutes became the fashion at this time. At first the body was smoothly plain, but more frequently the panels were handsomely embossed or chased with motifs such as flowers or fruit. The rim might be strengthened with smooth surfaced ribbon, and the handle moulded in a single graceful curve.

The 1830s brought a return of the rococo designs of the previous mid-century such as the footed pear-shaped jug, fluted and chased, the handle once more of double scroll outline, and the rounded base raised above the tea tray on four short moulded scroll feet.

Early Victorian master silversmiths made few milk or cream jugs, the factory silversmiths having captured virtually the whole of such trade in silver tea-ware as was left by the competition of exquisitely coloured and gilded bone china. So numerous and bewildering is the variety of patterns that it is impossible to classify them into well-defined groups.

The George I pear-shape continued in prolific production, followed in numbers by the melon-shape and the hexagonal, strangely known as the Elizabethan pattern. The nine-sided form returned but with in-sloping sides, standing flat upon the tray; there was a squat baluster with ungraceful bulging curves on a low, moulded foot; a pear-shaped jug with wide lobes, on four cast shell or scroll feet; a hexagonal jug of baluster form on a low cast pedestal foot. These might be left without surface ornament; they might be engraved all over with festoons, scrolls and foliage, strap-work, or game bird designs; embossed by mechanical raising which was considerably less costly than engraving; or chased. A distinguishing feature of the period was the deeply channelled lip with bold uprising curve and outward sweep. Some jugs were made with hinged covers at an extra cost of approximately thirty shillings.

A quaint conceit of the third quarter of the eighteenth century was the milk jug modelled in the form of a cow (5). Although the name of John Schuppe is particularly associated with these jugs there is the evidence of hall-marks that David Willaume the younger was making them before Schuppe, who remains an obscure figure, dying in 1773. Silver cows, as they were listed at the assay office, were made in sections. The sides of the head and body were made separately as were legs and hooves, horns, ears, and the tail handle which looped upward over the haunches. The top of the hollow body was fitted with a curved hinged lid, like a saddle, either plain or bordered with chased flowers and foliage, and with a lifting knob in the form of a large fly modelled in the round. The jug was filled through this lidded opening, the milk being poured into the tea-cup from the animal's mouth. Head and body might be tooled to represent the cow's hair, but others were left smooth-surfaced except for some tool work representing hair beneath horns and eyes, and along the back bone, this being applied with the intention of concealing joins.

Silver cows approximate 4 inches in height: an example by Schuppe sold at Christie's weighed 4 oz. 15 dwt. In modelling, as in general design, the style is naive but lively. Many were gilded and a crest might be engraved on the side of the body. In some instances the neck was engraved with an inscribed collar.

By the mid-century dessert tables were brilliantly set out (see Chapter Five). A trade card issued by D. Negri, confectioner at the Pine Apple in Berkeley Square, listed ice-cream whips, custards, trifles, jellies, blancmanges, and similar spoon-requiring confections served individually in small glass containers, and there were also candied fruits, boiled sweets, orange chips, comfits and flowered candies offered in small silver baskets or shallow glass bowls. Fruit was handed in large silver baskets or porcelain bowls accompanied by cream in small silver cream-boats.

The shapely outline of the silver cream-boat contributed to the graceful elegance of the dessert. The earliest of these vessels date to about 1720, the body formed as a nautilus shell, with a dolphin handle, on a stem formed as a dragon or grotesque animal figure and an oval or octagonal foot. Before 1725 such a body stood on four feet terminating in dolphin heads. This shape of cream-boat was revived early in George III's period.

The typical cream-boat, however, followed the same general lines as the single-spouted sauceboat introduced at the same period. Its low body emphasised the wide forward-sweeping lip projecting far beyond the body, usually a compressed oval with an outward expanding rim which might be scalloped or in cyma outline.

At first a double-scroll handle rose above the rim, being attached to it by a forked unit. This handle extended far to the rear, returning to join the body in such a way that the lower scroll extended below the base. A later example might have the outer curve of such a handle capped with scroll or leaf ornament. Another alternative feature was a free-standing scroll handle, terminating in a chased bust, ram's head, serpent, amorine, or other motif modelled in the round.

In some early examples the cream-boat was supported by four legs. Three legs were usual, however, cast and chased, one immediately below the spout, the other two towards the back, flanking the handle. Each joined the body with an expansive ornamental flange, sometimes a lion mask ending in a paw, claw-and-ball, shell, or flower. Scroll, hoof and pad feet were frequent. The rim might be slightly everted and a cast mask or other motif applied beneath the lip.

Hand-raised cream-boats might be ornamented with engraved scrollwork and flowers, and a crest beneath the spout. Light chasing is also found. By the 1740s low-embossing had become established, typical motifs being scrollwork, flowers and foliage against a matted ground. In some instances a hand-raised cream-boat might be ornamented with applied motifs such as flowers, foliage, shellwork, and other rococo curiosities. The interior thus remained smooth and easy to clean, a style always preferred. The collector should carefully inspect hand-raised cream-boats.

for it has proved simple and highly profitable to convert hall-marked punch ladles into heavier, more costly cream-boats.

Cream-boats cast in silver were made from the late 1720s, elaborately ornamented in relief, the chased and burnished motifs rising sharp and bold. The body was made in two separate halves, the handle and the feet separately, and all were finished by chasing and burnishing. Fashionable motifs included cows grazing or lying in a pasture, sometimes accompanied by a goat. In these the rim was shaped in deep curves and the back of the body might curve forward upon itself. The handle was cast, often in the form of a pair of writhing serpents, or a dolphin with its tail attached to the back of the vessel, rising upward from the rim, and curving forward over the body.

Such a cream-boat might stand upon an irregular, round or oval moulded foot with a spool-shaped stem bearing the additional ornament of applied cast motifs. Another design had a low tripod foot, each member springing from the centre of the base. Dolphins' heads with their mouths resting upon escallop shells were frequent. Yet another type consisted of three feet formed from the convolutions of a snake.

Cream-boats were usually sold in pairs, but hall-marks have proved the existence of sets of a dozen. The raising of cream-boat bodies from the plate was a specialist branch of the early Georgian silversmith's craft. Other small silver vessels such as punch ladles, salt-cellars, and sauce-boats were wrought in the same workshops. Sir Ambrose Heal possesses a trade card issued by David Hennell who worked at the Flower de Lis and Star, Gutter Lane, from 1736 to 1758, announcing that he "Makes and Sells all Sorts of Salts, Punch Ladles, Cream Boats, Sauce Boats."

As porcelain dessert services, decorated in gold and a wide range of colours, came into use in the wealthiest households, cream-boats in silver were superseded by porcelain tureens and ladles. In various catalogues of Christie's sales dating to about 1780 these were described as "oval cream basons, covers, plates, and spoons." A Chelsea-Derby dessert service, sold in 1783 for £26, consisted of 36 plates, 17 compotiers, and a pair of cream bowls, covers, stands, and spoons, and at the sale of Derby porcelain a year later "a cream pail and ladle" were catalogued.

The service of clotted cream in miniature pails of silver had become a fashionable conceit in the late 1740s. Mrs. Delany, in June 1752, expressed her delight at having been presented with "a cream pail and a spoon." A few months later she wrote to the Duchess of Portland, "my cream-pail is now before me in my china case, and makes a very considerable figure."

Clotted cream had great advantages in the days before refrigeration, and should not be confused with quickly-souring fresh cream: as early as 1542 Borde in his *Dyetary* distinguished between "rawe crayme" and "clowted crayme," the latter made by scalding or heating milk until its cream became thick or clotted. The Georgian cream pail in which it was served was bucket-shaped with a swing bail handle of twisted or corded wire and might be chased with sprays of flowers and foliage or encircled with chased lines representing hoops (2).

Cream pails from the early 1770s were given a new splendour by piercing the silver and lining it with a cream container in Bristol blue glass (1). At first the piercing was cut by hand-saw in such encircling open-work designs as landscapes with figures, farmhouses, and grazing cows, the entire pattern being worked in low relief repoussé. In some instances the tiny pail, measuring between $2\frac{1}{2}$ and 3 inches in height, consisted of three vertical panels each displaying a motif of pastoral life. There were also cream pails pierced and chased with Chinoiserie designs. Others were pierced flat in scroll, flower and leaf patterns: the surface might be lightly engraved. A cartouche was incorporated upon which a crest could be engraved. The top rim was strengthened with knurled or other moulding, the base with thick plain moulding. By the 1780s the vessel might be cylindrical with a free-standing scroll-handle and blue glass liner. Late cream pails were press-pierced, usually with lattice-work, bands of vertical pales, crosses, circles, urns, and husks, with beaded borders. In some instances a ground of open-work trellis was enriched by the application of embossed and chased ornament pressed separately and soldered into position. From about 1785 the main ornamental features such as classic swags were incorporated in the open-work silhouette, mechanically cut. Only surface detail such as bright-cut engraving required hand-finishing. Rims were usually encircled with beading impressed by a special tool. Other cream pails fitted with blue glass liners were built from silver wire, with corded rims and applied decoration such as swags and foliage.

Small silver ladles were used for lifting the clotted cream from the pail. Seldom are these now discovered *en suite*, such tiny ladles having been mistaken for mustard ladles. Usually the bowls of cream pail ladles were smoothly plain, for the essential scrupulous cleaning, and frequently in the shape of well-rounded escallop shells. Handles and finials matched those of fashionable dessert services of forks and spoons. Stem decoration was rare until the 1760s. An example made in 1765 by William Plummer and still with its chased pail, has a floral finial.

Cream baskets matching accompanying sugar baskets and containing blue glass liners had become fashionable by the 1770s. In an otherwise matching pair there would be a difference in size, the larger vessel being intended for cream.

II SUGAR BOXES, BOWLS, VASES, BASKETS, AND TONGS

SPECIAL vessels for serving fine sugar were being made as early as the sixteenth century when sugar box and spoon accompanied the wine. Plate inventories, such as the Unton inventory of 1620, usually entered them as "a suger boxe, and one suger boxe spoon," or as "scollop suger boxes." The earliest escallop-shell sugar box so far noted bears the London hall-mark for 1601 and is in the collection of Earl Beauchamp. A number of James I examples exist, all following the same design, hall-marked at the London assay office, and weighing about 9 ounces each (47).

The hinged lid was raised from the plate and embossed in the form of a highly domed fan-shaped escallop shell, deeply grooved and ridged, with undulating edges, squared at the back to make provision for the hinge. This hinge might be attached directly to the shell shaping but more usually there was a square, flat-surfaced extension between, ornamented with an embossed motif such as a dolphin. The edge of the lid was strengthened with moulded egg-and-tongue ribbon, and a downward rim of sturdy flat ribbon, cut from the plate, fitted closely over the top of the box. This was a shallow, plain-surfaced box following the lid outline and ornamented around the base with similar wide mouldings. The design was completed with four shell feet.

On the lid, opposite the hinged back edge, was a three-lug hasp hinged to the extreme front. This secured the lid, but for lifting it there might be a small moulded shell matching the feet, outward pointing and soldered to the lid's lower edge; alternatively a loop fitted with a loose ring served this purpose. The curve of the body to the right of the hasp might be engraved with the owner's crest.

Sugar had become more plentiful in England by 1660, when in London alone about fifty master sugar bakers or refiners were working, in comparison with but one a century earlier. Nine qualities of sugar were now on sale, ranging from refined loaf sugar at three shillings a pound to a coarse dross at threepence a pound.

Sugar boxes in the years succeeding the Restoration were oval caskets with convex sides, measuring about 7 inches by 6 inches and 2 inches deep. The body and single-step hinged cover were usually smoothly plain, supported by four small scroll feet. Alternatively the casket was enriched with embossed and pounced ornament and a scrolled wire handle was soldered to the lid.

Double-lidded sugar boxes were made during this period, one compartment containing refined white sugar, the other ambered sugar used for tempering the roughness of many wines. Ambered sugar was prepared by grinding together twenty parts sugar, four parts ambergris, and one part musk. The body of such a sugar box was usually without ornament, the lids, opening on a central double hinge, being elaborately embossed and each fitted with a moulded knob for lifting. To each of the long sides, in a line with the hinge, was soldered a swan-neck handle to facilitate passing from hand to hand. The shell, scroll, or claw-and-ball feet were longer in the leg than those on single-lidded boxes, thus permitting the handles to be curved

26, 27, 28   HOT-MILK JUG (26) by Richard Bayley, 1720; (27) OCTAGONAL BALUSTER
MILK JUG by Gabriel Sleath, 1719; (28) HELMET MILK JUG with free-standing handle, by
Isaac Ribouleau. *In the collection of Mrs. William B. Munro*

29, 30, 31   MILK JUGS: (29) heavy pyriform, cast in sections, *c.* 1745; (30) embossed
ovoid body by Peter Taylor, 1750; (31) helmet-shaped with dolphin handle, supported on
sea-horse, *c.* 1750. *In the collection of Mrs. William B. Munro*

32, 33, 34, 35   BALUSTER-SHAPED MILK JUG (32) by Thomas Heming, 1770; (33)
PYRIFORM MILK JUG by John Walker, 1740; (34) CREAM BOAT by John Jacob, 1737;
(35) MILK JUG by John Kentenber, 1769. *In the collection of Mrs. William B. Munro*

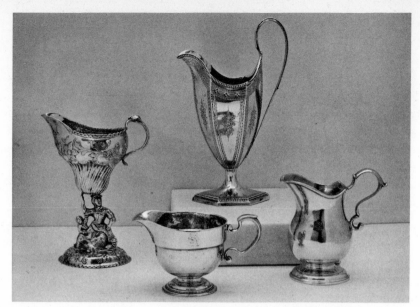

36, 37, 38, 39   MILK JUGS: (36) with cast support, by John Schüppe, 1763;
(37) by John Hamilton, Dublin, *c.* 1730; (38) hexagonal helmet-shaped by
C. Chesterman, 1786; (39) baluster, by George Wickes, 1729
In the collection of Mrs. William B. Munro

40, 41, 42   CREAM BOAT (40) with writhen snake handle, by John Schüppe, 1755; (41) CREAM
BOAT with chased flowers, by John Schüppe, 1762; (42) HELMET MILK JUG by Edward
Wakelin, 1757. *In the collection of Mrs. William B. Munro*

43, 44, 45   CREAM BOAT (43), cast and gilded, *c.* 1735; (44) ENGRAVED MILK JUG, *c.* 1725;
(45) PLAIN MILK JUG by George Wickes, 1729. *In the collection of Mrs. William B. Munro*

boldly. The seventeenth-century sugar box was accompanied by a small ladle, kept within the box.

By the end of the century fine wines were so much improved that the silver sugar box ceased to be an essential part of the wine service, but by then the new ritual of tea-drinking demanded the serving of sugar with equal elegance. A hemispherical sugar bowl surmounted by a domed loose cover became fashionable during the last quarter of the seventeenth century (*50*). This formed a part of the silver tea equipage, then a new challenge to the skill and originality of the silversmith. It was required for lumps of sugar royal, the finest sugar then obtainable, trebly refined to make it white throughout its texture and free of the treacly flavour that hostesses less well supplied had to disguise with saffron or peach leaves.

Cone-shaped loaves of sugar royal weighing about 6 pounds were favoured gifts for more than a century. Lumps were broken from the loaf with a sugar chopper and cracked into small pieces by the sharp semicircular blades of polished steel sugar nippers. Silver tongs lifted the small pieces of sugar from bowl to tea cup.

Known as a sugar dish, this bowl, 4 to 5 inches high, copied the covered bowls of Chinese porcelain and red earthenware then being imported from the East and for which demand exceeded supply. It might stand upon a vertical rim foot, or upon a spreading moulded ring. The closely fitting cover resembled an inverted saucer. It was smoothly shaped into a low flattened dome, and its only handle was an applied moulded ring about half an inch deep and one-third the diameter of the bowl rim, so that the whole lid was often just an inverted shallower version of the bowl. The rim of the cover was horizontal and its lower surface encircled by deep moulding. When in position the cover rested upon a ring of moulding soldered a little below the bowl rim. Moulding of matching pattern might strengthen bowl and cover rims.

This design was continued and modified in the eighteenth century, the low, flat-domed cover usually topped with a rim foot or moulded ring having an everted rim. An example hall-marked in 1728, with a diameter of $4\frac{1}{4}$ inches, weighed 7 ounces; another, of the same size and same year, weighed 10 ounces. Sometimes the design was modified by the substitution of three moulded lugs on the lid instead of the moulded ring, more obviously declaring the lid's secondary purpose as a dish upon the tea table, possibly to serve as a rest for the mote-skimmer (*48*).

A notable alternative style throughout the reigns of William III and Anne was enriched with that period's widely-favoured light-twinkling gadrooning. This might transform the design, being introduced around the cover rim and rise, the lower body, and the foot. A boss on the lid supported a vase-shaped knop (*50*). By Anne's reign, too, and for the first twenty years of the eighteenth century, the bowl might conform to another current vogue that made the most of tea-table candlelight, being sharply angular on plan, often hexagonal or octagonal, with a spreading moulded foot, and with a baluster finial to the cover. It is rare, however, to find a covered sugar bowl of this period surface-ornamented with more than an engraved coat of arms on the side of the bowl, a crest on the cover, and a pair of chased or engraved lines encircling the cover's dome.

The sugar box continued in production, too, throughout these periods. In the early eighteenth century this, too, might be octagonal and of bombé form, on a moulded octagonal foot, and with a lift-off cover surmounted by a baluster finial.

By about 1725 the sugar bowl tended to lose its graceful hemispherical shape in favour of a heavier, more capacious line, and 10 years later surface decoration might be introduced, with shallow chasing or engraving in symmetrical designs, and a cartouche enclosing a coat of arms. Circular sugar bowls on rim feet continued until the end of the century, later examples being edged with bands of bright-cut engraving: they might be as much as 6 or 7 inches in diameter. A few examples have been noted during the 1740s with bold lion mask and paw feet and their bodies chased with festoons of flowers in matt panels. By then silversmiths were in the throes of rococo design and sugar bowls inevitably appeared in strange asymmetrical designs, loaded with shell and scroll ornament. But these were extreme specimens. More frequent was the bowl in ogee outline, with a deep ringed cover shaped to match. The 1750s saw the beginning of a twenty-year popularity for a swirling, spirally fluted sugar bowl on three hoof feet; in a late example the body might be chased above and fluted below, and the rim beaded.

To this period, too, belongs the covered sugar vase on a high circular foot (52): sets of three are sometimes noted. Here, too, the upper part of the body was chased, with fluting below and on the foot. Reflecting the period's liking for taller, more impressive designs, the vase had shell and scroll handles rising from the shoulders, and a cast pineapple or strawberry, flower or urn finial topped the cover (53). Such a vase might be accompanied by a silver sugar sifter, its bowl in the form of a pierced escallop shell and with a shell finial to the stem. The vase shape continued until sugar bowls began to be fitted with loose linings of blue glass instead of the customary interior gilding.

These features all reflected current vogues among other pieces of tea-table silver, but it must be emphasised that the sugar bowl so far had been designed as an individual piece, harmonising with the rest of the tea equipage but seldom matching it. From the early 1730s, however, it had been customary for the fashionable hostess to keep her silver canisters of precious tea in a casket or tea-chest. In many instances such a pair of canisters was accompanied by a silver sugar vessel, designed as part of the set (57). This canister, with a lid fitting tightly into an opening that covered the full extent of the top, was more capacious than the accompanying tea canisters with their small openings and domed lids.

These sugar canisters followed the changing fashions in tea caddy design, early Georgian, rococo, and neo-classic. During the 1770s, however, the manufacturing silversmiths began to replace the neo-classic sugar vases with covered jars of cut-glass, and later with open bowls. It is arguable that these bowls were often intended for blending the dry tea leaves as part of the tea-making ritual, for by then the silver tea service usually included a matching sugar bowl. Hall-marks show, however, that silver sugar vessels might be included in tea-chests until the end of the century.

Meanwhile, the trend of fashion was beginning to give the comfortable English tea table the stately grace of Grecian design. Inevitably the sugar bowl conformed to the neo-classic craze, appearing in the guise of a Greco-Roman vase, wide at the shoulder where two short handles might support swag ornament, and tapering to a spool-shaped stem above a round foot. The lid was highly domed with a decorative finial (52). The classic mood was responsible for the development of the wide-brimmed sugar bowl, often elliptical, with a pair of long narrow handles rising from the rim at its widest part, and recurving down to the base of the body (53). Such handles might be strengthened with narrow moulding applied down the centre. The cover was highly domed.

Delicate hand-pierced ornament, magnificent against a ground of Bristol blue glass, was introduced in the early 1750s. The design might be an all-over scene encircling the vessel, but more frequently consisted of a band of geometrical piercing above embossed and chased ornament, which might be in the form of thin leaves extending upward from the foot junction. The cover and foot ornament matched that of the body and both might be encircled with gadrooning. Many sugar vases were unpierced, but fretted designs continued in production with round feet on square plinths until early in the nineteenth century.

Piercing to the silversmith has always tended to suggest graceful basket designs. Already, by the 1750s, pierced sugar vases were being made without covers, and mounted on short-stemmed feet. These were fitted with swing handles, and early examples measured slightly more in width than in height: the normal size approximated $4\frac{1}{2}$ inches high and 5 inches in diameter. From the late 1770s they became taller and more slender. Handles were usually pierced. At first these vessels were hand-pierced in panels of varying trellis work, with corded rims, and were fitted with detachable silver liners. The pattern included a cartouche engraved with the owner's coat of arms or crest (1).

Sugar buckets, without feet, pierced and fitted with Bristol blue-glass liners, were made to accompany matching cream pails, with chasing to suggest hoops and staves. Sugar buckets were also made in open wirework on high spreading bases.

Pierced sugar baskets and buckets were made in large numbers during the 1770s and 1780s, the piercing restricted to vertical pales on body and foot.

A circular sugar basket of the 1770s might be pierced and chased with festoons of flowers and foliage, arabesque scrolls and a medallion bust, and have a beaded rim which might be punched or in the form of moulded ribbon. A vase-shaped sugar basket with swing handles, pierced or beaded, is occasionally found with three scroll feet and a triangular base. From the 1770s until about 1790 the popular type of sugar basket was canoe-shaped on a stemmed or oval foot (55). Here, too, an early example may be found with a cream pail pierced to match, such as a pair hall-marked 1778, with beaded rims, pierced with bands of vertical pales, urns, and husks. In the 1780s and later the rim and foot might be encircled with drawn reeded ribbon, with a reeded swing handle, and the body might be pierced with a band of ovolos and foliage. The light chasing hitherto sometimes associated with piercing was now replaced by bright-cut engraving, festoons and rosettes being favourite motifs.

The canoe-shaped sugar basket with unpierced body, stemmed foot, and swing handle dates from about 1780. This, like the greater part of the pierced work, was basically a factory product, machine-shaped and press-pierced parts being bought by the master silversmiths who assembled and finished them. For the first time an inexpensive three-piece set could be marketed—teapot, milk jug, and sugar bowl *en suite*. In early work the bowl was undecorated, its rim strengthened with applied beading or drawn reeded ribbon to take the stresses of the swing handle. Similar ornament was applied centrally over the loop of the handle. A short, spool-shaped stem linked the bowl to a foot in an outline corresponding to that of the rim.

The solid body soon became a field for decoration and was given wide upward-flaring flutes to a wavy edge, the foot rim being scalloped or shaped to harmonise. The surface was enriched with bands of bright-cut engraving. Few canoe-shaped sugar baskets bear date letters later than about 1805.

Sugar baskets continued to be made throughout the nineteenth century, at first following the late eighteenth-century style and of the thinnest plate possible until the 1830s. Subsequently body and handle were loaded with unrelated ornament, embossed, chased, or in the form of applied casting or stamping: designs were innumerable. Usually the vessel was raised on three slender cast feet, thin scrolled work being most frequent. The rim was widely everted and the handle attached to the outer edge, giving the bow the appearance of being lower and wider than the pre-1830 style. From the late 1840s ruby glass became fashionable for liners, the cost being five shillings more than for blue glass. Pierced lattice work was common, being simple to produce mechanically, and the liner might be silver-gilt. By the end of the century sugar baskets had become mere stamped toys adapted from styles introduced a century earlier.

As a more substantial vessel than the basket, a low, flat-bottomed sugar bowl was approved in the final decade of the eighteenth century. In this the oval-shape was sometimes squared up so that on plan the vessel was a round-cornered rectangle. The sides bulged, but a balanced design was achieved with a flat-topped handle at each end, curving from rim to base. Some examples had narrow foot-rims of moulding, and from about 1800 the bowl was raised on four ball feet in harmony with the teapot. Early decoration consisted of wide vertical flutes encircling the lower part of the bowl, with a wide raised band of engraved ornament placed midway on the plain space above. The rim, shaped slightly off the horizontal, was decorated with moulding cast in ornate designs. D-shaped handles were fixed horizontally on the narrow ends.

During the Regency years the lower part of the bowl might be fluted and the ornamental band moulded in low relief with floral motifs. The rim was more widely everted and ornamented with chased, gadrooned, or shell-and-foliage moulding, and the ball feet might be replaced with four paw feet or, more commonly, with a moulded foot ring. Handles were of the vertically scrolled type and might terminate in busts. Some bowls were chased all over with bands of flowers, vines, scrolls, and foliage on a matted ground. From about 1815 the bowl might be oval or circular with a low-domed cover bearing an elaborately cast and chased finial. Matching pairs were now made and weight increased owing to the lavish use of applied castings. The compressed spherical body appeared at about the same time, and might be chased with vertical panels of flowers on a matted ground with floral borders, a style which continued until the 1830s.

With the accession of George IV and a general return to rich versions of the rococo, came the widely fluted, melon-shaped sugar bowl ornately embossed or chased with flowers and foliage. Shell and scroll ornament was popular on the widely everted mouth. There might be a pair of elaborately moulded upcurving handles, claw or paw and foliage feet, and a flower finial on the cover. Often a base ring was applied to the bowl, designed to include four ornamental cast feet. The cover finial might be in the form of an armorial crest, chased and burnished.

Some sugar bowls were now being catalogued as sugar basins and made without covers. For several decades to come the basin was decorated with a mass of embossed, chased, or engraved ornament, and fitted with a pair of handles that might take any of the forms used by earlier silversmiths. The most frequent shapes were: octagonal with a waisted rim; a compressed sphere; melon-shaped, waisted at the rim; urn-shaped; cup-shaped. It might be flat-based, but more usually was raised either on four ornamental cast and chased feet, on a moulded, stamped, or cast foot ring with four cast feet below, or on an openwork cast foot. The glass liner was for the most part abandoned owing to the fashion for an incurving line at the neck, and the interior was gilded.

Sugar tongs were introduced in the 1690s and resembled steel ember tongs. A typical pattern was made with a wide horseshoe-shaped bow of springy silver linking a pair of slender round arms with wide, escallop-shell grips. The arms might be double or treble knopped at ends and centre, but the whole design was essentially delicate, intended for lifting the tiny fragments of sugar suited to the small tea-cups of the period. Hall-marked examples are extremely rare.

A somewhat better grip on the small sugar lump was obtained with the scissor design evolved during the late 1730s, but it was still a delicate little tool, of small use to clumsy fingers (235). These sugar tongs had scroll arms and shell grips. The finger and thumb in the round bows had to maintain a firm hold while conveying the sugar lump cracked unevenly from the loaf. In 1749, however, Benjamin Cart-wright patented a spring device that controlled the movement of the arms, obviating the unintentional opening of the grips that would let the sugar fall before reaching the cup. The pivoting joint was concealed in a flat circular box containing a coiled spring so arranged that it closed, and held closed, the shell-shaped grips. The grips themselves were improved when their interior surfaces were hollowed instead of flat. The plain side of the spring box might be engraved with the owner's crest, monogram, or initials: the other side was covered with a convex boss, usually in the form of a finely worked rosette. Few scissor sugar tongs bearing hall-marks later than 1755 failed to incorporate the spring.

The less costly tea tongs date from about 1760. As tea became less prohibitively expensive and tea-cups larger, the accompanying sugar lumps required sturdier, simpler tongs. The arms of these sugar tongs extended from a U-shaped spring arch hammered from flat plate and convex on its outer surface. The fact that this arch was of flat plate distinguishes it at once from the round-section arch of the earliest tongs. For thirty years the arms were soldered to the ends of the spring, and were cast in complex scroll and openwork designs finished with chasing and burnishing. Such arms might include shell-shaped grips, but just as frequently these were cast as separate units and soldered in position.

In harmony with the rest of the silver tea equipage, from the mid-1780s spring tea tongs were forged from single strips of silver, the tapering arms press-pierced. Then press-piercing in its turn was abandoned after the early 1790s, in favour of simple chasing or bright-cut engraving. The grips were now spoon-shaped, occasionally stamped in the form of tea leaves.

Regency tea tongs were ornamented with little more than threaded edges, but from 1815 the arms were made to match tea spoons with old English or fiddle ends. After 1820 sugar tongs were of more massive design, of thicker silver, made to harmonise with the period's large sugar bowls of enamelled bone china. The name sugar tongs was revived in pattern books of this period. This form continued throughout the nineteenth century with arms matching spoon finials in such patterns as the king's, Victoria and Albert, fiddle, threaded, threaded and shell, lily, beaded, and French.

III   TEA-CADDY LADLES AND MOTE-SKIMMERS

SOMETHING of the grace of the early Georgian tea-table ritual is caught in Hogarth's conversation piece "The Walpole Family," believed to have been painted in the late 1730s. This painting illustrates a complete tea equipage: the small cabriole-legged table of mahogany; a tray set with porcelain cups and saucers, and silver teapot and sugar bowl; and on the floor a shagreen tea-chest, its open lid revealing a silver tea-canister in the rectangular dome-and-neck design. Lady Walpole is seen measuring dry tea leaves from a second canister into the domed lid, forerunner of the caddy-ladle. In the centre of the picture a servant waits with a steaming kettle; behind stands a low tripod supporting the silver kettle-stand and spirit lamp.

After the dome-and-neck design for tea-canisters had been superseded by hinged and sliding lids, stemmed ladles were used to spoon the tea into the pot. The first of these had a deep, escallop-shell bowl with the stem rising from it almost at right angles, its terminal matching those of contemporary teaspoons. To the back of the stem might be soldered a small hook fitting an appropriate loop within the tea-chest. Ladle bowls were generally hand-raised, rarely cast, and in some instances the handle might be of turned ivory, ebony, or stained boxwood. A vase-shaped tea-canister of the mid-eighteenth century might have a pair of upward-curving D-handles, one of them bearing the ladle hanging by its scroll or Onslow finial, its stem following the curve of the canister body.

The short-stemmed silver tea-scoop, known to most collectors as a caddy-spoon (59), dates from the late 1770s onwards, when it was the invariable accompaniment to a single tea-canister in silver, ivory, tortoiseshell, mother of pearl, exotic wood, or other material. Such canisters were termed tea caddies and the small scoops were caddy-ladles. The earliest use of the name caddy-ladle so far noted appears in the Assay Act of 1790. They were advertised as late as 1839 by David Cope, Birmingham, and other silversmiths as "caddee shells" and by 1860 as caddy-spoons. Such a ladle was kept in the caddy with the tea and was therefore necessarily short-stemmed. In some instances a recess in the lid, or a small drawer in the side of the chest, contained the ladle.

Caddy-ladles were never exempt from hall-marking as were the majority of small articles of silver weighing less than 5 pennyweights. They were not made until long after the passing of the Act in 1739 in which certain articles were exempted from the obligation to be submitted for assay, and they were not even included in the assay office price list of 1777. This omission suggests that caddy-ladles were rare objects of assay until after that date. It is unusual to find a caddy-ladle bearing a hall-mark earlier than 1780. The Assay Act of 1790 specifically excluded "caddy-ladles" of 5 pennyweights or less from the list of exemptions.

The earliest caddy-ladles were in the form of shallow escallop shells, the hand-raised bowl and short, broad, flat thumbpiece being made from a single piece of plate (59). The shell flutings were exquisitely embossed, and the thumbpiece enriched with bright-cut engraving and a line-engraved crest or cypher on the reverse, sometimes in a bright-cut border. A typical example made in 1785 by Thomas Shepherd, Aldersgate, measured 3 inches long, 1½ inches wide, and weighed 10 pennyweights.

By far the greater number of caddy-ladles were made from thinly rolled plate by factory processes, thus creating a half-century demand for these dainty trifles as inexpensive presents. Most of these bore the anchor of the Birmingham assay office, others were struck with the hall-marks of Sheffield, London, and Dublin. These were shaped by gradual raising in a hand-operated ball-press using tools made from a hard steel not widely available until the early 1790s. In some instances bowl and thumbpiece were pressed in a single piece: in others the bowl and handle were made separately and joined by hard soldering a roman joint.

Because of competition in smooth-bowled and shell-shaped caddy-ladles in Sheffield plate from about 1790, the silversmiths introduced greater individuality into their productions. Shape of bowl and handle were apparently designed to be as unlike the conventional teaspoon as possible. Plated caddy-ladles were necessarily bordered with narrow beading or thread moulding, so this feature was quickly abandoned by the silversmiths.

Smooth and shell-shaped caddy-ladles were the least costly to make, speed of production being high and tools lasting well: other designs were often exquisite little masterpieces of the silversmith's craft. Some were gilded. So fragile were some eighteenth-century caddy-ladles that the bowl-stem junction was liable to fracture; such breakages have often been almost invisibly repaired, although careful inspection through a magnifying glass will reveal traces of this. A series of ornate caddy-ladles displaying the duty marks of George IV and William IV were cast and chased, sometimes also enriched with engraving.

Most desirable of all caddy-ladles to the collector is the rare eagle pattern, first issued in the early 1790s by Joseph Taylor of Birmingham. Stamped from a single piece of rolled plate, the bowl formed the outline of an eagle, the neck constituting the handle and terminating in the bird's head with a burnished eye. Delicate

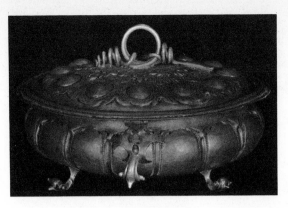

46, 47   SUGAR BOXES: (46) oval, raised from the plate, London, 1677. *Courtesy of Mr. S. J. Phillips.*
(47) Escallop-shell shape, maker's mark T.I., London, 1610
Courtesy of Messrs. William Bruford and Son Ltd.

48, 49   HEMISPHERICAL SUGAR BOWL (48) on moulded foot with low-domed ringed cover, by G. Jones,
1727. *Courtesy of Messrs. Spink and Son Ltd.* (49) SUGAR BOWL by Eliza Godfrey, 1747
Courtesy of Messrs. E. T. Biggs and Sons Ltd.

50   SUGAR BOWL with hemispherical gadrooned body and cover supporting boss and
finial; in Britannia standard silver, by J.
Leach, 1699. *Courtesy of Messrs. William
Bruford and Son Ltd.*

51, 52, 53   COVERED SUGAR BOWLS: (51) embossed foot-rim encircled with applied flowers, by Samuel Taylor, 1760. *Courtesy of Mr. J. Parkes.* (52) Fluted ovoid body, moulded figure handles, London, 1771. *Courtesy of Messrs. Harvey and Gore.* (53) Leaf motifs on body and cover, London, 1783. *Courtesy of Messrs. Harvey and Gore*

54, 55   OPEN SUGAR BOWLS: (54) gadrooned and with ornamental band in low relief, by Paul Storr, 1814; (55) canoe-shaped with swing handle, by Hester Bateman, 1790
Courtesy of Messrs. Harvey and Gore

56, 57, 58   TEA CANISTERS with MATCHING SUGAR CANISTER (57), its lid covering the full extent of the top; engraved with busts and shell motifs; London, 1735. *Courtesy of Messrs. Harvey and Gore*

embossing and chasing of the bowl suggested plumage. A second series, made perhaps from the same worn tools and poorly finished, bear hall-marks of the 1830s. A third well-made series issued during the present century may be recognised immediately by the absence of the duty mark.

The jockey cap, now also rare, is an attractive ladle (59); the cap itself, with a tiny bow of silver wire at the back, acted as the scoop, the visor as a thumbpiece. Like the eagle this pattern has been reproduced: Georgian specimens had the hallmark, including a duty mark, struck on the visor; modern versions have the hallmark struck on the back of the cap and lack the duty mark. An attractive series of jockey cap caddy-ladles was hand-worked in silver filigree: the finest of these bore William IV hall-marks, less carefully made versions belonging to the 1850s. Associated with the jockey cap are stirrup patterns and semicircular scoops with their outer rims engraved to suggest horse-shoes. The half-closed hand is another scarce variety, its flat wrist, engraved with the edge of a lace cuff, forming the thumbpiece. This and the eagle pattern formed scoops somewhat more capacious than other caddy-ladles. Another desirable pattern is in the form of a fish engraved with arcs to simulate overlapping scales.

A series of caddy-ladles embossed on the scoop with a design of war trophies bear Birmingham hall-marks ranging from 1804 until 1815. The design incorporates a standard, pennon, cannon with ramming irons, drum and fife, bayonet and sword, and in some instances the stem is engraved with the name of a battle and a date. "Trafalgar" has been noted in script letters. The earliest example noted dates to 1804, when the dies were probably cut in celebration of General Wellesley's victories at Assaye and Arguam.

Caddy-ladle bowls embossed with designs composed of vine-leaves and bunches of grapes were popular between the 1790s and about 1820, a silver wire shaped as a vine tendril forming the handle. These were first issued as a fashionable accessory for use at the after-dinner tea-table where cordials were served to the ladies. In another popular pattern the scoop itself was in the shape of a tea-leaf, fine chasing showing the leaf structure, from the thick central vein. The stalk handle of silver wire ended in a circular or oval loop (59).

The most frequent shape in caddy-ladles was the escallop shell made in innumerable sizes and outlines throughout the period. An exquisite series was issued by Joseph Taylor in the 1790s, in which the flutes of the scalloped ladle were delicately embossed with floral sprays. The rectangular ladle was among the early patterns, bordered with engraved ornament on inner and outer surfaces, and with a short handle cut from the same piece of plate. Some display evidence of being hand-made throughout.

The handle of a caddy-ladle might be decorated on both sides with bright-cut engraving and the expanded finial bordered to surround a line-engraved crest or cypher: thumbpieces were similarly ornamented. If the bowl were smooth the engraving might be carried down into it. Fiddle-shaped handles date from about 1805 (59). In rare early instances a handle is found bordered with narrow beading or thread moulding as with Sheffield plate.

The demand for rareties has produced a crop of spurious examples. As early as 1926 a writer on this subject was marvelling at the number then existing. In the most costly of these it has been found worth while to take the hall-marked section cut from a small teaspoon handle and weld it to a new bowl. These are sometimes to be recognised by a peculiar thumbprint indentation at the bowl-handle junction. Other fakes are those imported with foreign hall-marks which, after removal of the English assay mark, are judiciously rubbed to produce an excellent imitation of the Birmingham hall-mark. The head resembles the duty mark of George III, and the lion bears a close likeness to the lion *passant gardant*; date letter and anchor are less clearly defined. Careful inspection reveals this fraud to the experienced collector.

Included in the Georgian silver tea equipage was a mote-skimmer or strainer tea-spoon (60). This had a long tapering stem with a barbed finial and an ornamentally pierced bowl. The stem was used for clearing tea-leaves from the teapot spout and the perforated bowl for skimming the infusion. Mote was the old English word for a minute solid particle of foreign matter in food or drink.

The bowl of the skimmer was used to remove these motes after the beverage had been poured into the cup. As they floated on the tea they were caught on the silver surface of the skimmer, the liquid draining through the perforations. The skimming was done by the maid in charge of the tea-table, or on less formal occasions by each individual. Sometimes a mote-skimmer was clipped into the lid of a tea-chest containing wide-mouthed canisters. It is never found in association with a caddy-ladle: it is probable, therefore, that it was also used for measuring tea-leaves from the canister.

The leaves of good-quality tea were plucked one by one, rolled, dried, and exported in air-tight containers. The Georgian hostess made her tea at table, the usual recipe being to "boyl a quart of clean water, add a few dry leaves, and let them stand in a covered Pot two or three minutes, in which time the leaves will be spread to their former breadth and shape, and yield their bitter yet pleasant taste." These outspread leaves were liable to block the perforated strainer at the entrance to the teapot spout, obstructing the flow of tea. The barb of the mote-skimmer was used to remove such leaves.

The earliest reference to mote-skimmers so far noted appeared in the *London Gazette*, 1697: "long or strainer tea spoons with narrow pointed handles." These were of rat-tail design and the bowl pierced with circular holes. Saw-pierced crosses arranged in closely spaced rows appeared in the Queen Anne period, and by about 1720 the rat-tail had been abandoned. The earliest hall-marked example so far noted is of Britannia standard silver made in 1719. More gracefully cut crosses arranged sparsely in diagonal lines date from about 1730 and by the mid-century the tip and shoulders might be pierced with scrolls. George III examples were pierced with attractive designs composed of small foliated scrolls, circles, diapers, crescents, and diamonds of various sizes. The early barb was short, about one-quarter of an inch in length; the early Georgian barb was double this length and from about 1760 it might be about an inch long. The shorter barb, however, was to be found throughout the period. Giant mote-skimmers, always with George III hall-marks, were intended for use with silver tea-urns.

Chapter Two

I SWEETMEAT BASKETS

THE gargantuan meals of earlier centuries have little appeal to modern tastes. The Georgian banquet or dessert, with dainty refreshments informally served to a moving, chattering throng, is far more in keeping with twentieth-century ideas of social pleasure. Similarly, the various charming accessories to this repast are particularly well suited to present-day living and are becoming notably popular among collectors.

The "dressing out of a dessert" for a banquet was a polite accomplishment of Georgian ladies, but when guests were numerous a professional confectioner would be engaged. The colourful sweetmeats were displayed in vessels of glowing silver and scintillating glass. Trade cards issued by Frederic Kuhff, confectioner to George III and the Princess Dowager of Wales, show a dessert table brilliantly set out. There were ice-creams, custards, trifles, jellies, syllabubs, and similar spoon-requiring confections served individually in small glass containers—"wet sweets" was the contemporary term—and there were also candied fruits, comfits, boiled sweets, orange chips, and other "dry" sweetmeats offered in silver baskets or shallow glass bowls. In 1752 Mrs. Hannah Glasse in *The Compleate Confectioner* described a number of magnificent arrangements for dressing out a dessert. In her table setting a vast array of sweetmeats and fruit were made the more daintily decorative, not only with colourful jellies, but with small vases of flowers and porcelain figures.

The silver and glass required for a well-attended banquet was costly, for at least three dozen four-tier glass pyramids were required, with hundreds of subsidiary glasses and many silver sweetmeat baskets. The graceful outward flare of the sweetmeat basket was designed to make the most of a display of sweetmeats and to make matters easy for those who wished to partake of them. Even in less opulent households where the sweetmeat course might be served in the dining-room the silver sweetmeat basket was much in demand, for the company moved to the drawing-room after dinner and was served with wine and baskets of nuts and raisins.

Table baskets and fruit baskets made from heavy silver plate graced dining-tables of the early seventeenth century, but the most notable feature, the arched and hinged handle, was only introduced in the early 1730s. The silver sweetmeat basket as best known today, its greatest measurement about 6 inches and its weight between 6 and 7 ounces, came into use during the late 1740s, a shallow, round, oval, or rectangular vessel with finely pierced and chased rims and graceful hinged, arching handle (68).

Sweetmeat baskets of the 1740s to 1750s were superb examples of the silver-smith's craft. The rim, in a curved outline, was expanded to display as much as possible of the inner surface of the hand-raised body, a field for elaborate pierced decoration with a wide border of rococo moulding, and a contrasting unpierced base (67). The basket was supported on four short cast and chased legs terminating in volute, claw-and-ball, or scroll feet. These might be linked to the body by masks or other soldered ornament, or the feet might be connected by aprons of shell and leaf ornament. Soon the entire combination of feet, masks, and aprons was merged into a single elaborate cast ring with motifs in high relief matching those encircling the basket rim. Into the ring fitted the lower part of the basket (65).

These early sweetmeat baskets were pierced by embossing the design and cutting away the background. More commonly, however, silversmiths employed the intri-cate saw-cut designs which had newly reached their greatest popularity on large table baskets. Shaped panels finely saw-cut with designs composed of scrolls, circles, crescents, and diamonds were succeeded by quatrefoils, spiral and arabesque diapers, ovals, and rows of small crosses arranged diagonally. Panels of such piercing alternated with others pierced with foliated scrollwork, the panels being separated by raised ribs, later by rows of punched beadwork (85). A dozen such panels might go to the making of a single basket. At this time sets of pierced sweetmeat, sugar, and cream baskets were made all in matching designs. Although sweetmeat baskets were made in sets of a dozen it is rare to find more than a matching pair.

Sweetmeat baskets constructed almost entirely of wirework were introduced after the invention of the swage block in 1762 (83): the surface of silver ribbon could then be given any desired contour. This type of basket continued to be made until the 1820s, often with wire in place of ribbon. A shallow oval base was raised from the plate and for a 6-inch basket about forty flat or reeded ribbons might radiate from this, shaped in an ogee outline, and soldered to a reeded or beaded rim. The swing handle might consist of two intertwined silver wires (83) or ribbon worked into the type of ornament known as the guilloche: this style is found in various forms on all kinds of sweetmeat baskets throughout the eighteenth century. The same pattern was sometimes pierced in the foot rim. In some instances the central bow of the handle consisted of a cast insertion with a smooth oval in the centre to receive an engraved crest, a coat of arms being engraved inside the basket.

By 1770 the swing handle might be pierced, a pair of recurving foliated scrolls supporting a widely expanding bow-shaped arch containing pierced ornament. In many instances the surface of the arch was plain or slightly chased. The pin of the hinge was sometimes concealed beneath a circular or shell-shaped boss. If the solid base were shaped, the rim followed the same outline and the arch of the handle was similarly curved. The basket stood upon a narrow foot-ring wrought from the plate, which became deeper during the 1770s. Inside at the hinges there might be soldered a pair of expansive ribband bows made from very thin plate (83).

A popular version of the wire sweetmeat basket was introduced in the late 1750s. The wire was fashioned into trellis work forming a background to applied hand-worked motifs of thinly beaten silver (82). These might represent sprays of wheat alternating with roses, chased trails of flowers, leaves, fruit, and other motifs, the vine-leaf and grape being the most frequent. The foot-ring was built from similar wire or ribbon with a stronger corded wire rim, and there was a matching bail handle. A light-weight series made at the end of the century had trellis sides composed of thinly drawn ribbon woven over-and-under to a corded edge.

Sweetmeat baskets bordered with mechanically pierced designs were common during the last quarter of the eighteenth century (81). Piercing intended to resemble saw-cutting was carried out in a fraction of the time by means of small fly-presses capable of producing work of extreme delicacy when used with tools of crucible cast steel, then difficult to obtain. The sweetmeat basket, usually oval, might be encircled with three rows of cusped pales, often further decorated with symmetrically superimposed swags pendant from tiny medallions, foliated scrolls, masks, insects, vine-leaves and grapes, wheat-ears, and other motifs cast in silver and enlivened with chasing and burnishing. The curve of the handle exactly coincided with the oval of the body and the design was completed by a pierced foot.

By about 1780 the oval became more pointed or canoe-shaped (82), with the ends higher than the sides where the handle hinged. Drawn reeded ribbon encircled rim and foot, and the wide-bowed handle was reeded to match. The rim was encircled with a narrow band of pierced ornament, such as alternating panels of vertical pales and scrollwork, above a row of rosettes, each perhaps enclosed in a chased swag. Press-piercing also included bands of Vitruvian foliated scrollwork and other ornament adapted from Greco-Roman sources. Applied foot-rims made from rolled silver plate were pierced to match. Some sweetmeat baskets were now circular and many were gilded.

Some delightful little baskets of this period were unpierced: these were either fluted or lobed in the style of escallop shells bordered with bands of chased foliage. Small, light-weight sweetmeat baskets might now be shaped with a hand-operated drop-hammer. These would be hand-finished by the master silversmiths. Early in the nineteenth century shell and gadroon mounts replaced the beaded rims.

Some lack of fine design and craftsmanship in sweetmeat baskets of the early nineteenth century suggests that they lost status as fashionable table accessories after the decline of the banquet service. The body was now invariably a factory product, with a border of gadroon and shell moulding and with the pierced ornament limited to a band of short pales encircling the rim. Mechanical embossing, hand-chasing, and engraving are to be noted on such work. These uninteresting pieces appeared on middle-class dining-tables until early Victorian times.

Victorian sweetmeat baskets displayed mechanical ugliness in form and ornament. When the latter was embossed, chased, or engraved the foot was a hollow pedestal, but, with the perversity of the period, delicate pierced ornament prompted the use of four heavy cast feet linked by aprons. The body was stamped in two halves and invisibly seamed, the rims strengthened with elaborate moulding, frequently the fruiting vine motif, and plain drawn reeding. The swing handle might be hinged to the end of the basket and might be stamped or cast with high-relief motifs, the centre of the hoop being expanded into a plain cartouche for an engraved coat of arms. The rim of the foot, whether oval or shaped to the outline of the body, was bordered with moulding to match that of the body rim. In some finely pierced boat-shaped examples with undulating rims the ends were ornamented with rams' masks. These highly decorative sweetmeat baskets continued until the 1870s, when there was another vogue for late eighteenth-century styles, until the development of the *art nouveau* of the 1890s ensured that there could be no further confusion between the eighteenth century's artistry and the nineteenth century's laboriousness.

II SPICE DREDGERS AND MUFFINEERS

PUNGENT aromatic flavours were essential to the Englishman's enjoyment of his food while dried and salted meat and fish constituted much of his main diet. Such a garnish was introduced either as a prepared piquant sauce or by sprinkling spices such as nutmeg, mace, and cinnamon, ground to flour fineness. Spices were tabled in small hinged boxes accompanied by tiny ladles until the late seventeenth century, when individual silver casters made their appearance. Their forerunner was the hollow ball finial of the late Tudor and early Stewart bell-salt which was pierced to serve as a tiny pepper caster. A silver salt-and-pepper vessel of this kind is mentioned more often in inventories than its rarity today might lead the collector to expect, but its vulnerability is obvious. More surprising, perhaps, is the fact that there is no evidence to suggest the making of separate pepper casters in England until after 1660.

During the post-Restoration epoch of extravagant display silversmiths busied themselves with the development of a new range of table ware. Much of this was concerned with the newly fashionable beverages tea, coffee, and chocolate, but dining, too, was becoming more gracious and the table set with an eye to elegance, even daintiness, rather than mere pomp and glitter. The sets of casters then coming into fashionable use typified the new approach. Such a set offered the diner sugar and two kinds of pepper, the pungent cayenne and the milder black pepper. But before the end of the century the service of spices with food and drink to suit individual tastes had become sufficiently widespread to have created a need for a distinctive container. This need was met with those silver spice casters which today suggest miniature flour dredgers, measure about 3 inches in height, and weigh 2 to 3 ounces (70 and 72).

The earliest of these silver spice dredgers were plainly cylindrical, shaped from flat metal and vertically seamed, the circular base being inserted and encircled with a spreading moulded or gadrooned foot ring. The flat scroll or S-shaped handle terminated in a short tail. The low-domed, pull-off sprinkler, pierced with fret-cut geometric and curved motifs or with circular holes, at first possessed a cylindrical extension overlapping and fitting tightly over the upper part of the body, an encircling moulded rib preventing it from sliding too far. The cover rim was edged with strengthening moulding. Such a lid was unsatisfactory, however, as it tended to spring off when the dredger was shaken and release the entire spicy contents.

This mishap was prevented from about 1700 by locking body and cover together with bayonet fasteners. Two lugs were soldered opposite to each other on the cover rim. These projected below the rim, to where corresponding notches were cut into the moulding encircling the rim of the body. The lugs were so shaped to the profile of the moulding that a slight twist of the cover made them grip it securely. The top of the domed cover might be drilled with circular holes within a narrow ring of fret-cut piercings, or the cover might be fret-cut all over.

Early Georgian spice dredgers were for the most part octagonal, with a slight inward slope from base to sprinkler (70). A deep, expansive foot-ring lifted the base considerably above the table. The octagonal domed cover was encircled almost midway by a raised rib separating circular holes and piercing of formal fret-cut scrolls. The scrolls might be made blind by an inner lining of silver plate, now seldom found in situ. The cover was topped by a cast baluster or vase-shaped finial. The S-handle might be plain, or its upper curve might be reeded, beaded, or notched.

The cylindrical spice dredger had returned by the end of the 1730s, when an alternative was a baluster shape ribbed at its widest diameter (73). These vessels were fitted with bun-shaped sprinklers pierced with round holes and culminating in low, smooth button finials. The piercing was usually arranged in attractive designs. The bayonet fastener continued as a safe means of attaching the cover, but in some examples the cover screwed on, a corresponding thread being cut into the top of the body, and others depended on exact workmanship to make a successful pull-off

59, 60   TEA-CADDY LADLES (59), including two of tea-leaf pattern, rare jockey cap, and shell shape, some with bright-cut decoration on the handles. *In the Victoria and Albert Museum.* (60) A SILVER MOTE-SKIMMER, back view; London, 1777. *In the Victoria and Albert Museum*

61, 62, 63 SIDE VIEWS OF THREE HAND-SAWN SWEETMEAT BASKETS WITH SWING HANDLES: *c. 1770, c. 1750, c. 1780. In the Victoria and Albert Museum*

64, 65, 66 SWEETMEAT BASKETS: silver-gilt wirework (64), with applied leaves and berries, *c.* 1770; (65) made by William Plummer, 1761; (66) silver-gilt wirework with applied fruiting vines, *c.* 1770. *In the Victoria and Albert Museum*

67, 68, 69 THREE SWEETMEAT BASKETS, London hall-marks: 1756, 1753, 1766. *In the Victoria and Albert Museum. Lent by J. H. Fitzhenry, Esq.*

cover. Cylindrical spice dredgers of this form continued to be made throughout the eighteenth century.

The handled spice dredger was superseded during the 1760s by the handleless caster used for cinnamon and known to collectors as the muffineer, a name brought into use for such a caster early in the nineteenth century. Cinnamon sprinkled on hot buttered toast was a tea-time delicacy of the late Georgian and Regency periods. The early eighteenth-century muffin was defined by Thoresby in 1703 as: "Moofin, a Wheat Cake bak'd upon a Bake-stone over the Fire, as Oat-cakes." Not until the 1760s did the muffin become a light, flat, circular, spongy cake, eaten toasted at the living-room fire, lavishly buttered and sprinkled with cinnamon or pepper and salt. These flavourings were tabled in silver containers which might be in sets of three identical casters, distinctly engraved with the names of their contents. More usually a single muffineer containing cinnamon was tabled with an ordinary salt cellar and pepper caster.

The finest cinnamon groves were in Ceylon, but had been found difficult to cultivate commercially until the mid-eighteenth century. The best flavouring was obtained from the bark of the upper shoots of these low trees and bushes. The branches were cut in April and November, and the bark peeled off in rolls thinner than paper and fitted together in long sticks containing hundreds of layers. The best quality was thin and brittle, taken from the middle of the branch. This was sent to London, where it was ground between stones and sifted through silk.

The silver muffineer designed for the tea-table of the early 1760s was a small vase-shaped or shouldered pyriform container, gilt-lined and with a tall-domed sprinkler pierced with circular perforations, in contrast to casters of the period which were fret-cut. The body seldom displayed such ornament as embossing or chasing, as a completely smooth interior was desirable to prevent stale accumulations of the spice in crevices.

From this form developed the stemmed muffineer, the majority of these being constructed from factory-spun units finished by master silversmiths (79). The body was shaped like an egg-cup on a pedestal stem, topped by a tall incurved neck. Into this neck screwed a tall-domed cover light-chased in narrow diagonal panels pierced with circular sprinkling holes and topped by a cast and burnished finial. The lower part of the body might be in ogee outline and the domed sprinkler lightly chased with a trellis-work pattern and encircled with six rows of piercing.

This style was succeeded by a less expensive form, thus widening scope of production and reducing prices. The neck was shortened to a mere spool—called by silversmiths a pulley—and fitted with a medium-domed sprinkler, spun and pierced in panel designs, and topped by a finial after the style of the taller sprinklers. The round pedestal foot stood upon a square plinth. More frequently, however, the neck finial and plinth were omitted and the muffineer was topped by a shallow-domed sprinkler pierced in four concentric circles. Sprinkler opening, rim, shoulder, and base were encircled with swaged reeding.

These types continued in production until the end of the century and beyond. In the late 1780s a breakfast-table muffineer was issued in the form of an egg on a pedestal foot, the opening placed about one-third down from the top, the joint being made by a pair of threaded insertions, as in the smooth egg-shaped nutmeg graters of this period. Body and lid consisted of spun units, smoothly plain, the lid being drilled at the apex with two or three concentric rows of piercing. The rim of the body was encircled by a swaged strengthening rib. These vessels measured about 3 inches in height. Early in the nineteenth century a beaker-shaped muffineer was made, cylindrical with an outward slope, and with a low-domed sprinkler screwed into a wide gadrooned rim. The factory-inspired muffineer was seldom made with anything more elaborate than a spring-fitting sprinkler, causing J. Beresford to complain in *Miseries of Human Life*, 1806, that "as you are shaking a muffineer the cover springs off."

By 1790 a purely cylindrical muffineer was being made with a flat base and a flat lid, its centre supporting a tall, narrow, straight-sided dome, pierced only upon the curved top (*78*). An example of this design may be found with a light scroll handle. At about the same time appeared the first of a long series of muffineers with a low, urn-shaped body, an incurved rim encircled with wide gadrooned moulding, and a flat lid centrally domed into a narrow sprinkler with a knop finial. A short-stemmed circular foot was usual. The fashionable body shape from about 1810 changed to a short, wide baluster on a taller, thicker stem rising from a small, round foot. A short spool neck was added, ornamented with wide moulding and fitted with a low-domed sprinkler.

Muffineers with bodies pierced in ornamental patterns and fitted with liners of Bristol blue glass were fashionable between 1775 and the early years of the nineteenth century. Early examples were made with small cylindrical bodies pierced with pales and arches interspersed with festooned drapery and chased with borders of lace-work. Later, the pierced sides were ornamented with applied festoons of thinly stamped silver or classic motifs. A caster in this style was usually encircled with a narrow strengthening girdle a little below the middle, and stood upon a plain moulded base.

The vase-shaped muffineer supported on a slender stem and round foot was spun. Piercing was usually carried out by the press, consisting perhaps of bands of pales with chased borders above and below; three narrow bands of chased piercing separated by rows of pales; or a double band of pales with a chased and pierced border of leaves above. The low-domed sprinkler, pierced with three or four concentric circles of round holes, was about half the width of the shoulder and mounted on a spool-shaped neck. The rim of the opening, the shoulder, and the foot were encircled with strengthening moulding, swaged or ball-stamped. In some early instances the round foot stood on a square or round plinth. Bright-cut engraving might ornament the pierced work. Height averaged 4 inches.

Muffineers in the main followed eighteenth-century forms until the 1830s. Victorian muffineers were catalogued in an extensive range of designs, stemmed, footed, and flat-based (248). They might be embossed, chased, engraved, or left smoothly plain, and bodies might be cylindrical, octagonal, or pyriform. Embossed work was carried out mechanically: a catalogue illustrating a 5-inch muffineer with an embossed body quotes an extra $16\frac{2}{3}$ per cent. for the embossed work. All sprinklers are illustrated with round perforations and topped by cast and burnished finials. Octagonal baluster-shaped muffineers with pedestal feet were made with tall sprinklers of the Queen Anne type. Interiors were gilded by the electro-deposit process. Such gilding was less permanent than the earlier mercury gilding.

A new style was designed for the Great Exhibition, 1851. This was a flat-based cylindrical muffineer with a slight inward slope, topped by a minaret-shaped sprinkler with a sharply pointed finial (248). It was chased with cinnamon plant designs—pepper casters with pepper plants. A pyriform muffineer measuring $7\frac{1}{2}$ inches in height might be lavishly embossed in the style of a century earlier, with an elaborate cartouche on the upper body for an engraved coat of arms and the swell embossed with swags in high relief. The tall cover was pierced in a spiral pattern (248). Only by the hall-mark and careful examination of the manufacturing processes is it possible to distinguish an example of the 1850s from a handsome raised caster of a century earlier.

Silver-mounted muffineers of crystal-clear flint-glass cut in a multiplicity of diamond patterns are found struck with hall-marks dating from the mid-1770s onwards. These ultimately proved to be formidable competitors of solid silver muffineers, and were advertised by the glass and china sellers. A silver collar was cemented upon the neck of the crystal and the sprinkler sprung into this. The collar might be encircled with three or four chased lines and the sprinkler followed prevailing styles set by the silversmiths.

The silver-mounted muffineer contained less cinnamon than its silver prototype owing to the thick section of the glass required for deep diamond cuttings. Early examples have been noted with square-cutting below and hollow-diamond cutting above, or cut all over with simple shallow facets. During the 1780s the body might be encircled with full-length flutings intersected by two or three horizontal prisms. In others the sharp edges of the flutes were softened with small oval facets, a style that continued until the mid-nineteenth century. In the early nineteenth century the thick, flat base might be cut with a star.

III NUTMEG GRATERS

THE fashion for highly spiced foods was widely adopted from early Elizabethan days by all who could afford the indulgence. Every small-town general dealer carried a considerable stock of pungent spices, including gilded nutmegs, which were popular gifts. In the inventory of James Backhouse, Lonsdale, Yorkshire, made in 1578, nutmegs were valued at eleven shillings a pound. Grated nutmegs, in considerable demand for flavouring ale, were thought to purify the breath. In 1380 Chaucer referred to "Notemuge to put in ale."

Pocket nutmeg graters, it appears, were not carried until the last quarter of the seventeenth century, when the powdered spice, then renowned for its stimulant and carminative properties, was sprinkled over a wide variety of foods and drinks. In 1695 Congreve in *Love for Love* spoke of "a little nutmeg grater which she had forgot in the caudlecup." Hot negus, mulled wine, and custards were rarely taken without a sprinkle of nutmeg, and until the early nineteenth century it continued to flavour ale. Warton in 1770 refers to "an old October [ale], nutmeg'd nice."

The heyday for nutmeg graters, however, was during the toddy-drinking period, from the 1770s to the 1830s: few existing specimens date earlier than this. So potent was the flavour of the nutmeg when brought out by the hot toddy that little was required. Today it is not uncommon to find a Georgian nutmeg grater containing an old nutmeg still highly scented. So definitely was the nutmeg associated with toddy that some Regency nutmeg graters were shaped in the form of rum kegs.

The keepers of taverns, punch houses, and so on seldom provided a sprinkling of nutmeg with their drinks, and were chary of making nutmegs available to customers lest they lose both nutmeg and grater. In consequence it became the fashion for the customer to carry his own nutmeg in a container fitted with a grater.

Nutmeg graters were made chiefly in ivory, bone, and hard wood, but the fashionable preferred silver. These were designed in such a way that flat plate could be used throughout with no more labour than cutting or bending, costly hand-raising being rare except in early egg-shaped examples. Joints were hard-soldered, and so carefully burnished as to be invisible on the outside, and almost so within. Some egg-shaped examples were hollowed by spinning, an inexpensive process competing with Sheffield plate.

The hall-marking of "very small nutmeg graters" was not required under the Act of Parliament of 1739, until this was repealed in 1790. The result was that from 1739 to 1790 silver nutmeg graters were made abnormally small to escape the obligation of presenting for assay. Those made between 1784 and 1790 also avoided the duty tax of sixpence an ounce. In rare instances silversmiths might send nutmeg graters to Goldsmiths' Hall for hall-marking: such marks struck between 1784 and 1790 do not include the monarch's head duty mark. Otherwise the only proof that a nutmeg grater was of sterling silver was the presence of the maker's mark as registered at Goldsmiths' Hall.

The London assay office price list for 1777 shows a charge of one penny each for hall-marking. Snuff rasps are absent from this list, suggesting that they had long been outmoded and should not be confused, therefore, with nutmeg graters. Snuff boxes remained on the assay list, twopence being charged for assaying.

From 1790 the London assay office struck the complete hall-mark of five punches within the lid: on the lower lid appeared the lion and date letter, while only the lion appeared on the body. The Birmingham assay office struck part of the mark on each lid, so that unscrupulous traders could not replace either with an inferior, unmarked replica. On the upper lid appeared the anchor, date letter, and maker's mark; on the lower lid the duty mark, lion, and often the maker's mark. The body was not marked. The silver cases were presented for hall-marking before insertion of their steel graters: hall-marks are often noted in positions where otherwise they could not have been struck.

The rasping surface of the grater consisted of a series of small protuberances roughly broken by punched holes (86). Until 1739 it was of silver hammered until springy and tough: with freedom from hall-marking, the sheet-metal grater came into use. This was usually framed in silver to lie snugly within the body of the box, resting upon a ledge formed by a narrow ribbon of silver encircling the interior rim. Hammered sheet steel was used until the 1770s, when rolled steel came into use. This was tinned to prevent rust, but friction of the nutmeg quickly removed the surface: French plating with silver leaf was even less permanent.

From the early 1790s the rolled steel used for graters was annealed in a bed of hot charcoal about 2 feet deep, the lower part of the fire being in a state of incandescence, the upper layer at a lower temperature. This produced conditions suitable for the development of oxide colours. After removal from the fire the steel was hardened by plunging into raw whale oil and then vigorously rubbed with an oil-soaked pad of beaver felt. This process surfaced the steel with a hard blue film capable of resisting the friction of the nutmeg. Signs of scaling are by now often visible, but numerous graters of the late 1790s are still in excellent condition.

In early steel graters the jagged-edged piercings were irregularly spaced and appear to have been forced into the metal by means of a sharp punch. Later the perforations were made by raising small hemispheres with a fly-press in such a way as to leave a perfectly flat ground: each hemisphere was then broken by a tool, giving a jagged edge.

Silversmiths appear to have bought graters by the sheet and cut it to fit as required, for many an oval grater shows severed perforations around the edge. In some instances the silversmith has obviously been his own piercer, the marks of a scriber being visible on the back of the grater, showing a network of squares pierced at each intersection of lines and in the centre of each square. In the finer pieces the perforations were hand-pierced in the form of concentric circles.

The earliest existing silver nutmeg graters so far noted were cylindrical, measuring $2\frac{1}{2}$ inches to $2\frac{3}{4}$ inches long by $\frac{7}{8}$ inch to 1 inch diameter (86). This design had a slip-on cover and contained a loose tubular grater made from a piece of silver plate invisibly seamed vertically. The lid was constructed from two pieces of silver, the circular end-piece extending a little beyond the body: the base was similarly extended. In some examples the cylinder was partitioned with a convex disc to form a separate container for the nutmeg, in which case slip-on covers were fitted at both ends.

The cylinder was encircled with raised ribbing below the cover to which it formed a stop, thus protecting the rim, and matching ribbing appeared a similar distance from the base. The inner sides of the ribbing were ornamented with bands of engraving; alternatively a band of simple engraving encircled the centre. The flat of the cover was engraved with a simple motif such as a star or tulip (86). Those made between 1697 and 1720 were of Britannia standard silver, the hall-mark encircling the rim and concealed by the slip-on cover.

The tubular graters contained in these cases were made from silver plate, seamed vertically and funnelled at each end to contain the nutmeg, and also to prevent rattling whilst being carried (86). As the graters were not hall-marked, the metal probably contained more copper in its composition than the Britannia standard thus producing rough edges capable of withstanding continual rasping. The piercing might be irregular or in spirals.

Box nutmeg graters preceded these and were probably small heart-shaped boxes such as are recorded as having been assayed from time to time during the late seventeenth century. Nutmeg graters fitted into heart-shaped silver boxes measuring about $1\frac{1}{2}$ inches in each direction have been noted with hall-marks of the 1730s (87). The steel grater fitted into a heart-shaped frame hinging immediately beneath the cover on the same seven-lug hinge. The outer lid consisted of a slightly convex silver plate soldered into a rim of reeded moulding: the base projected a trifle from the body to which it was soldered. The body was shaped into a heart from a single strip of plate and soldered vertically.

From the 1750s heart-shaped nutmeg graters were made with top and bottom lids, each working on a projecting three-lug hinge. One lid opened to reveal a permanently fixed steel grater: the other gave access to the nutmeg. In some of these the perforations are in concentric heart-shaped designs. Circular, oval, rectangular, and square boxes were made to this design: seldom are these hall-marked or provided with a blued grater.

Small egg-shaped nutmeg graters were made from the 1770s to 1790, when they tended to become larger owing to the obligation to present them for hall-marking (86). Such a design unscrewed into two sections, the lower usually a little less than twice the depth of the upper section. A circular grater in a silver frame fitted into the lower rim by pressure. Surfaces were usually perfectly smooth apart from ribbing around the screw-joint. The pre-1790 series was struck with a maker's mark inside the apex of each section.

Some were hand-raised from the plate and the rims thickened to take the threads for screwing together. Others, surprisingly for this period, were spun, the vertical marks caused by pressure of the wooden tool and circular marks brought about by revolving in the lathe being visible on the interior surface.

The mark of Samuel Massey, 8 Foster Lane, London, entered at Goldsmiths' Hall in 1773, is found on many egg-shaped nutmeg graters, hand-raised and spun, as well as on delicate examples finely embossed and chased all over with flowers, foliage, and scrollwork, around the small cartouche left to display the owner's crest. The London hall-marks are struck inside the covers of such nutmeg graters, the maker's mark only in the base.

Associated with the egg-shaped series were the acorn nutmeg graters, the majority being the work of Samuel Pemberton, Birmingham (87). They had small slip-on covers and might be ornamented with bright-cutting. Walnut and nutmeg-shaped graters have also been noted.

Nutmeg graters resembling official maces were so shaped as a play upon the name mace, a spice ground from the dried outer covering of the nutmeg (86). The stem of the mace unscrewed from the crown to reveal a steel wire corkscrew in the form of a helix screw spiral. After about 1790 the worm of the corkscrew was usually fluted, a refinement considered to ease the passage of the spiral through the cork. The base of the raised or cast crown was strengthened with a socket through which the shank of the corkscrew passed and was rivetted over inside. The rim was strengthened and threaded to take the circular grater, over which was screwed a domed cap with a knop finial. The maker's mark on this series is DT and none has been noted with a hall-mark. In some examples the corkscrew cover also contained a tubular grater which was tinned to prevent rusting. In these the domed cover unscrewed to give direct access to the nutmeg in its container, which was cast and lathe finished.

Nutmeg graters in the form of oval or cylindrical boxes with slip-on interchange-able lids top and bottom are also small and light in weight (*87*). The upper lid, which might be slightly domed, gave access to the fixed grater, the lower to the nutmeg and also to the powdered nutmeg. Most of these bear the marks of the Birmingham silversmiths Thomas Willmore and Samuel Pemberton. The hall-mark is struck in full on each lid and omitted from the body. The majority bear date letters from 1795 to 1800 and may be undecorated or ornamented with bright-cutting.

A series of somewhat larger square and rectangular nutmeg graters had a top lid opening on a hinge to reveal a fixed grater, and the base lid opening sideways to give access to the box (*87*). This lid extended a little beyond the box at the end opposite the hinge to facilitate opening. The hinges are virtually invisible when the box is closed, the lower being so designed that the lid opens at right angles and no more.

The bodies of these and other boxes were usually strengthened by the addition of a band of plate encircling the interior of the upper lid, the hinges being concealed in a narrow box-like projection running the length of the lid within the box. Some of these nutmeg graters are plain, others are decorated with bright-cut engraving, occasionally in such a way as to give an all-over scintillating effect, or with designs carried out entirely by punches of various sizes. Nutmeg graters of this type were made considerably heavier from about 1810 and all surfaces might be engine-turned. The lids of outwardly similar boxes, sometimes oval, dating from about 1790, open to reveal a steel grater fitted into a silver frame hinging to the right and slightly beyond the vertical.

Urn-shaped nutmeg graters, oval on plan and split down the sides from rim to square or round foot where they hinged, date from about 1780 (*87*). The oval lid was domed with a moulded rim and a ball finial. Lid and foot had three-lug hinges. The sides were shaped from the plate; the foot and stem cast; the lid hand-raised. When opened a steel grater came into view, shaped to follow the outline of the urn.

In the early nineteenth century appeared the round or oval cylinder with a long, narrow steel grater set in one side of the tube and covered with a silver lid, to one end of which was hinged a cover fitting over the cylinder top and hinged at the base (*87*). In some instances a third hinge permitted the base to be opened also, so that the nutmeg could be more easily grated, with base, lid, and cover lying flat. Most of these split cylinders were plain surfaced, but late examples might be engine-turned.

Large table nutmeg graters in the shape of a half-cylinder with a silver frame including a semicircular handle were accompaniments of the toddy bowl from about 1800: these enabled the nutmeg to be powdered more speedily. They resemble a kitchen grater, 4 to 10 inches in length, with top and bottom ends covered, the

70, 71, 72 SPICE DREDGERS with octagonal containers, by Glover Johnson, London, 1716, 1718, and 1726

73, 74, 75 BALUSTER-SHAPED SPICE DREDGERS with domed covers; London hall-marks for 1740, 1754, and 1727 *Courtesy of Messrs. William Bruford and Son Ltd.*

76, 77, 78, 79   A PAIR OF VASE-SHAPED CASTERS with low-domed sprinklers, for pepper and salt (76, 77), by T. and J. C. Creswick, Sheffield, 1812. (78) CYLINDRICAL MUFFINEER with flat lid, Scottish provincial, 1795. (79) STEMMED MUFFINEER assembled from factory-made units, London, 1790
All by courtesy of Mr. John Bell

80, 81   SWEETMEAT BASKET (80) with silver wire sides, by William Vincent, 1771; (81) SWEETMEAT BASKET with borders composed of hand-cut scrollwork and pales, London, 1792. *Courtesy of Messrs. Harvey and Gore*

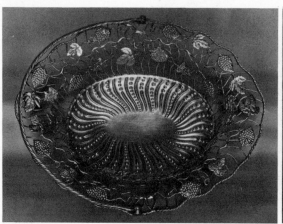
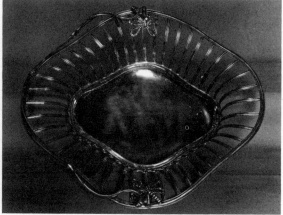

82, 83   SWEETMEAT BASKET (82) with wirework frame overlaid with chased fruiting vines, London 1762; (83) SWEETMEAT BASKET with wire framework and applied bows below the hinges, by W. Plummer, 1762

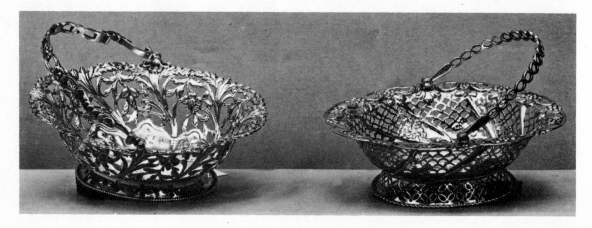

84, 85   SWEETMEAT BASKETS raised from the plate and hand pierced, with collet feet and swing handles
In the Victoria and Albert Museum

lower being hinged to permit removal of the ground nutmeg. The steel grater per-forations formed a pattern of concentric circles and might be concealed beneath a sliding cover of silver.

The majority of the frames had gadrooned rims; in small examples the frames were gadrooned across their entire width, or reeded. Occasionally there was an orna-mental cast and chased motif at the centre of the bow. In others a cylindrical steel grater was set in silver rims top and bottom, with silver side pieces continuing over the top to form a semicircular handle. A rare late-eighteenth-century type of nut-meg grater resembled a rectangular bat set in a silver wire frame extended at one end and shaped to form a handle.

Although numerous nutmeg graters are monogrammed or initialed, few are found with crests, suggesting that those who drank more costly wines did not find it necessary to add the nutmeg's aromatic flavour.

Chapter Three

I THE SERVICE OF SAUCE: SAUCERS, BOATS, TUREENS, LADLES

IQUANT sauces, relishes, and pickles supplemented the powdered spices required for flavouring the dried foods of much everyday fare in earlier centuries. These were prepared by specialists in a household department known as the saucery under the superintendence of the Yeoman of the Sauces. The *Household Ordinances*, 1440, laid down that "there is none that dyneth in their offyces, savinge onely the cookes, the scullery and the saucery." The *Survey of Nonesuch*, 1650, records "one little Timber building, commonly called the Saucery House, conteyning foure little roomes used by the Yeoman of the Sauces."

The Yeoman was an important household official dressed in distinctive livery who attended table "redye with vyneger and colde water" to counteract the fiery tang associated with the lavish use of his sauces. Elizabethan and Stewart diners cooled their mouths with lumps of ice served on small glass plates, a custom vigorously condemned in 1723 by Sir Richard Steele as "fashionable though vulgar." For the same reason wines and other drinks were served as cold as possible.

Sauces were brought to table in deep, rimless circular dishes of silver, tin, or pewter, none of these metals imparting an unpleasant flavour to foods. These little dishes, averaging about 6 inches in diameter, were called saucers, a term defined in *Bailey's Dictionary* 1728, as "a Little Dish to hold Sauce." The word's common use in association with tea and coffee cups dates from the following decade.

Silver saucers were included in every service of plate. They were never gilded, because the film of gold was liable to be damaged by certain food acids such as lemon juice and vinegar. These saucers were hand-raised from the plate with shallow sides slightly rounded and their rims strengthened with thin moulding. The Earl of Northampton possessed "half a dozen sawcers 24 oz" in white silver when his plate was inventoried in 1614. When Charles I was captured by the Cromwellians in September 1647 he was supplied with "one gilt salt, Tobias; 12 gilt trencher plates crowned E; 2 knives; one fork gilt; 2 spoons gilt; two saucers white." The inclusion of two ungilded saucers in this gilded service emphasises the important part played by sauces in giving zest to foods at this period.

A saucer might be fitted with a pair of vertical ring handles in the reign of James I and later with two flat or shell-shaped handles soldered diametrically opposite to each other (*88*). Such saucers were of thinly beaten silver embossed with

66

simple punch-work patterns, usually six or eight panels divided by radiating borders encircling a central design or shield engraved with a coat of arms or initials, and sometimes a date: the rim might be serrated. These saucers might also be used for the service of soft fruit.

Handles began to be omitted from the early 1660s and by the mid-1670s had been abandoned. The centre of the saucer was now left with a smooth surface, the concave bouge being divided by embossed ridges into plain panels, often eighteen in number. The rim might be scalloped, serrated, or shaped in cyma outline (89).

Georgian saucers might be of a design embossed with ridges radiating from the centre to the outer edge of the rim. This rim might now be wide and flat, made as a separate entity and soldered horizontally to the top of the bouge. Its upper surface might be reeded after the fashion of plates, or encircled with a wide band of applied cast and chased ornament. Saucers remained part of the silver table service for pickles and other highly flavoured relishes throughout the reigns of the first two Georges. They might be incorporated in the silver epergne, one being supported by each of the several outspreading branches, and often containing a flint-glass liner.

Boat-shaped saucers were also used for flavouring foods with semi-liquid sauces. In 1630 several "boat saucers" were submitted to the London assay office for hall-marking. This is the earliest reference so far noted to the sauce-boat and it may be assumed to have been fitted with a pair of vertical ring handles. Nothing further is heard of the sauce-boat, although it no doubt existed side by side with the saucer, until the Hanoverians popularised those smooth semi-liquid sauces in which a single distinctive flavour predominated. These sauces were tabled cold in small boat-shaped vessels from which each individual could serve himself. Saucers containing pickles and other relishes continued as part of the table service. The inventory of plate taken at His Majesty's Jewel House in 1725 describes a magnificent gilt epergne "containing one Table Basket and Cover, one Foote, four Salt Boxes, four small Salts, four Branches with Saucers, six Casters, four Sauceboats."

The silver sauce-boat was lipped at each end and had a cast scroll handle attached vertically to the centre of each side, to facilitate passing at table (90). The rim on each side was shaped with a double cyma divided by an outcurving semicircle, its surface supporting the upper terminal of the handle. The rim was strengthened with narrow moulding to prevent accidental bending whilst being cleaned, and the boat was carried on a low oval moulded foot.

Early George I sauce-boats were of Britannia standard and were notably weighty. This weight was reduced by about a third when sterling silver was restored in 1720. The centres of the side rims were now raised rather higher than the two lips: later in the decade the outcurving semicircles were widened and the curves of the cyma accentuated. Soon after 1727 the centres of the side rims were made considerably higher than the two lips, and the lower surface of each lip might now be strengthened with a thin cast ornament such as an escallop shell. Double-scroll handles were usual and might be capped with palm leaves.

Double-lipped sauce-boats were made in six parts: a central oval body, hand-raised from the plate; two moulded lips soldered to its ends resembling those on jugs; a pair of cast scroll or double-scroll handles; and an oval moulded foot. Occasionally the lips were shaped in a piece with the body, which was devoid of decoration apart from an engraved coat of arms or crest. These sauce-boats were sold in matching pairs measuring approximately 8½ inches long by 5 inches wide.

A second series of double-lipped sauce-boats was made early in the nineteenth century, some cast with florid ornament in relief, others with bodies stamped in two halves from rolled plate and tool-embossed. The style was repeated by mid-Victorian silversmiths using mechanical processes although hand-made examples of very light weight have been noted.

Single-spouted sauce-boats date from the early 1720s, but George I examples are extremely rare. In this design a wide upcurved spout projected beyond the body, designed to facilitate the pouring of slow-moving semi-liquid sauce (92). The body, left severely smooth, as embossed work would act as a brake against pouring, was hand-raised from the plate into ogee outline above an oval moulded foot. A double-scroll handle rising above the rim, edged with narrow moulding and extending half-way down the body, was attached to the rim by means of a forked unit. This type of sauce-boat continued to be made until the 1760s. A later specimen might have a scalloped rim and a double-scroll handle capped with scroll ornament. Some of these weighed as little as 7 ounces.

Early in the 1730s the moulded foot might be replaced by four elaborately designed legs, cast and chased, a pair below each side of the spout and handle (93). Each joined the body with an expansive mask, usually a lion, the short leg ending in a paw, claw-and-ball, or shell foot. Soon it became customary to attach three legs, one beneath the spout, two at the back (95). Scroll feet and hoof or shell feet with scrolling knees were frequent on these.

The rim of the body was slightly everted, the outer surface encircled with engraved scrollwork, matching ornament on the inner rim, but not continuing over the spout which remained smoothly plain. The sides were engraved with a coat of arms or crest. In some instances the sides of the container were further ornamented with applied swags of cast and chased flowers, foliage, shellwork, scrolls, and other rococo curiosities, extending between the masks. In such circumstances the crest was engraved beneath the spout. The sauce-boat interior thus remained smooth and easy to clean, a style always preferred. The rising double-scroll handle, now heavier, extended outward 3 or 4 inches, capped with leaves and sometimes scaled. By about

86   NUTMEG GRATERS: (*upper row*) cylindrical with tubular rasps, 1704–7; (*lower row*) two in the form of maces with corkscrews concealed in the stems ; centre example by Samuel Massey, 1780s
Courtesy of Messrs. Bracher and Sydenham

87   NUTMEG GRATERS, the top row engraved with bright-cutting; the lowest row cylindrical and vase-shaped, shown open and closed. *Courtesy of Messrs. Bracher and Sydenham*

88   SAUCER with punched decoration and flat ears. Dated 1664. *Courtesy of Messrs E. T. Biggs and Son Ltd.*
89   THREE FROM A SET OF SIX TWENTY-LOBED SAUCE DISHES, by Edmund Pearce, 1710. Diameter 4¼ inches
In the collection of Mrs. William B. Munro

90, 91   DOUBLE-LIPPED SAUCE BOATS with shaped rims, double-scroll handles and oval moulded feet: (90) by Thomas Tearle, 1728; (91) by Sarah Holoday, 1791. *Courtesy of Messrs. Christie, Manson, and Woods Ltd.*

92   SINGLE-LIPPED SAUCE BOAT by Joseph Daniel, 1732. *Courtesy of Messrs. Garrard and Co. Ltd.*

93, 94 PAIR OF ENGRAVED SAUCE BOATS with paw feet, by Paul de Lamerie, 1739 *Courtesy of Messrs. Bracher and Sydenham*

95 SAUCE BOAT with gadrooned body, three lion-mask and paw legs, and double-scroll handle capped with a leaf, by Edward Feline, 1735 *Courtesy of Messrs. D. & J. Wellby, Ltd.*

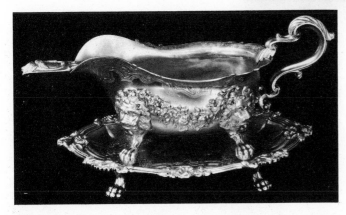

96, 97 ONE OF A PAIR OF SAUCE BOATS (96) with lion-mask and claw-and-ball feet, stands, and ladles, by Paul de Lamerie, 1735. *Courtesy of Mr. S. J. Phillips.* (97) ONE OF A SET OF FOUR SHELL-SHAPED SAUCE BOATS with short-stemmed moulded feet, London, 1753. *Courtesy of Messrs. Harvey and Gore*

98, 99 SAUCE BOAT (98) with shell-shaped body and handle in the form of a lamprey, by Paul Storr, 1819. *Courtesy of Messrs. Holmes (Jewellers) Ltd.* (99) ONE OF A PAIR OF SAUCE BOATS by Fuller White, 1748 *Courtesy of Messrs. Spink and Son Ltd.*

100 ARGYLE heated with a central box-iron in a cylindrical sleeve; the upper lid is for inserting the box-iron, the lower one gives access to the gravy; London, 1789. *Courtesy of Messrs. Harvey and Gore*

101 CYLINDRICAL ARGYLE with hot-water jacket; decorated with bright-cut engraving; by Hester Bateman, London, 1783
Courtesy of Messrs. Birch and Gaydon Ltd.

102 ARGYLE with lower hot-water compartment of the early type, by W. Gundry, London, 1776
Courtesy of Messrs. Birch and Gaydon Ltd.

1740 the handle might be cast and chased in the form of a dolphin, lamprey, or snake, its tail attached to the back of the vessel, rising upward from the rim, and curving forward over the body.

The sauce-boat might be made less expensively at this period by shaping three pieces of plate into spout, back, and sides and base, joining them invisibly and strengthening with four narrow flutes. The metal was of thicker gauge than formerly and the rim needed no strengthening moulding. The rim might now be encircled with deep rococo design, a matching motif extending beneath the lip. The scroll rim was more frequent, however, with a chased shell beneath the lip.

Sauce-boats in repoussé and chased work were in the minority, their interior surface irregularities being difficult to keep clean. They were used for serving melted butter, then a fashionable sauce particularly associated with fish (95). They date from the 1730s and at first a single row of bold gadrooning might encircle the body (95): then came delicately embossed rococo work, often a medley of flowers and foliage motifs enclosing a reserve to be engraved with a coat of arms. Other designs are found such as a goat and sheep jumping hurdles. Early plain examples have been noted in which embossed decoration has been carried out at a much later date, converting sauce-boats into butter-boats.

From about 1750 the rim might be enriched with gadrooned or knurled moulding, and short legs with shell-shaped feet might extend from expansive shells soldered to the body (99). Later in the century the rim might be edged with beading which in factory work was stamped into the body. The loop handle was reeded. The sauce-boat body by now might be incurved towards the everted rim, but more usually was helmet-shaped. There was little variation in shape from this period, although fluted bodies with hoof feet similar to earlier hand-raised examples are found bearing hall-marks of the early nineteenth century. Applied festoons of flowers and panels of trellis work date from about 1820.

The Victorian single-lipped sauce-boat often had a plain body with bulging sides, a gadrooned rim which might be scalloped, a double-scroll handle and three hoof feet. Another design had a high uprising spout, almost vertical, and an uprising scroll handle, on an elaborately moulded stem with four scroll feet. Variants were innumerable.

The sizes of sauce-boats varied, large, medium, and small in the same pattern being catalogued in the late eighteenth century. In a price list it has been noted that footed sauce-boats were at least 30 per cent. more costly than those with three legs— sometimes as much as 50 per cent. more. They were always sold in pairs, but from 1750 there were double and triple pairs and occasional sets of a dozen.

Shell-shaped sauce-boats with graceful, hand-raised bodies and short-stemmed moulded feet date between the 1740s and 1760s (98). The back of the body, when not in a true shell spiral, curved over upon itself with a leaf-capped double-scroll handle. The rim was strengthened with moulded ornament and a cast and chased shell or other appropriate motif applied below the spout lip. Shell-shaped sauce-boats on shaped moulded oval feet appear to have been intended for the fish course, as the handle was frequently cast in the form of an appropriate device such as a heron catching a fish, a lamprey, or a dolphin. An elaborate cast loop may also be found, sometimes terminating in the head of a sea-monster. Diarists at this period have noted that each person was served with "an almost entire fish."

The oval moulded foot was sometimes chased with scrollwork and shells. More frequently the oval was outlined with eight scallops and the instep chased with simple ornament. Occasionally the foot was ornamented with a group of applied motifs matching chased or engraved foliage encircling the rim, which was usually strengthened with narrow scroll moulding. A pair of shell-shaped sauce-boats is sometimes found with stands, ladles, and a matching cream-boat, all struck with the same hall-mark (96).

The shell-shaped sauce-boat continued well into the period of classical design in silversmithing. There was a revival of this form early in the nineteenth century in a heavier, florid style consisting of highly elaborate casting applied to a factory-made body.

A change in culinary fashion during the early 1750s required sauces to be less spicy but served piping hot, bringing into use the covered sauce-tureen, sometimes accompanied by a silver stand. The stand had a raised centre, the better to protect the table surface from damage by heat. The earliest of these tureens had a canoe-shaped body with a pair of handles rising from the rim and recurving downward to the base of the body (103). The body rim, the edge of the short-stemmed oval or shaped foot and the rim of the stand were strengthened by simple moulding in a matching design. The lid was centrally domed, and an urn or berry finial might rise from a rosette of palm leaves. Ring finials were corded, accompanying handles similarly decorated. The majority were smooth-surfaced: others might be gadrooned on bowl and cover, engraved, or ornamented with applied swags and medallions.

A sauce-tureen and its stand from about 1800 might have a circular or rounded oblong body with D-handles, supported by a short-stemmed round or square foot, or by four cast and chased feet perhaps in the form of dolphin heads, animal paws, or scrolls (105). At this period the more lavish sauce-tureens were gilded. Most of these tureens were assembled from factory-made carcasses, smooth inside, while ornamented with a wide variety of chased castings. An alternative was a partly fluted body, flat-based, with lion's mask and ring handles. This might be ornamented with bands of bright-cut engraving below the rim.

From the opening of the nineteenth century a series of covered sauce-boats appeared in which the rounded-oblong tureen with bulging sides was supported on four wide scroll feet. Except for early examples these were factory-built from strips of plate. They continued to be made until Victorian times, when they might have gadrooned feet and rims and ring handles to the covers. It was a fashionable conceit at this time for crest handles to be fitted, cast and chased. Few were made after the 1860s, when the sauce-boat came into its own again.

Although sauce-boats were shaped with spouts for pouring sauce or melted butter, it soon became fashionable to spoon out the sauce with a ladle, one ladle to each sauce-boat, the handle shaped to the curve of the spout against which it rested. A pair of sauce-boats with ladles bearing the mark of Paul de Lamerie and the date letter for 1739 have escallop shell bowls and eagle-head finials.

From the middle of the eighteenth century sauce ladles were usually included in the table service of forks, spoons, and so on. Bowls were commonly in the shape of escallop shells or smoothly plain. Finial design followed a chronological sequence. A pair of sauce ladles hall-marked in 1752 have escallop shell bowls with corkscrew finials; another pair of the same year have similar finials with plain ladles. This design was followed by the old English pattern which from about 1780 to the 1820s might have a feather edge or a border of bright-cut engraving. The fiddle pattern, which might be reeded and display a shell motif, dated from the 1760s; then came, in this order, thread and shell, king's pattern, queen's pattern, and husk. In the nineteenth century these were joined by the shell and hour-glass motif. The popular feather edge consisted of a border chased with short oblique lines resembling the barbs of a feather. Such a stem often terminated in an embossed escutcheon engraved with crest or cypher. Stem decoration, emphasising the graceful outline of sauce ladles, dates from the 1760s.

II ARGYLES

Carving at the dining-table was an early Georgian innovation influenced by the introduction of white salt-glaze carving dishes by the Staffordshire potters. Formerly meat and poultry had been carved on silver or pewter dishes at the side table by the butler. Carving at table for more than two decades was a privilege of the hostess or a lady deputy. At the wedding of the Princess Royal to the Prince of Orange in 1733 the Countess of Hertford carved at the high table. By the 1740s, however, the host customarily undertook the duties associated with carving. Inevitably, however, in a large gathering, the meal was served slowly. The hot gravy that had taken the place of the old pungent sauces gradually cooled and congealed while he wrestled with the joints, since the customary design for a sauce vessel was still an open boat of silver, porcelain, or pottery.

This semi-cold gravy was heartily disliked by John, 4th Duke of Argyll (*d.* 1770), who emphasised his opinion by designing his own gravy containers for his table. These were internally heated. The silversmiths appear to have taken note of this vessel in the early 1760s, and under the duke's name, mis-spelt, it was used on fashionable dining-tables, keeping gravy hot throughout the meat course. The vessel somewhat resembled a small teapot with an excessively long, narrow swan-neck spout, and continued in fashionable and general use for about a century: argyles were illustrated in a silversmith's catalogue of the early 1860s. A long series was made in silver, more in Sheffield plate, and also in electroplate. Present-day owners of these somewhat quaint-looking little vessels are often perplexed regarding their original purpose, although in their heyday every well-equipped dinner-table was furnished with at least one pair of argyles.

Collectors will find that four distinct methods were used for keeping the gravy hot within its silver container: a hot-water jacket (*101*); a central box-iron (*100*); a central hot-water chamber; a lower hot-water compartment (*102*). It appears from the hall-marks on existing examples that the earliest type was made with the hot-water jacket: an example has been noted hall-marked in 1769. The box-iron heater was only patented in 1774 by John Wadham, a brazier of St. George-in-the-East, London, and no example of the type with a lower hot-water compartment has been noted hall-marked earlier than 1776. Argyles were extensively produced at this time, for they were entered on the assay office price list, the charge being two-pence each for hall-marking. The vessel contained two gills of gravy and measured about 7 inches in height.

Argyles for the most part were made from rolled plate by factory methods, being so designed that costly hand-raising was avoided, although the argyle with a lower hot-water compartment might be hand-raised. The vase-shaped body was stamped in two halves and invisibly seamed. Lid, foot, and handle were stock components found in other articles of silver plate.

The argyle with a hot-water jacket (*101*) had a cylindrical body with a detachable cover. This was fitted with a double lining or outer jacket to contain boiling water inserted through a socket at the time near the handle and sealed with a screwed stopper. In later examples a less expensive self-closing hinged cover was substituted for the screwed cap. Opposite, or at right angles to the upcurved ebony or hard-wood handle, rose a swan-neck spout, long and thin. This was set low on the body and passed through the hot-water jacket into the bottom of the gravy container where the gravy would be richest. The inner vessel might be of silver or of Sheffield plate to avoid the hazards associated with the use of copper as a container for acidic foods where careless cleaning might result in an accumulation of poisonous verdigris. The long, curved, and extremely slender spout, designed to prevent

103, 104 PAIR OF FLUTED SAUCE TUREENS WITH COVERS AND STANDS, by Daniel Smith and Robert Sharp, 1784. *Courtesy of Messrs. Spink and Son Ltd.*

105 SAUCE TUREEN WITH COVER AND STAND by Paul Storr and Benjamin Smith, London, 1805 *Courtesy of Messrs. Harvey and Gore*

106 SET OF FOUR SAUCE TUREENS with four scroll legs, by Paul Storr, 1802 *Courtesy of Messrs. William Bruford and Son Ltd.*

107 OCTAGONAL SAUCE TUREENS, 1789; TWO SUGAR BASKETS, gilt-lined, with swing handles, 1790; FOUR GILT-LINED SALT-CELLARS, 1792–4. All by Henry Chawner, London *Courtesy of Messrs. William Bruford and Son Ltd.*

108, 109, 110   SAUCEPAN (108) with domed lid and ivory finial, by J. Franklin, London, 1835. *Courtesy of Mr. John Bell.* (109) SPOUTED SAUCEPAN with flat cap cover and three claw-and-ball legs, London, 1685; (110) SILVER SKILLET with the pot raised from the plate, and three cast and turned legs. Maker D.W., London, 1645
In the collection of Mrs. William B. Munro

111, 112   SKILLET AND COVER (111) with flat thumbpiece, on three paw feet, by James Birkby, Hull, *c.* 1650. *Courtesy of Messrs. Sotheby and Co. Ltd.* (112) SCOTTISH SAUCEPAN, by William Jamieson, Aberdeen, 1810. Diameter 4 inches, length overall 9 inches, weight 7¼ ounces. *Courtesy of Mr. John Bell*

113   SAUCEPAN with cylindrical body and everted rim, by William Fleming, 1702. *Courtesy of Mr. John Bell*

114, 115   SAUCEPAN with beak-spout (114), hinged lid, and stand with lamp; by J. Wakelin and W. Taylor, 1786. *Courtesy of Messrs. E. T. Biggs and Sons Ltd.* (115) CYLINDRICAL SAUCEPAN with hinged cover for spout: the handle fits into a slot and can be removed. By Hamilton and Co., Inverness, 1790. *Courtesy of Mr. John Bell*

over-large servings of the rich liquid, was particularly difficult to clean. This type of argyle was made throughout the period and is still a satisfactory coffee jug for one or two people.

Body shapes followed the chronological sequence of teapots, the low domed, detachable cover being succeeded by hinged lids of current highly domed patterns and decorated with plainly turned vase-shaped or knopped finials. The body usually remained plain but might be delicately engraved with festoons and garlands, or decorated with bright-cut engraving. On an undecorated example a crest or cypher might be engraved on the side of the body to the right of the handle: on an engraved body a cartouche was usually included in the design for this purpose. The rims of lid and base might be strengthened with moulded reeding, beading, or gadrooning.

Early examples of these hot-water-jacket argyles were fitted with neither foot-ring nor feet to lift the flat base, heated by the hot gravy, above the polished table, which was thus liable to be disfigured. The same difficulty was encountered in the design of many late eighteenth-century teapots, and in each case the immediate solution—a separate stand—and the subsequent development of a single-unit design, was the same. The stand consisted of a simple design in silver or Sheffield plate supported by four ball feet or four short moulded feet. Seldom, however, has the stand remained with the argyle. The stand was discarded from about 1800 and replaced by a flaring foot-rim of deep moulding attached to the argyle.

The argyle containing a box-iron heater inside was usually designed with a vase-shaped body rising from a low stem in the form of a slender spool expanding towards a square or circular foot (*100*). Within, rising vertically from the base, was a lidded socket of silver or Sheffield plate designed to contain a cylinder of hot iron. The argyle lid was shaped with a high dome so as to accommodate the largest box-iron possible for such a small vessel. Such an argyle was, of course, nothing more than a miniature tea-urn with a spout in place of a tap. It was usually plain-surfaced. Some early examples had the upper body encircled with applied or engraved classic ornament and festoons: after 1785 the lower part of the body might be fluted, and from 1790 this decoration might cover the entire body. Some vase-shaped argyles have beak-shaped spouts like jugs: these are rare.

During the mid-1770s a more capacious water-heated argyle was evolved, having a baluster-shaped body expanding into a spreading base (*102*). The interior was divided horizontally, only the swelling upper portion containing gravy. The lower section was filled with boiling water through a projecting socket covered by a hinged lid. A narrow moulded foot-ring lifted the body above the table. Handle and spout in this type of argyle were placed at right angles to each other, the thin spout emerging from the bottom of the gravy container opposite the socket. In most argyles of this type made from about 1785 the body was constructed in two sections and raised upon a deep-spreading foot-ring with the edge strengthened by beaded or gadrooned moulding.

The argyle with a central hot-water chamber was made during the two final decades of the eighteenth century with an oval or hexagonal body and a straight, tapering spout rising exactly to the height of the body rim. The cylindrical hot-water container rose centrally from the base and was sealed with a screwed stopper. The gravy was poured around this. The domed cover was detachable. Such argyles might be decorated all over with bright-cut engraving.

Sheffield plate competition took the bulk of the argyle trade in the early nineteenth century: those made in silver were usually of the hot-water-jacket type. The demand for silver argyles revived with the invention of electroplated copper and a more elaborate series was made. In this design a cylindrical body had a cast and chased spout attached with an expansive scalloped edged junction: the spout opening was sealed with a self-closing lid. The handle was of silver, double-scroll design, with ivory insulators and leaf flanges with sockets joining them to the body. The lid was of the double dome type with an ivory finial, and the flat base was encircled with expansive moulding. It was usually plain, but simple engraving might be added for about eight shillings extra.

III SAUCEPANS AND BRAZIERS

Elizabethan apothecaries recommended wealthy patients to drink from silver cups and cook in silver skillets or saucepans. Scientists of the period were aware of the food poisoning hazards associated with brass or copper utensils left in the charge of careless servants. Less scientifically, laymen such as Jonathan Swift in his *Directions to Servants*, 1729, advocated the use of a silver saucepan for such duties as melting butter for the very good reason that brass gave it a ''taste.''

Particularly important were silver saucepans in the preparation of piquant sauces which disguised the unpalatable flavours of preserved foods (see p. 66). The acids contained in many of these sauces were liable to act upon the surface of base metal and affect the flavour as well as endangering health. Silver saucepans had long been considered essential, however, by those who could afford the precious metal. The cooked foods, still in the covered saucepans from which they were served, were carried into the dining-room on burning charcoal braziers.

The *Oxford English Dictionary* defines a saucepan as ''a small skillet with a long handle in which sauce and other small things are boiled,'' and early inventories associate these skillets, known also as chafers, with such charcoal braziers termed chafing dishes. These burned special court charcoal prepared from flexible woods stripped of their bark, which might crackle and fly about whilst burning. Such coals required little draught, yet emitted an intense, glowing heat until entirely consumed. A silver blow-pipe was used to revive the fire if necessary. Not until the second half of the seventeenth century did the term "sawce-pan" come into use. Such vessels are usually referred to by present-day collectors as brandy saucepans, but there seems no adequate reason for this.

Silver saucepans were in continual use for nearly three centuries. Existing examples bear hall-marks dating from the early years of James I until mid-Victorian times: saucepans dating from the 1740s are plentiful.

Three types of saucepan were made, in six sizes of $\frac{1}{4}$, $\frac{1}{2}$, $\frac{3}{4}$, 1 and $1\frac{1}{2}$ pints, and 1 quart capacity: (a) hand-raised from the plate, the shape from the 1660s being slightly bellied with a smoothly rounded base rim (109); (b) a similar type spun from the plate and dating from the 1780s onwards (108); (c) a slightly tapering cylindrical body made from sheet silver and seamed vertically, with an inserted base and a moulded foot ring (113).

The forerunner of these familiar types, made until about 1660, was a cylindrical saucepan, hand-raised from plate of heavy gauge, and lacking a pouring spout. It stood upon three or four vertical, stumpy, pear-shaped legs, cast and turned. The ebony or hard-wood handle fitted into a thick, lengthy socket and rose only slightly above the horizontal (110). A flat cap cover was usual and the only ornament was a coat of arms engraved opposite to the handle. In one mid-seventeenth-century type the deep cap lid had a flat thumbpiece soldered horizontally to it, close to the rim, enabling it to be used, inverted, as a porringer.

Thinner plate was used from about 1650 and a small saucepan complete with flat feet might weigh no more than 4 ounces. The rim of the base was rounded and fitted with three outspanning cast feet, often of the claw-and-ball variety, the points of attachment being reinforced by discs cut from plate. A tubular swan-neck spout might rise from near the base (119). More frequently a pouring lip was made by expanding the rim slightly outward into a V-shape at a point at right angles to the handle. This was later replaced by the beak spout, more expansive than could be made by raising the metal. A V-shaped section was cut from the rim, extending almost halfway down the body, and a triangular beak lip was applied, the lower point of this spout sometimes displaying a decorative terminal. These two types of spout continued in use throughout the period. From about 1700 a hinged flap might cover the opening of the beak spout.

The handle was placed at right angles to the spout and rose at an angle of about forty-five degrees. A single socket was attached to the saucepan on a small reinforcement plate soldered immediately below the rim and was fitted with a turned handle of ivory, ebony, or black-stained hard-wood. An occasional example has been recorded with a flat-pierced handle of silver extending almost horizontally from the side of the body.

The slight inward slope to the saucepan body became an established feature in the 1660s. The lid was a flat cap with a central handle, either a knop finial or a wire scroll. The William and Mary saucepan was distinctly bellied and might stand upon three short vertical or outspanning legs terminating in scroll feet (109). The handle socket was frequently joined to the body by a cut-card cartouche. By Anne's reign, however, the vessel was without legs, being intended for use in association with the spirit-lamp that now outmoded the brazier. The cover was low-domed with a knob finial, a style that continued until about 1820, when it might have an extension covering the spout opening. Towards the end of the eighteenth century the cover became highly domed with an ivory or ebony knob, and spread a little beyond the edge of the pan. Lids have been supplied to early saucepans at later periods and these usually lack hall-marks: rim moulding was often added at the same time.

The handle socket was an important feature of a silver saucepan, for the pan's life of useful service depended upon its stability. Sockets were made from the plate, shaped at first in cylindrical form, then slightly tapering, this becoming more pronounced during the late eighteenth century. The wood handle fitted firmly into the socket, a silver rivet being driven through socket and handle as an additional safeguard. At first the handle was turned with a collar to fit flush against the plain rim of the socket. By 1700 the socket was made of thinner plate and its rim strengthened with rounded moulding. The pan attachment was at first soldered directly to a reinforcement disc with a supporting bracket beneath. It was soon found that the socket was inclined to separate from this. Thereupon the plate was made much thicker and shaped in the form of a shield or heart, the socket being inserted and hammered over a slight depression encircling the hole. This was welded and could not pull away. Later a cast socket with an expanded flange was soldered to the pan and the handle inserted.

The smooth surface of the plainly curved hand-raised saucepan possessed no crevices for the lodgment of food left by careless cleaning. Even the rim was substantially thickened in the plate to avoid the necessity of encircling it with strengthening moulding and thus producing a crevice. Usually the only ornament was the expansive coat of arms engraved on the majority of such pans, so that a stolen vessel could only be melted down for disposal; the cover was crested. A few saucepans have been noted with fluted sides and wavy rims: these bear mid-George II hall-marks. From the 1780s saucepans were infrequently hand-raised, the less costly process of spinning being used instead.

The cylindrical saucepan was used concurrently with the hand-raised and subsequent spun types from about 1690 (*113*). The body tapered outward with an inserted base and heavy moulded foot-ring to ensure stability should the base eventually bulge. The rim might be slightly everted, a feature more accentuated from about 1720, and was without spout or lip. Socket and handle resemble those of contemporaneous hand-raised saucepans. A typical size for such a saucepan was 3½ inches in diameter by 2¼ inches in height. By 1750 the depth might be increased. At this time green-stained ivory handles were not unusual.

Cylindrical saucepans were made in considerable numbers during the first half of the nineteenth century. In some instances they might be fitted with loose linings of silver for making soufflés. By the 1820s the pan might be shallow and the handle replaced by a pair of moulded horizontal loops. Double saucepans in silver date from the 1840s, the lower part with a spun body and the upper of cylindrical form: the cover was interchangeable.

As already noted it had been found convenient by the end of the seventeenth century to discard charcoal from the brazier and put a spirit lamp there instead. The brazier bowl with a wide pierced rim was held slightly above table level by a tripod with three double-scroll legs: later, claw-and-ball or hoof feet were usual. The upper scrolls of the legs were connected to a ring upon which the saucepan rested.

The costly hand-raised brazier bowl was soon abandoned and the upper scrolls of the legs connected by a pierced ring to support the saucepan base. The feet were insulated from the table by small buns or cushions of ebony or hard-wood. A horizontal branch curving from each leg held a smaller ring which fitted a spirit lamp, its wick covered by a hinged dome. One example struck with the London hall-mark for 1703 measured 5¾ inches in diameter and had a circular detachable lamp with three burners.

The spirit lamp at first was slightly more than hemispherical and was raised from the plate, fitted with a flat top containing a wick aperture covered by a hinged dome. A moulded rim encircled the body: this rested upon the supporting ring in the stand. From the 1720s the spirit container was made more capacious, its depth being increased until it almost touched the table. Later the container might be in ogee outline. The less costly cylindrical spirit lamp dates from the 1760s onwards, shaped from a rectangular sheet of silver, a disc base, and a loose-fitting concave cap without a hinged dome to the wick opening (*114*).

The saucepan stand was a simpler contrivance after about 1780, consisting of a plain, deep pan-ring supported by three legs which at first ended in paw feet, and later were connected by a second ring. A slightly smaller ring held between the three legs contained a plain, cylindrical spirit lamp. From the early 1790s the stand, apart from the saucepan ring, might be composed of swage-drawn ribbon, usually reeded.

The cylindrical lamp might contain a large mortar light instead of spirits after about 1800. These mortars were specially made for the purpose. Their wicks were of flax, as cotton could not stand up to the long-continued heat and was not so uniform in its capillary action.

Chapter Four

I MUSTARD POTS

USTARD-MAKING was an established trade at least five centuries ago. Caxton knew "Nicholas the Mustard Maker" in 1483, and a century later Thomas More wrote of "a musterde maker in Cambridge." Mustard-makers, members of the Grocers' Guild, were engaged in growing mustard seed, drying and grinding it in a mill, and mixing the pungent powder with peaflour. This was sold dry, and for table use was made into a paste with the unfermented juice of grapes or with vinegar. A Tudor cookery book described mustard as "a sharp, biting sauce made of small seed bruised and mixed with vinegar." Mustard and sugar formed the gourmet's sauce for pheasant, and mustard sauce was recommended as a relish for brawn, beef, chive, bacon, and mutton.

The earliest reference to the mustard pot so far noted dates to 1380, when John Wycliffe, writing from Oxford, remarked that he always kept at hand a pot of ready-mixed mustard covered with parchment to exclude the air. The Halliwell inventory of 1610 refers to "two silvar musterd pottes." Mustard pots of silver were frequently noted during the 1670s, such as an advertisement in the *London Gazette*, 1676, offering a reward for the recovery of silver plate including a silver mustard pot. It is somewhat surprising to note that only a very few mustard pots were recorded for half a century from the late seventeenth century, suggesting that mustard temporarily lost favour to the period's notably pungent sauces, mustard sauce being a favourite.

The shape of mustard pots until the mid-eighteenth century is a matter of conjecture. The London assay office then listed them as "mustard cans" and charged three-halfpence for the assay. The term "can" had for centuries meant a cylindrical drinking vessel with a handle, the inference being that the mustard pot followed this form. A set of eight mustard pots made by George Methuen, London, and hall-marked 1752 have been noted included in a cruet frame with casters and oil bottles. These have cylindrical bodies, with highly domed and finialled lift-off covers: they have no handles.

Hall-marked examples show that from the early 1760s the mustard pot resembled a small lidded tankard measuring about 3 inches in height and 2 inches in diameter, its flat hinged lid cut with a spoon aperture. Silversmiths for more than half a century listed "mustard tankards." The lid was opened by means of a thumbpiece which hinged backward over a scroll, S- or D-handle of flat silver strip. The cylindrical body was shaped from solid plate seamed invisibly under the handle. Moulding strengthened the outer rim and moulding of similar silhouette, but rather deeper, encircled the base, lifting it slightly above table level: these mouldings were known to silversmiths as hoops. The pot was fitted with a glass liner to simplify cleaning. This basic form has continued uninterruptedly until today with a sequence of minor variations.

Pierced mustard pots in this form were soon in production, fitted with Bristol blue-glass liners against which the brilliance of the silver piercing was displayed to perfection (141). Trellis and large honeycomb piercing resembling fish netting have been noted with hall-marks dating from 1767 until the 1790s. At first these were all hand-made in widely spaced designs cut into plate of a gauge strong enough to accept the stresses caused when lifting by the handle. Designs made from flat silver ribbon extending between rim and base moulding were arranged in all-over repeat patterns such as outlined leaves and pointed ovals. The lid might be flat, highly domed, or double domed, with or without a spoon aperture, which might be cut diametrically opposite to the thumbpiece or at the side. The handle curved from below the rim moulding with the tail ending immediately above table level.

The thumbpiece, known to contemporary silversmiths as the purchase or lever, possessed a hinge attachment resembling that used on ordinary tankards. This rose vertically from a three-lug hinge soldered to the surface of the lid and extended to the upper curve of the handle. Collectors will find several variations during the period. The thumbpiece itself was cast and chased and appeared in several standard designs, the most frequent being the pierced type, with the escallop shell only slightly less popular.

By 1770 fine hand-worked flat piercing appeared on mustard pots, displaying all-over scenes with figures of men, women, animals, and birds prominently embodied in the pattern. Their features and dress were accentuated by engraving, as were the background motifs. A cartouche for engraving a crest was included in the design below the spoon aperture of the lid. Such a mustard pot might be fitted with a low domed lid curving down to the rim. More frequently the lid was flat, its edge encircled with ornamental moulding. Lids were always solid and close-fitting to expose as little as possible of the mixed mustard to the air.

Piercing cut by the hand-press soon followed, the majority of this work being of factory origin, so that workers became thoroughly skilled in producing perfectly formed patterns (147). Some master-silversmiths are known to have employed hand-presses, but these were infrequent until about 1790 owing to the difficulty of obtaining suitable tool steel. Factory piercing appears chiefly in the form of narrow bands composed of repeating motifs. There might be narrow bands of circles or other geometrical motifs top and bottom, with a wider band of upright pales between,

116, 117   OCTAGONAL SCROLL SALT-CELLAR (116) of capstan form with shallow well, by Joseph Sutton, 1681. *Courtesy of Messrs. Christie, Manson, and Woods, Ltd.*; (117) CAPSTAN SALT with expanded base and top and three scroll handles, London, 1656. *Courtesy of Messrs. Christie, Manson, and Woods Ltd.*

118, 119, 120   TRENCHER SALTS with shallow hand-raised wells: (118) gilded, *c.* 1690; (119) capstan type, London, 1695; (120) twelve-sided baluster by Matthew Cooper, 1707. *In the Victoria and Albert Museum*

121, 122, 123   LONDON-MADE SALT-CELLARS: (121) small standing salt, gilded, *c.* 1577; (122) trencher salt, 1639; (123) gilded bell salt, 1596. *In the Victoria and Albert Museum*

124, 125, 126, 127   PIGGIN-SHAPED SALT-CELLAR (124), by R. Dattle and J. Barber, York, 1808. *In the Victoria and Albert Museum.* (125) SALT-CELLAR with hand-raised bowl, four double-tailed mermaid feet, London, 1745. *In the Victoria and Albert Museum.* (126) ONE OF A SET OF FOUR SALT-CELLARS with applied festoons and lion-mask feet. By Paul de Lamerie, 1729; (127) SALT-CELLAR by Augustine Courtauld, made in 1730 for the Lord Mayor of London. *Courtesy of the Corporation of the City of London*

128   ONE OF A SET OF FOUR SALT-CELLARS by Emes and Barnard, 1791. *Courtesy of Messrs. D. and J. Wellby, Ltd.*
129   REGENCY SALT-CELLAR with gadrooned body and moulded feet, 1816. *Courtesy of Messrs. Harvey and Gore*

130   TWO OF A SET OF FOUR TRENCHER SALT-CELLARS with recessed corners and oval wells, London, 1736. With contemporaneous shovel salt spoons. *Courtesy of Messrs. E. T. Biggs and Sons Ltd.*

interspersed with little urns in outline. The variety of pierced patterns made with only a few tools reached many hundreds. The hoops were usually gadrooned or beaded. Most frequently the lid was highly domed in the centre, two or three concentric circles being incised on the flat flange. The surface of the outer curve of the handle was usually smooth, but might be ornamented with a line of balls in decreasing sizes; the lower attachment of the double-scroll handle was now placed about two-thirds of the way down the body.

From about 1780 a mustard pot might be made *en suite* with four or more cylindrical pierced salt cellars. The latter had short-legged claw-and-ball feet, but the mustard pot remained flat based. Piercing might consist of narrow top and bottom bands such as pierced and engraved flat shells, with three expansive motifs between—one in front and two at the sides—or with a midway band of alternating star and urn motifs numbering seven in all.

A pierced mustard pot from about 1790 might be raised on claw-and-ball, scroll, or pillar feet, with a double dome lid and a loop thumbpiece (*140*). A short strut might connect the lower terminal of the handle with the body. Unpierced parts of the body and the surface of the lid might be ornamented with bright-cut engraving. Mustard pots with solid cylindrical bodies and flat lids might be similarly decorated, the designs sometimes resembling those of hand-cut pierced work.

Vase-shaped mustard pots date from the 1770s. An example struck with the London hall-mark for 1779 measures $6\frac{3}{4}$ inches in height and has a hinged cover. The body, in the form of a graceful classical vase, is embossed on each side with an oval medallion in relief, and examples have been noted with fluting encircling the body base. The tall bell-shaped lid has a cast and chased pineapple finial. The round pedestal foot, encircled with ball moulding to match the rim, stands on a square plinth. Two reeded handles rise high above the lid and recurve down to the base of the body immediately above the foot junction.

The majority of vase-shaped mustard pots, however, were pierced: this might consist of wide rim bands of geometrical designs and three equidistant motifs below with engraving on the intervening plain area, or of all-over pierced beading on the body rim and rimming the hollow pedestal foot. The lid, always with a cast and turned finial, might be low-domed, tall-domed, or bell-shaped with a domed top. In some instances a thumbpiece was fitted, but more usually the hinge extended from the top of the body and was curved to fit the rise of the handle. The spoon aperture was cut opposite the hinge and midway between the handles.

Oval mustard pots became fashionable at this time following the vogue for oval forms among more impressive pieces of plate such as teapots and tea-caddies (*148*). This design was shorter than the cylindrical type, but of about the same capacity, the body length being about equal to the height to the top of the lid dome. The handle of flat ribbon was attached to one of the long sides with the spoon aperture opposite. The majority were made with uprising ends and the lid, curved to the shape of the body rim, might lack any other shaping, or might be highly domed and topped by a cast and turned finial. The oval body might be encircled with two bands of pressed piercing with repeat motifs throughout and bright-cut ornament between. Late in the 1790s the harp-shaped handle appeared on oval mustard pots with short strut attachments: the spoon aperture was cut at the opposite end of the lid. The centrally domed cover might be topped with a ball finial, less frequently a vase. In some instances the thumbpiece was omitted, the hinge then being five-lugged, but both thumbpiece and finial are usually found.

The oval mustard pot by about 1800 might have convex sides, a low-domed lid and an S-handle. The barrel-shaped body in mustard pots dated from about the same time, the flat lid being opened with a thumbpiece. Top and bottom of the body were encircled with numerous incised rings and other ornament.

Rectangular, hexagonal, and octagonal mustard pots were made between about 1790 and the 1820s and were seldom pierced (*140*). The rectangular series was usually made with canted corners vertically corrugated, wide moulding encircling rim and base. The lid was double domed, with a plain turned finial and a thumb-piece. The harp-shaped handle was usual, rising above the body of the pot, and was attached to one of the long sides. By 1800 the rectangular mustard pot might have an oval collet foot and a boldly convex body, the rim ornamented with wide mould-ing, the pattern laid horizontally. The body might be enriched with bright cutting, matching ornament decorating the flat surface of the handle and the vertical edge of the foot. In later examples the lower part of the body might be widely gadrooned and the rim incurved and decorated with wide gadrooned moulding.

The cylindrical or tankard mustard pot continued to be made, and by the end of the eighteenth century the body might taper slightly upward and in many instances the flat or slightly convex lid had no spoon aperture. By the 1820s the cylindrical mustard pot might be vertically fluted, with rim and base encircled by heavy moulding, and with a bun-lid and a bold D-shaped handle. In the 1830s the cast S-shaped handle was thicker and heavier than formerly and the moulding around rim and base was wider and more elaborate than ever.

A change in the form of the cylinder now took place, its diameter measuring only half as much as its height, and its lid usually flat (*142*). A harp-shaped handle was usual, to which the thumbpiece was hinged. A coat of arms, crest, or other identi-fication motif was engraved on the lid, which was sunk into a square-cut recess in the rim moulding, the two surfaces being level when the lid was closed.

The Victorian tankard mustard pot (*248*) normally measured about 3 inches in height. Its surface might be all-over engraved, most probably with intricate scrollwork; pierced with patterns of similar design; or embossed. The base moulding became even more expansive, but the cast design upon its surface was coarse; the lid overhung the rim to the same extent. Handles of all former types were used and the flat tops of the harp-shaped handles were in line with the flat lids.

Gothic motifs were fashionable from the 1830s, constructed from cast and chased Gothic openwork arches applied over octagonal bodies. Lids extended upward in the form of Gothic domes with tall finials (248). Smooth-faced hexagonal and octagonal mustard pots might be engraved with two designs repeated on alternating panels. These stood upon four heavy scroll feet, cast and chased. A rare octagonal type had a collet foot, the body sloping inward and terminating in an irregular rim edged with elaborate cast moulding (248). Embossed bodies were produced mechanically, with six vertical panels displaying flower and foliage motifs between vertical double corrugations (248). Many Victorian pierced mustard pots were composed from cast motifs in high relief soldered together, such as a dozen rings, each containing a flower, arranged into four vertical panels. The later Victorian mustard pots were issued in many hundreds of patterns too various to collate here.

II SALT-CELLARS

A STANDING salt, magnificently wrought and double gilt, adorned the dining-table of the medieval noble. This ancient ceremonial salt has always received in full measure from collectors the attention merited by its splendour and rarity. But more immediately interesting, perhaps, is the more direct forerunner of the silver salt-cellar, the trencher salt of the medieval gentry.

In great households trencher salts were numerous. Edward III in 1329 possessed more than five hundred of them. The Elizabethan trencher salt was cylindrical, about 1 inch in height, the top consisting of a silver plate with a shallow well hammered into the centre. This was set within the upper rim of a vertical-sided carcase, the lower rim of which rested upon the table. Trencher salts were double gilt to protect the silver from the effect of damp salt which caused disfiguring black stains difficult to remove. Hall-marks show early Stewart trencher salts to have been circular, square, triangular, octagonal, or quatrefoil, with sides vertical, sloping inward from the base, or concave.

Even in rich mansions the impressive great salt by this time had become as rare as the ritual that had accompanied its display. For daily meals in the dining parlour the master salt was a spool-shaped container (116), measuring up to 8 inches in height, with three scroll branches curving upward from the rim.

Several reason for the presence of the scrolls have been conjectured, but it does not appear to have been noted that they were but a relic of past ceremony, designed to aid the host when he lifted the salt and offered it to the chief guest on his right as a gesture of friendship. Such a salt was made in 1730 for the Lord Mayor of London by Augustine Courtauld, and is still preserved with the City plate. This elaborate salt has an open-topped near-spherical bowl with uprising everted rim and is supported by four cast and chased dolphin legs, above which rise four double-scroll handles terminating in cherubs' heads (127).

These spool or capstan salts may be regarded as the last relic of medieval table ceremony. Even by Charles II's reign emphasis was upon the smaller version of this waisted design, measuring no more than 3 inches in height, its base diameter approximating one-and-a-half times that of the top, and with a more capacious salt well. The edges of rim and foot were encircled with wide, highly convex bands of gadrooned ornament, the body remaining plain or decorated with a band of simple punched or incised pattern immediately above the lower gadrooning (119). Salts of this type have been noted with hall-marks dating from the 1660s to the reign of George II.

The plain circular trencher salt, hammered from a single disc of plate in such a way that its circumference supports a shallow well for the salt, is found with hall-marks dating from about 1670 until the end of the century. A contemporaneous trencher salt, measuring rather more than an inch in height, had its well enclosed in a roundly convex body embossed with fluting or ovolo ornament, plain moulding encircling rim and base (118). From about 1690 such a salt was made deeper and stood upon a spreading domed foot ornamented with gadrooning, or built from strips of narrow moulding in various widths and patterns.

When Britannia standard silver temporarily displaced sterling silver plate, between 1697 and 1720, the fashionable trencher salt was eight or twelve sided, the carcase containing a deep, circular well, the base encircled with wide moulding (120). The silhouette might be convex or concave, and in some instances resembled a squat baluster.

Early Georgian trencher salts, at first in Britannia standard metal, and from 1720 in sterling silver, were rectangular, with clipped or rounded corners containing an oval well. Concave sides extended outward to the foot, rim and base often encircled with moulding (130). This pattern continued to be made until the early 1730s and there was a revival in the early nineteenth century.

Ornamental salt-cellars superseded trencher salts on fashionable tables from the early 1720s, the deep well no longer being enclosed in a silver carcase. The expansive gilt-lined bowl, raised from the plate, was almost hemispherical, with a diameter of about $2\frac{1}{2}$ inches, its outer surface either smooth or ornamented with an applied calyx of boldly formed palm leaves, usually twelve (136). The rim until about 1730 was strengthened by plain moulding, then wide gadrooning became more usual.

131, 132   TWO OF A SET OF FOUR SALT-CELLARS WITH STANDS (131), by B. Smith and Digby Scott, 1804. *Courtesy of Messrs. Cavendish House Ltd.* (132) CANOE-SHAPED SALT-CELLAR with bright-cut engraving; by Matthew Boulton, Birmingham, 1775. *Courtesy of Mr. John Bell*

133, 134, 135 · PIERCED SALT-CELLARS WITH BLUE LINERS: (133) by R. and D. Hennell, 1770; (134) vertical piercing with applied swags and medallions by R. Hennell, 1775; (135) with bright-cut engraving, by John Wren, 1799. *In the Victoria and Albert Museum*

136, 137, 138   SALT-CELLARS, each from a set of four: (136, 138) with cut-card leaf work and round collet feet, by Paul Crespin, 1730, and Louis Cuny, 1728; (137) oval with saw-cut ornament, by Patrick Robertson, Edinburgh, 1771. *In the Victoria and Albert Museum*

139, 140, 141 MUSTARD POTS: (139) by Henry Chawner, *c.* 1800; (140) octagonal, pierced and bright-cut, London, 1796; (141) pierced, by Charles Aldridge and Henry Green, 1769. *Courtesy of Mr John Bell*

142, 143 MUSTARD POTS: (142) by Emes and Barnard, 1790. *Courtesy of Mr. John Bell;* (143) with London hall-mark, 1724. *Courtesy of Messrs. Christie, Manson, and Woods Ltd.*

144, 145 SILVER CONDIMENT SET including mustard pot (144), by S. Hennell, 1801. *Courtesy of Mr. John Bell.* (145) MUSTARD POT by Emes and Barnard, 1800. *Courtesy of Messrs. Harvey and Gore*

146, 147, 148 MUSTARD POTS: (146) by Anne Robertson, Newcastle, 1803; (147) by Hester Bateman, 1777; (148) by John, Henry, and Charles Lias, 1828. *Courtesy of Mrs. Josephine Grahame-Ballin*

The bowl rested on a low collet foot of slightly lesser diameter. This was built from a series of five mouldings in various shapes and widths, soldered one upon the other, the broader "stem" and "spread" sections enriched with chased ornament in relief, a band of guilloche ornament being frequent. This pattern continued in production until the mid-century, when the design was elaborated with a wavy, gadrooned, knurled or corded rim, the spreading foot enriched with matching ornament.

Salt-cellars of identical shape were copied during the first quarter of the nineteenth century, but bowls were not hand-raised. Some were cast in a piece with the encircling calyx of palm leaves in relief and then chased: others were spun and the leaf ornament applied in a series of castings. The spun bowl was noticeably lighter in weight than the cast. The nineteenth-century foot was composed from three sections of mouldings, the "spread" moulded and chased with palm leaves. The foot rim measured about two-thirds the diameter of the bowl rim and might stand upon a square or circular plinth. These salt-cellars might be entirely gilt, or only the bowl interior gilded.

The salt-cellar standing on three slender legs placed equidistantly around the bulge of a flattened hemispherical bowl raised from the plate was in use by 1725. The legs expanded in a foliated motif at the bowl junction and terminated in scroll feet. The rim of such a salt-cellar, about $2\frac{1}{2}$ inches in diameter, was strengthened with gadrooned moulding. The surface at first was plainly smooth, but by 1727 Paul de Lamerie was applying heavily cast and chased festoons to the spaces between the legs, which he increased to four. These he designed with lions' masks, their manes extending to the rim, and legs terminating in paw feet, all in high relief (126). The rim was now made separately and soldered to the bowl opening, rising in a curve to a horizontal surface ornamented with deep gadrooning. By the 1740s rims were shaped at an angle of about forty-five degrees and gadrooned or knurled, with the upper line of the masks rising no higher than the bowl-rim joint and terminating in claw-and-ball, paw, or hoof feet. Masks were also cast in the form of mermaids, amorini, rams' heads, or escallop shells with feet to harmonise. Festoons of drapery or foliage and flowers extended between the masks, except in the case of escallop shells, when the surface remained plain.

The body of a mask salt-cellar might be either cast and turned, or spun from the beginning of the nineteenth century. The everted rim was given a deep convex curve, its wide upper surface ornamented with broad gadrooning interspersed with shells or other motifs placed at points immediately above the masks. From about 1815 clusters of shell ornament might occupy the space on the body between the mask and claw-and-ball or paw legs, now more efficiently cast and chased. Such a salt-cellar might be fitted with a cylindrical gilt liner, fully hall-marked.

From this time a series was made with a shallower body, spun and lightly embossed by mechanical means, with three shell feet. From the 1850s again the body might be hand-raised from the plate and its surface hand-embossed, although mechanical embossing continued throughout the century.

Georgian pierced and chased salt-cellars with liners of Bristol blue glass date from the early 1760s, when master-silversmiths discovered this rich smalt blue to be a superb ground for displaying intricate openwork patterns, at first in hand-worked floral arabesques and rococo and chinoiserie styles (137). Silversmiths specialising in pierced work produced some exquisitely intricate salt-cellar galleries by means of the hand-operated fret-saw and chasing tools. Original Bristol blue liners have been noted in a set of pierced salt-cellars bearing the 1762 hall-mark. These were oval with bodies about one inch deep raised upon four short legs terminating in claw-and-ball feet; rims were strengthened with knurled moulding. Wavy rims date from about 1770 with hand-worked piercing in a pattern of foliated scrolls wherein birds are sometimes discovered (133). Some early pierced salt-cellars were fitted with bail handles, a small cartouche beneath each hinge being ornamented with an engraved motif.

These styles were followed by classical patterns mostly designed by factory silversmiths. Many master-silversmiths included factory-pierced galleries in their salt-cellars, the hall-mark containing only their own registered mark as maker of the finished piece. Matthew Boulton, Birmingham, and Tudor and Leader, Sheffield, issued vast numbers of ready-pierced salt-cellar galleries, as well as making complete vessels struck with their own hall-marks. The factory silversmiths used fly-presses, and in the large number of flat-surfaced formal designs the same groups of geometrical motifs may be detected over and over again, arranged with consummate skill (132). An early favourite consisted of rows of vertical Gothic arch motifs, others including vertical pales, light trellis work, cross patterns, circles, crescents, diamonds, and conventionalised scrollwork.

Bands of bright-cut engraving encircled the bodies of many pierced salt-cellars from about 1780, either above a row of narrow piercing or between two narrow bands of geometric piercing. Four taper or scroll feet might replace the claw-and-ball pattern (135). The gallery was sometimes taller at the narrow ends than at the centre.

This was a reflection from the canoe- or boat-shaped salt-cellar dating from the 1770s, supported by a slender stem rising from a spreading foot. An early specimen would be pierced and ornamented with applied swags, the foot rising in a high instep and pierced to match the body. In some instances a bail handle of twisted silver wire might be fitted (132).

The majority of boat-shaped salt-cellars had bowls ornamented with bright-cut work: some had an ogee outline. The ends of the body were usually plainly pointed; others terminated in scrolls from which might swing loose rings. These were abandoned from about 1780 in favour of loop handles rising high above the rim, then curving or bending squarely over and extending beneath the body towards the stem. At about the same time the boat-shaped body might be ornamented with eight or ten batswing flutes, the rim scalloped in harmony with the outline. Each flute was ornamented with an individual motif in bright-cutting. The edge of the foot was shaped in scallops following those of the bowl rim.

Salt-cellars with hemispherical or oval bowls, supported on short slender stems rising from spreading feet, preceded the boat-shape by about ten years. Early examples were hand-pierced with chased festoons and medallions, the highly domed foot pierced in a matching design. After 1770 the bowl might be press-pierced with a rim border, a similar band of piercing encircling the body, the space between engraved with swags and pierced pendant urns. The rim was strengthened with knurled, ball, or reeded moulding.

These were followed by a series of stemmed salt-cellars in which the top of a plain hemispherical bowl was encircled by a tall pierced rim with a scalloped edge, stem and foot being plain. A contemporary type supported a hemispherical or double-ogee bowl upon a hollow pedestal foot, rims of bowl and foot encircled with reeded moulding and edged with bright-cutting.

A two-piece salt-cellar was made during the 1790s and early nineteenth century, a small flat rectangular dish or stand supporting an oval salt container and serving also to carry the silver salt spoon. In early examples the dish measured about 3 inches long, with a central depression for the shallow oval salt bowl which had a collet foot. Bowl and dish might be enriched with bright-cutting. Various more elaborate forms dating from about 1800, cast and chased by the master-silversmiths, were usually double gilt (131).

The plain oblong salt-cellar with a low collet foot of similar outline was introduced in the late 1790s. The narrow ends of the bowl were slightly higher than the centre and the sides were usually roundly convex. The corners of the bowl rim were ornamented with moulded motifs lying horizontally, and joined by gadrooning or other moulding.

Master-silversmiths by the accession of George IV were including salt-cellars in the luxurious dinner services then being made. These were usually miniature versions of the tureens in the sauce service, and appear to have been the first attempt at matching. At about the same time appeared the melon-shaped salt-cellar, lobes alternately wide and narrow, mechanically raised on a spun bowl. The expansive masks of the four legs were attached to the narrow lobes.

The rococo shell pattern in salt-cellars came into fashion during the 1830s, starting a vogue which continued until the 1870s. These were identified at the time as the spotted tridacna shell; the spinous cassidaria shell; the Triton and shell, with a cast and chased Triton forming a handle, whilst the shell itself rests on a rock; the dolphin and shell; and the echinous shell with a coral foot. A best-selling theme at this period, also copied in electroplate, represented an eagle standing on a rock, its outstretched wings supporting a shell for containing salt.

Victorian salt-cellars were made in many hundreds of designs, the majority of which fall into one of the three main groups continued from the eighteenth century: hemispherical body with mask legs; rectangular body with collet foot; pierced with flat base. A fourth group was extensively produced, those which stood upon four short ornamental feet cast in high relief and chased. These were either fitted with blue-glass liners or gilded inside. The hexagonal Gothic style was favoured from the early 1830s until the late 1860s. The body, embossed in relief, was pierced with Gothic arches, the blue liners forming windows.

The most popular of early Victorian salt-cellars were circular, pierced with arabesque scrollwork. The rim was widely everted with a wavy outline and gadrooned or knurled edge, its base raised upon four elaborately cast, outcurving feet. Less expensive salt-cellars were made of about half the normal height, the vertical gallery pierced with pales, sometimes alternating with other geometrical motifs. The rim might be straight or wavy and three low shell feet were usual.

Twin and triple salt-cellars were made from the mid-George II period. These were the work of master-silversmiths and are infrequent. Some early double salts were basket-shaped with corded borders and handles. A set of four triple salt-cellars sold at Christie's were made in 1821. These had three shell bowls on spool-shaped stems chased at the top with rams' masks and with sexfoil bases chased with dolphins' masks and shell fish. A set of twelve double salt-cellars with cylindrical containers and guilloche rims and handles, in the personal collection of H.M. the Queen, was made by Robert Garrard in 1867. See *The Queen's Silver* by A. G. Grimwade.

Salt spoons might accompany salt-cellars from early Georgian days. Until about 1750 the Strood salt spoon was used to the exclusion of all others: this was a miniature shovel with a flat-faced scoop and a rat-tail stem terminal, the interior of the scoop being gilded (*130*). This was superseded by the more practical deep-bowled oval salt ladle, the stem finial following the fashion of table spoons. The majority of examples, however, possess the old English pattern handle chased with shells. The Strood salt spoon had returned by 1840, often with a heart-shaped scoop and a D-handle. Shell-bowled spoons also belong to the period.

Chapter Five

I FISH SLICES AND KNIVES

THE Duchess of Northumberland in her *Diary* of the 1760s shed many interesting sidelights upon the home-life of George III and his newly married queen. In April 1762 she recorded that "Their Majesty's constant [dinner] Table at this Time was as follows: a soup removed with a large joynt of Meat and two other Dishes such as a Pye or a broyl'd fowl and the like. On the side table was a large joynt, for example, a large Sirloin of Beef cold and also a Boar's Head and a Sallad; 2nd Course always one Roast, one of Pastry and Spinage and Sweetbreads, Macaron, Scollopt Oysters, Whitebait or the like. . . . ''

The fashion for whitebait spread and the special table accessory which silversmiths had designed by 1760 was used for serving this dainty. The London assay office listed this as a fish trowel, the cost of assay being three-halfpence. It is known to present-day collectors as a fish slice. Service at the table was a comparatively new fashion, the host assuming the duty of carver, hitherto performed by a servant at the sideboard. This necessitated the introduction of such accessories to the table as knife rests, marrow spoons, and the fish trowel.

Rarely is an example seen of the original exquisitely worked fish trowel (*149*). This resembled a builder's mortar trowel with a triangular blade, its length about one-eighth greater than its breadth, the silversmith cutting six from a circular plate of silver. By working six potential blades at a time on a single plate, the silversmith was able to ensure greater stability whilst saw-cutting and filing. Each triangle was pierced with an elaborate and delicate all-over openwork design of foliated scrolls and other motifs, enclosed within a narrow border. The disc was then cut into six sections and the points rounded off. Even the flat surface of the remaining silver was then enriched with engraving.

This decoration was achieved by saw-cutting and removing the background, leaving the pattern in solid, flat-surfaced silver. Fish trowel blades were so delicately pierced and so ambitiously worked that to the casual observer they might appear to lack strength. The metal, however, was compensatingly strong to withstand strain in use and during cleaning, and the scrolls reinforced each other at cleverly designed points of contact. The curved edge of the blade to which the handle was to be fixed was given a wavy outline, its curve being an arc of the original circular plate. At this time the edges were still squared off, not bevelled.

The slender handle was of solid silver worked in a single piece from the plate. In form it resembled contemporary spoons with an expansive shell- or fan-shaped bracket joining it to the blade, the rim of which was feather-edged to match (*149*).

During the 1770s the hand-pierced fish trowel gave way to the fish slice on which the edges were bevelled (*149*). Such a scoop more easily served small fish, or prepared portions of a large fish, the piercing allowing surplus liquor to be strained off, but for dividing a large fish at table two matching slices would have been required. These triangular blades were less expansive than those of fish trowels, eight being cut from a single circular plate. Piercing also was less costly, hand-cut designs being simpler with less silver cut away (*149*). Designs might contain rows of conventional neo-classic motifs in repeat. Many of these were produced by press piercing, often finished by file to give the appearance of hand-work. The head of the blade might be engraved with a crest or ornamental motif. Both sides of the blade were similarly engraved and the hall-mark was usually struck on the underside.

Press-piercing on fish slices was composed of simple decorations such as vertical and horizontal pales (*149*). Some highly effective piercing was achieved by repeating such simple motifs as bands of lunettes, shells, semicircles, and so on, with a narrow engraved band encircling the bevelled edges. The pierced outline was usually accentuated by the addition of rows of engraved dots and simple classic ornament bordering the curves. More elaborate was an adaptation of the honeysuckle motif, a series of running scrolls terminating at each end of the pattern with an individual scrolled foliated motif.

The fish slice with a fish-shaped blade had become fashionable by 1780 (*149*) and for the remainder of the century this was the most frequent shape. In this the conventional motifs were usual, but often there was a central full-length motif resembling the backbone and ribs of a fish. A blade of this shape might be engraved with a motif of crossed fish included in foliated scrollwork, the surrounding ground being cut away to form a pierced design. In later instances the fish-shaped blade was wide, in the form of a headless plaice, so that the point of the blade was considerably to the right of the handle.

The factory-made fish slice of the eighteenth century was more or less standardised to a fish-shaped blade with a border of pales following its outline and an oval central rosette: the pales themselves were bordered by ornamental engraving or other pierced motifs. The pierced design was enriched with engraving.

Diamond-shaped blades were made from about 1780. Three rows of pressed pales alternated with circles around the long edges and points of the diamond outline, the centre being ornamented with a single classic motif in the bright-cut engraving that also ornamented the solid areas between the piercing. Rectangular blades were made with rounded edges from the 1790s to the 1820s (*150*), mostly decorated with pressed piercing in a coarse style. Decoration was confined to simple geometric motifs following the blade outline and enclosed in a frame of engraved lines, a similar feature encircling the edge of the blade itself. These are usually found in Sheffield-made hafts, even though the blades bear the marks of master-silversmiths. It appears that such silversmiths bought factory-made parts and finished and assembled them in various fish-slice designs.

Fish-slice blades were always symmetrical until the 1790s, when the form later perpetuated in fish knives was acquired (150): this shape has been used for knife blades from Anglo-Saxon times. There was now only one cutting edge to the blade, a smoothly curved outline bordered with a single or double incised line. The blunt edge was undulating and incurved, meeting the cutting edge with a blunt point. The centre of the blade was pierced with a simple motif and the field might be engraved with flower and foliage motifs. This asymmetrical blade, pierced only with heavy openwork, could be made with silver of thinner gauge at a time when silver was costly. The shape continued to be made throughout the nineteenth century, however, usually from stout metal, with but slight variations of outline.

The solid bolster joining the blade with a silver, ivory, or wood handle was a simple casting, usually with a short upcurving shank ending in a tang for insertion in the handle. A silver ferrule fitted over this handle end to keep it from splitting whilst in use. Ivory handles were frequent, at first plain surfaced, stained green and polished; they might be turned or turned and carved. Later the ivory was preferred in its natural colour with a smooth surface, and the haft might be round, rectangular, or octagonal in section, tapering towards the blade.

Hafts in silver occasionally resembled the handles of contemporary spoons. The vast majority, however, were factory made, stamped from thinly rolled sterling silver plate. The two halves of the shaft were struck from dies and invisibly soldered together: even with a magnifying glass the join is difficult to detect. The central cavity was filled with a mixture of shellac strengthened with powdered pumice, poured in whilst semi-liquid. The tang of the bolster was then inserted and when this cement had hardened the handle was securely fixed. The cost of producing such hafts was about one-thirtieth that of hand-made specimens. The weight of silver varied from 15 to 20 pennyweights a dozen.

A statute of 1790 so amended the law of assaying silver that among very small pieces weighing less than 5 pennyweights hall-marking was compulsory on only a few specified articles. Knife and fork hafts were not specified and were, therefore, optionally exempt from hall-marking. Silver handles made towards the end of the eighteenth century and lacking a hall-mark are often marked STER LING, the only other device being the maker's mark. No duty was paid on such silver. These handles were usually made in Sheffield, and from about 1820 this type was used on fish slices and forks to the virtual exclusion of all other silver handles (150).

The development of asymmetrical blades was not at once marked by the intro-duction of fish forks. The collector will notice the existence of such slices designed for the server's left hand. But the most elaborate development was the fish server intended to lift the portion of fish between two slices attached one above the other to be held in the one hand. These dated from the opening of the nineteenth century and were eventually superseded by pairs of fish carvers consisting of a fish slice and a matching wide-bladed fork. The fish server was constructed from a fish slice with a long bolster-shank and a second smaller blade of similar shape and piercing, fixed above it and fitted with a solid silver handle wrought from flat plate. This upper handle extended slightly beyond the lower bolster-shank, and was linked to it by a fixed lever hinging from front to rear in a slot cut in the bolster-shank, or less frequently by a spring attachment. By pushing the upper handle forward with thumb-pressure upon its scrolled terminal, the upper blade was lowered on to the larger blade to secure the fish while lifting it from dish to plate.

Some authorities consider fish servers to have been used also for the service of asparagus. Catalogues from 1790 to 1900, however, illustrate and name the aspara-gus server as large, bow-spring tongs with a pair of wide rectangular blades measur-ing about two-thirds the length of the bow. The blades were pierced in geometrical all-over patterns or with expansive single motifs, surface engraving usually being carried over to the bow. From the middle of the century illustrations showed other asparagus servers resembling early fish slices with symmetrical blades rather coarsely pierced: these are sometimes mistaken for fish slices, but the hall-mark date reveals their original purpose. By the 1880s the blade might be squarer with up-curved sides and an embossed design covering most of its surface.

When at last the fish slice was given a matching fork the pair were catalogued in the 1820s as fish carvers and were often associated with sets of fish knives, which were now introduced to table service. The handles of fish carvers matched, usually in silver or, between the 1840s and 1870s, in mother of pearl. The fork had four broad, flat prongs and the curved base might be pierced with a motif matching the piercing on the slice blade. From the late 1880s the slice blade might again be symmetrical, but more usually remained asymmetrical with an ivory or silver handle.

Fish knives appear to have been included in fashionable table appointments no earlier than the reign of George IV, although steel-bladed knives must have ruined many a fish delicacy. These knives were miniature editions of the asymmetrical fish slice, but with solid blades engraved on both sides. The earliest to be noted are a set of six, their blades struck with the London hall-mark for 1821. The earliest literary reference to fish knives appears to be in T. Cosnett's *Footman's Directory*, 1825. In a comprehensive trade catalogue of silverware published in 1862, fish forks

149 (*upper row*) FISH TROWELS hand-pierced in all-over foliated scrollwork, squared edges, handles worked from the plate: 1769, 1772, 1770. (*lower row*) FISH SLICES with symmetrical bevel-edged blades and silver handles: 1784, 1794, 1795
In the Victoria and Albert Museum

150 FISH SLICES: (*upper row*) pierced symmetrical blade with bright-cut engraving, 1797; plain asymmetrical blade with carved ivory handle, 1797; fish-shaped blade with pressed handle, 1796; (*lower row*) 1791, 1800, 1800
In the Victoria and Albert Museum

151   (top) PAIR OF EGG-STANDS each containing four egg-cups and spoons, by Paul Storr;   (bottom) PAIR OF
TOAST-RACKS, by Paul Storr, 1810. Courtesy of Messrs. D. and J. Wellby Ltd.

had not yet made their appearance. Until the early 1870s table forks were used with fish knives, which perhaps accounts for the fact that these might number twenty-four in sets of tableware otherwise composed of a dozen of a kind. Fish forks to match the knives made their appearance in the 1870s, catalogues illustrating pairs as "fish eaters," surely the least inspired title ever applied to appointments of gracious living.

II EGG-CUP FRAMES, TOAST-RACKS, AND TOASTING FORKS

FOR centuries boiled eggs have garnished the English breakfast table. The early custom was to cook them over a charcoal brazier on a side-table; then, for a century from the 1770s, it was fashionable to have them carried to the breakfast room in an egg-cup frame which had been warmed before the fire and placed beneath a warmed oval dish cover. An example in the Harewood collection, bearing the hall-mark for 1770, is in the form of an oval wirework basket with claw-and-ball feet and a corded bale handle and containing six silver egg-cups. This form continued throughout the 1770s, made from circular or oval wire. Wires shaped in the swage block might then be used, and from the domed centre rose a pillar handle terminating in a pineapple or other cast and chased finial. Neither egg-cup stands nor silver egg-cups were frequent before 1777, for the assay office price list of that year makes no mention of them.

A frame with four circular guard-rings holding egg-cups was introduced at about the same time. Between each ring was a loop for an egg spoon, held vertically, bowl upward. On the central dome was a circular salt-cellar with a spoon. At first these frames were square, but almost immediately a sexfoil outline became fashionable, holding six egg-cups, the central dome supporting either a salt-cellar or a pepper caster. By 1790 the salt-cellar might be of cut-glass, or might consist of a spool-shaped wire frame fitted with a glass liner, sometimes in Bristol blue-glass. Another contemporaneous form consisted of an oval wire-based frame from which rose eight upright supports, four guard-rings around a central pillar handle. A boat-shaped egg-cup frame with round wires was made, too, with six egg-cup rings and a vertical heart-shaped handle at one side.

Silver egg-cugs were included in the set. These were made from two spun sections, the plain-surfaced cup and the hollow pedestal foot joined together. A rib with a flat or rounded surface encircled the egg-cup a little below the rim to allow for suspension in the guard-ring. In some early examples the rib was omitted and the guard-ring shaped inside to the curve of the egg-cup. The interiors of egg-cups and spoon bowls might be gilded.

Early nineteenth-century egg-cup frames had horizontal members of wide beaded or gadrooned moulding joined vertically by slender ornamental pillars with cast paw feet. By 1810 gadroon and shell moulding was preferred. The upper member was fitted with egg-cup rings and slots for spoons, and supported a stemmed salt-cellar in the centre. The rims of egg-cups and salt-cellar were encircled with a matching moulding of reduced size. The handle consisted of crossed arches of moulding with a finial at the join.

Customarily a man might eat two boiled eggs and a woman one. Special frames were evolved, therefore, to contain two egg-cups with a loop for a single spoon. Examples have been noted containing three egg-cups and two spoons, suggesting their use by man and wife. A collector may even find a specimen with two spoons attached to pillars and guard-rings that can be extended to receive two additional egg-cups. The rims of such egg-cups were widely everted with slender stems to the pedestal feet, matching a salt-cellar on a central raised platform. The frame was supported on four ball or scroll feet.

Egg-cup frames between about 1790 and 1825 were designed in patterns too varied and numerous to be tabulated: one firm alone issued sixty-four patterns between 1788 and 1815. The Sheffield platers possessed the monopoly in light plain styles and in some instances the frames were in Sheffield plate and the egg-cups of silver, the hall-marks conspicuously encircling the egg-cup rims to give the visitor the impression that the entire set was in silver.

Among designs may be mentioned the triangular egg-cup stand with wire-work baskets holding the egg-cups, a central pillar handle, and shell and hour-glass pattern spoons. The base consisted of a solid platform built from plate and moulding. The upper part of the egg-cup might be decorated with a band of applied cast ornament chased in relief on a matted ground. Other stands were of hexagonal form.

Heavier moulding was used for the frame from about 1820. The feet were elaborate cast and chased paws, and the supporting columns floridly designed. The egg-cups in some instances were turned from castings. The central salt-cellar was fashionably urn-shaped with a bail handle and a ladle. One pattern of this period included an oblong tray with moulded D-shaped handle and scroll feet as a basis for the six openwork egg-cups fitting into their openwork containers, supported by moulded columns with a central pillar handle. Foliage supports were a new feature. The lozenge-shaped basket egg-cup frame dates to the same period, with four egg-cups and spoons.

The early Victorian egg-cup frame was a florid, over-decorated affair difficult to clean, and thus creating a preference for bone china to the virtual exclusion of silver. It was catalogued as an egg-frame, although it was now really a stand from which egg-cup guard-rings had been discarded (*249*). In many instances a flat circular platform with a pierced gallery or a deep moulded rim was supported by four cast claw-and-ball feet. There was a central loop pillar handle, and the egg-cup borders were pierced or encircled with heavy moulded rims to match. The spoons were placed with their bowls on the stand and their finials projecting beyond the rim (*249*).

Other Victorian egg-cup frames were shallow dishes on four cast feet, with pillar handles topped by oval loop finials. The boat-shaped pattern was again fashionable, with four or six egg-cups, the rims of stand and egg-cups cut in a repeating cyma outline. In most early Victorian egg-frames both stand and egg-cups were smothered with ornament such as chased flowers and birds, intricate and closely engraved scroll-work, or pierced work in trellis designs (*949*).

An egg-cup frame combined with an egg-boiler, including spirit lamp and sand-glass egg-timer, was but one among many elaborate domestic devices dating to the 1790s and early nineteenth century. Craftsmen were then finding it more and more difficult to hold their own against the factory products that flooded their market. They sought, therefore, to create a fashionable demand for ingenious elaborations that would provide as many associated objects as possible within a small space. Even furniture designers, such as Thomas Sheraton in *The Cabinet Maker and Upholsterer's Drawing Book*, 1791–94, devised numerous pieces with this object in view.

The silversmiths and Sheffield platers produced a range of egg boilers in which the vessel was filled with boiling water before being brought into the breakfast room, and then kept boiling over the spirit lamp. Each person could boil eggs to his individual liking. In the majority of these contrivances there was a two-handled or vase-shaped hot-water vessel with a lid divided centrally and opening in two sections. This was supported on a spirit-lamp stand, the whole being a single entity. Fitting within the water pan was a frame of drawn silver wire arranged to hold four or six eggs while they boiled. This was lifted by a central wire pillar handle with a loop at the top framing an hour-glass. Such was the egg-boiling unit as at first conceived and made throughout the 1790s. Before 1795 it was generally encircled with guard-rings for eight egg-cups, alternating with loops for suspending the spoons. By the 1820s the boiler might be fluted, and raised on four footed legs, cast and chased, and holding a spirit lamp in a ring between them. Such a boiler was fitted with the period's lion and ring handles, and a domed, centrally divided lid.

Alternatively an egg-cup stand might be combined with a toast rack, a salt-cellar and a pair of pepper casters. Toast racks in silver appear to date no earlier than the early 1780s, when they were known as toast trays. They are not entered in a plater's list of 1774 nor in the assay office price list of 1777. Among the earliest noted were two bearing the London hall-marks of 1784. One was a nine-rack example of oval wire rising from a flat plate, with a ring handle and claw-and-ball feet. The other had seven racks of double looped wires and a pierced and beaded rim. By the end of the century the ends of the base might be upcurved.

At about this time appeared the arched base of wire on four paw or scroll feet, holding the toast more loosely than the customary design. The central rack might be reduced in height and fitted with a cage to hold a pepper or cinnamon caster of cut-glass with a silver mount. By 1810 the rim of the plate might be gadrooned and a shell and foliage handle attached. This type, but with a ring handle, was usual during the next two decades, either oval or rectangular, and made in matching pairs. Seven racks were usual and some later Georgian examples were provided with stands and spirit lamps for keeping the toast warm.

Folding toast racks were made, the first being patented in 1807 by Samuel Roberts, Arundel Street, Sheffield. In Sheffield plate they were marked "R. C. & Co. Patent." These folded lengthwise on the lazy-tongs principle, the wires forming the racks rising from the hinged junctions. A ball foot was fitted at each corner. Another type closed across its width, the apex of each rack being hinged so that when knobs at the end of the base were slightly unscrewed the toast rack would fold flat. The handle swivelled from the central rack. Folding toast racks included an egg-cup combination. The top of every alternate rack was shaped into a vertical circular hoop swivelling across the horizontal diameter so that it could be converted into a guard-ring at a touch. Such a rack would hold either four egg-cups or four slices of toast and two egg-cups.

A Victorian toast rack normally held six slices of toast, the racks rising from a rectangular base made from round rod with a central strengthening bar and four ball feet. In others the base might be of plate hand-pierced in scroll and foliage designs and engraved, with cast and chased openwork corner feet. The racks were shaped as Gothic cusps and from the apex of the central one rose a short loop handle. The Gothic curves continued until the end of the century. By the 1880s the base might be a rectangular plate into which fitted five or seven rings forming racks, the handle being a matching loop rising from the central rack.

By the end of the century toast racks were pressed from rolled sheets of plate silver. A row of five or seven long rectangular spaces with rounded ends were press-cut from the plate. This left a flat frame containing a row of bars which was bent into an inverted U-shape. The toast rack was completed by joining the short ends with flat strengthening bars. A flat ear was attached to each end or a loop handle soldered to the middle of the central rack. In some instances the bars were fitted into a rectangular stand with a gadrooned rim and four feet.

Silver toasting forks date from the late seventeenth century. One example sold at Christie's bore the London hall-mark for 1680, measured $39\frac{1}{2}$ inches in length, and was engraved with the weight of silver, 3 oz. 11 dwt. This specimen was

152 SILVER-GILT TRAVELLING SET: inscribed around the rim of the tumbler, "A Bartlemew Fairing sent by His Grace the Duke of Ormond to Fridasweed Lady Stephens, 1686"
Courtesy of Messrs. E. T. Biggs and Sons Ltd.

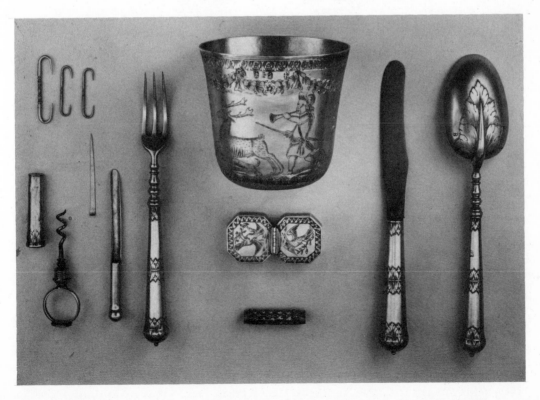

153 TRAVELLING SET with oval tumbler, knife, fork, and spoon with detachable handles, spice box, nutmeg grater, marrow scoop, corkscrew, and toothpick. By Charles Overing, 1701
Courtesy of Messrs. E. T. Biggs and Sons Ltd.

154, 155, 156 FOX-MASK STIRRUP CUP with erect ears (154); Edinburgh, 1828. *Courtesy of Messrs. E. T. Biggs and Sons Ltd.* (155, 156) SILVER-GILT FOX-HEAD CUP WITH STAND FOR DISPLAY, inscribed April 1820
Courtesy of Messrs. Bracher and Sydenham

157 HOUND-HEAD CUP by S. Hennell, 1813. *Courtesy of Messrs. E. T. Biggs and Sons Ltd.*

158 HAND-RAISED SILVER-GILT FOX-MASK CUP by Samuel Wood, 1776. *Courtesy of Messrs. E. T. Biggs and Sons Ltd.*

159, 160, 161 HAND-WORKED FOX HEAD (159), by John Lantier, 1773. (160) GREYHOUND-MASK CUP by Edward Mason, Birmingham, 1828. (161) FOX-MASK CUP by Thomas Powell, 1775. *All by courtesy of Messrs. Lewis and Kaye Ltd.*

typical of the form used for more than a century to come. The curved silver prongs were attached to a handle of polished wood and more metal was introduced in ring and ball finial and a central band, all the mounts having ornamental borders, typically foliage, and perhaps serrated edges. From about 1770 the handle might be of black japanned beech wood.

Early in the nineteenth century there was a vogue for telescopic toasting forks. These were intended for the use of travellers to the Continent, where, according to Lady Caroline Capel, writing in June 1816, such a toasting fork was "an inestimable treasure and made many a bit of sour, coarse bread go down, that would otherwise have stuck in the throat" (*The Capel Letters 1814–1817*, Cape, 1956).

Sir Edward Thomason, the celebrated Birmingham silversmith, claimed in his *Memoirs* that "in 1809 I invented the sliding toasting fork, some with one, two, or three slides, within a handsome japanned handle common now in all the shops. I also invented one that by the action of drawing the slide, the same movement raised a shield from off the prongs, and upon shutting up again of the slides this action moved the shield over the prongs. I also invented a third kind, which was that the three prongs collapsed together, which, on the shutting up of the slides of the fork, drew the same into the mouth of a snake, the head of a silver snake being attached to one end of the outer slide or handle. These were made in silver, gilt and plated and large quantities were sold even by me: but as I did not protect this invention by patent, thousands were made and sold by other manufacturer silversmiths." Examples have been seen with hall-marks for as late as 1861.

Chapter Six

I BEAKERS, TUMBLERS, TRAVELLING SETS, AND STIRRUP CUPS

FOR nearly a thousand years silver beakers graced the tables of princes and pre-
lates, in castles and manor houses. In its shape the beaker was the simplest, most
serviceable of drinking vessels, a deep cylinder, widening slightly towards the
everted rim and uncomplicated by either spout or handle. In its fabric it was sweet
and pleasant to use, infinitely preferable to the wood or clay of the commoner.
This was the vessel for the rich merchant's wines and his children's spiced ales, for
the rough ciders and pungent hippocras customary until Henry VIII set the fashion
for French wines laced with spices from the newly discovered West Indies.

Moreover, it was the silversmith's remedy for the health hazards of promiscuous
drinking from vessels of porous wood and base metals. Henry VIII was an enthusi-
astic dabbler in the art of pharmacy and compounded grisly potions such as dragon's
blood mixed with the powdered skulls of Irishmen. But he was persistent in his
advocacy of silver drinking vessels. "The cups whereof you drinke, should be of
silver, or silver and gilt" advised Doctor Vaughan in his celebrated *Fifteen Directions
for Health*, 1602. The less affluent compromised by using wood or metal vessels
with rims protected by thin silver plate, but the number of delightful little specimens that remain today testify to the immense popularity of the silver beaker.

Collectors find particular pleasure in the rich workmanship of late seventeenth-
century beakers, but the vessel continued in constant use throughout the eighteenth
and early nineteenth centuries. Beginner-collectors have to bear in mind that many
in the nineteenth century were designed to cater for the current orgy of historical
romance. The catalogue of the Great Exhibition of 1851 noticed the pseudo-
Elizabethan beakers on view: these might bear dates of the 1570s and 1580s and
once their hall-marks became worn and duty marks removed they would no longer
give the lie to such dating. However, details of manufacture should prove adequately
revealing to the wary.

The accounts of Edward, Prince of Wales, for 1348 included thirty-two silver
beakers: "32 magne pecie argenti, vocate Bikers." These were probably tall
narrow vessels such as is suggested by the inventory of a silversmith's stock taken
in 1399, which included "two bikers of silver gilt, 29½ oz., one other biker gilt,
16 oz." Cripps points out that this silversmith's entire stock weighed but 132 oz.,
valued at 2s. 4d. an ounce. Early in the Elizabethan period the spelling "beaker" is

noted, and the vessels were made in four sizes, great, middle, small, and children's, the great beaker being known as a stoop. A middle-size beaker measured about 6 inches in depth.

A typical late Elizabethan beaker had a wide everted lip, making the rim diameter about one and a half times as great as that of the base, which was encircled by a spreading moulded foot ring. This served to lift the flat base above table level, ensuring stability even if it developed a bulge. Such a foot was formed from three or four moulded rings, two of which might be decorated with punched ornament. The body might be ornamented with a lively pictorial design in flat chasing, the rim encircled with strapwork intersected with scrolling flower, foliage, and fruit pendants extending as far as halfway down the beaker. The name of the owner and a date might also be chased or a coat of arms engraved beneath. Early in the seventeenth century the foot-ring might be more massive, built from punched ornamental mouldings with corded moulding topmost, and with the central, vertical moulding ornamented to match the flat moulding below (*168*).

In some instances, from as early as Elizabethan days, the beaker was given a stemmed foot. The brief stem might be knopped or spool-shaped, the circular foot highly domed and moulded. The upper portion continued in the characteristic beaker style but the vessel was listed by its users as a goblet. Particularly delightful nests of these beaker-goblets were made, in which five of the footed vessels fitted into each other. Each vessel was encircled half an inch or so below the rim with a narrow rib which rested upon the lip of the beaker below. The lowest beaker stood upon a short spool-stemmed foot, making it taller than the other four, which had collet feet. The top beaker was fitted with a flat lid supporting a high steeple finial. When assembled such a nest of footed beakers gave the impression of a steeple cup. These were inventoried as nests of goblets and might be gilt or parcel gilt. The inventory of Sir Thomas Ramsey's plate in 1590 listed one great nest of goblets and six ordinary nests, all gilt: the great nest weighed approximately twice as much as each of the others.

The majority of seventeenth-century beakers were made without decoration other than an engraved coat of arms or other form of identification, and might have gilded interiors. The base was usually encircled with spreading foot moulding. Examples are known without this moulding, however, such beakers being wider and squatter than others and their bases of heavier plate than usual. One rare type is the beaker of Charles II's reign. Beneath an ordinary beaker and acting as a foot is a secondary drinking vessel intended for dramming. This measures about half the depth of the upper section and has an outward curve towards the base to ensure stability. The joint between is encircled with corded moulding.

The wide, squat beaker now became the standard form, with the body flat chased or chased in relief and the base banded closely with reeded moulding (*166*). Repoussé flowers and foliage might cover the entire field to within three-quarters of an inch of the thickened lip. Initials and date might be pounced below the rim. A typical example would measure between 3 and 4 inches in height and weigh between 2 and 4 ounces. Later in the seventeenth century a band of relief work in flowers and foliage encircled the body, the plain band above measuring twice the depth of the one below the ornament. The lip was less everted than formerly (*167*).

Hall-marks show that fewer were made towards the end of the seventeenth century, wealthy homes abandoning silver beakers in favour of costly porcelain drinking vessels from China, and goblets of tough, clear flint-glass. Presentation beakers date from this period. They were favourite gifts from merchant companies to ambassadors and others able to influence trade. Such beakers might be in gold and possess covers.

Wide, shallow beakers continued to be made throughout the eighteenth century. Many Georgian examples are engraved, bright-cut engraving and matting dating from the 1780s. Nests of small closely fitting beakers, the outermost measuring $2\frac{1}{4}$ inches in height, were made at the end of the eighteenth century for serving spirits. Silver beakers continued to be made throughout the first half of the nineteenth century, those mentioned in the Great Exhibition catalogue being ornamental beakers with hand-raised repoussé work in so-called Elizabethan designs. These would be of rolled plate and could be rounded into the beaker shape without distorting the raised ornament, but might be expected to lack the gradual thickening that strengthened the rim of the genuine Elizabethan vessel.

Beakers were made from flat plate. This needed to be of sturdy gauge and because no strengthening moulding could encircle the rim, the silversmith gradually tapered the rectangular sheet, making it thick at the rim, thinner at the base. Ornament, usually flat chasing, might then be applied to the metal. The vertical edges were then cut into a dovetail form known as the cramped seam and the sheet was turned up into a cylindrical shape and soldered. The seam was hammered until all sign of the joint had vanished, and the base was soldered into position. Soldering was carried out with an L-shaped blow-pipe applied to the open flame of a lamp burning whale oil, the beaker lying on a bowl of red-hot charcoal. The beaker was whitened by boiling in a solution of salts of tartar, burnished with oil and whitening, and given a final high polish with powder and cloth.

As decoration was applied to the beaker whilst in the plate form, the most convenient method consisted of flat chasing. This was easily executed on a flat surface and the subsequent shaping of the vessel would not distort it, despite the varying thickness of the metal. The flat, hammered plate, annealed until quite soft, was anchored on specially prepared warm pitch. When cold, this held the plate firmly, preventing vibration and distortion whilst the silversmith worked, yet cushioning the blows of the chasing tools.

The plate was smeared with grease or oil and sprinkled with powdered chalk, so that the design could be sketched upon it with a pencil. In the case of stock designs the chaser covered the greased surface with a parchment pricked with the pattern. Chalk rubbed over this registered the design upon the silver until it was outlined permanently with a pointed tool lightly hammered. The design was then impressed into the metal by means of tiny punches selected from a wide range, struck with hammer blows of varying force.

For travellers, the obvious variant of the beaker was the silver tumbler, with its characteristic rounded and weighted base (*162*). William Harrison in his *Description of England*, 1587, recorded that drinking vessels were seldom set upon the table in the sixteenth century, "but each one, as necessity urgeth, calleth for a cup of such drink as him listeth to have, so that, when he has tasted of it he delivereth the cup again to some one of the standers by." These silver cups were inventoried either as "bowles for wine" or as "quaffing cups," intended to be drained at a single draught, which accounted for their small size, their diameter exceeding their depth, which varied from $1\frac{3}{4}$ inches to 3 inches. As early as 1533 Sir Thomas More distinguished between vessels for sipping and for quaffing. Dekker in 1607 declared "I quaffe full bowles of hot wine," referring to the highly spiced liquor of the period.

The silver tumbler, raised from a single disc of plate, must be differentiated from the much deeper beaker in which the body was joined vertically with an invisible seam, and the base inserted. In the tumbler the rounded base was proportionately thicker than its vertical or slightly outward sloping sides, so that even if the vessel rocked from side to side in a swaying coach or were placed on an uneven surface, it would retain its balance like an acrobat—hence its name.

To carry a pair of tumblers, one nesting within the other, enclosed in a small gilt-enriched leather case, became a modish conceit among seventeenth-century nobility and gentry then acquiring a taste for coach travel, with its nightly discomfort of boarding and lodging in taverns or inns. The few newly established coaching inns provided wealthy patrons with a side table of silver plate. In the summer of 1664 Pepys confided in his *Diary*, "Thence home, taking two silver tumblers which I have bought." The magazine *Apollo*, 1704, advertised the loss of "a gold tumbler of £100 value."

Silver tumblers, now assiduously collected and catalogued as tumbler cups, remained an essential part of travelling equipment until towards the close of the eighteenth century, when drinking vessels of lead-glazed cream-coloured earthenware had been introduced in every coaching house and tavern.

The smooth outer surface of a tumbler was usually engraved for identification.

There might be an expansive coat of arms (*163*), a crest or a cypher, or the owner's name and a date might be inscribed in a narrow band immediately below the rim. In some instances an engraved design ornamented the base of a tumbler, suggesting that when empty the vessel was placed rim downward.

The earliest tumbler so far noted was formerly in the Riley Smith collection. This bears the London hall-mark for 1625, measures $2\frac{5}{8}$ inches in diameter and weighs 1 oz. 17 dwt. The body is engraved with the following inscription: "Ye guift of Humphrey Whistler gent somtymes Bailiffe of ye Cittie of Oxon to ye Maior of ye same Cittie for ye use of ye Master and Wardens of ye Company of Taylers there 1637." The diameters of eleven silver tumblers in the Riley Smith collection varied from $2\frac{1}{2}$ inches to $3\frac{3}{8}$ inches.

The Noble collection of twenty-one silver tumblers, dating between 1671 and 1740, included a set of four struck with the London hall-mark of 1707, and two pairs hall-marked 1671 and 1725. Their height ranged from $1\frac{5}{8}$ inches to 3 inches, and weights from 2 oz. 2 dwt. for each of the set of four to 7 oz. 5 dwt. for the Charles II pair of 1671. Twelve were plain and decoration on the remainder extended from coats of arms in elaborate cartouches to an example merely pricked with initials. One made at York in 1671 was worked in repoussé and chased with large flowers and foliage and two cartouches. The Duke of Hamilton possessed a set of three tumblers with matted grounds, plain narrow bands encircling their lips. These were struck with London hall-marks 1677 and 1683.

It is noticeable that from Charles II's reign, when a tumbler measuring $2\frac{1}{4}$ inches in height weighed 1 oz. 19 dwt., the weight of these vessels tended to increase progressively: an example of the same height struck with the 1713 hall-mark weighed 4 ounces, and a pair of tumblers assayed for Matthew Boulton on the occasion of the opening of the Birmingham assay office in August 1773 weighed 8 oz. 16 dwt. From the 1790s the production of silver tumblers decreased, greater numbers being made in Sheffield plate.

Tumblers made for practical use were always severely smooth inside. Some mid-nineteenth-century tumblers, made only for decoration, were raised in relief, such a pair made in 1841 "in repoussé" and chased with strapwork and foliage and engraved with Latin inscriptions, the royal arms of Scotland, crests, and the date 1567.

Silver tumblers were included in the pocket travelling sets fashionable from the 1680s until early Georgian days and carried by men and women alike. Such a tumbler was usually enclosed in a shagreen case, silver-mounted and velvet-lined, together with knife, fork, spoon, spice-box, nutmeg grater, corkscrew, marrow scoop, and toothpick, all in silver. The tumblers were usually engraved with picturesque all-over sporting scenes or with patterns of closely scrolled flowers and foliage (*153*).

A silver-gilt set (*152*) formerly in the collection of Viscount Monck was described in Christie's catalogue as ''comprising an oval beaker, engraved with a piping figure and birds amid scrolling foliage, and, round the rim, with the inscription 'A Bartlemew Fairing sent by His Grace the Duke of Ormond to Fridasweed Lady Stephen 1686,' a small double spice-box, engraved with winged caryatid figures blowing trumpets, and a rat-tailed spoon, four-pronged fork and steel knife with detachable handles engraved with foliage, circa 1685, in shagreen case.'' This set is struck with the maker's mark only, FS with a small S below and a coronet above, showing it to have been made to commission and not offered for sale on the open market.

Bartholomew Fair had long been established for trading purposes during two weeks of August. It was patronised by royalty and the nobility, the booths being weatherproof erections of timber framework, walled and roofed with planks. Leading silversmiths rented booths and specialised in the sale of gift ware made for the occasion. Pepys went often and once he noted Lady Castlemaine among the visitors.

The travelling set made by Charles Overington, 1701 (*153*), illustrates the numerous accessories carried by the epicure of the period to make his food palatable, much of it cured or otherwise preserved. His delight in flavouring it with pungent spices is recalled by the inclusion of a tiny spice-box. Such a box was hexagonal and opened into two sections revealing a pair of engraved lids covering tiny spice receptacles. Lids and boxes all hinged on a single pin. The cylindrical nutmeg grater enabled him to powder his own nutmeg over the ill-served foods in a public dining-room. Its chief purpose, however, was to add zest to wine and other drinks. It is surprising to find in this set a miniature corkscrew, then known as a worm or bottle screw, protected by a sheath: this is probably the earliest authenticated example. The flat plate on the thumb-ring enabled it to be used as a tobacco stopper. The long-bladed scoop was used for extracting marrow from cooked bones, and was a common table accessory from the late seventeenth century until Victorian days (see p. 199). These together with a rat-tailed spoon, three-pronged fork, and steel-bladed knife, all with detachable silver handles engraved with bands of foliage, a small knife with a plain handle, and a toothpick comprise the set. But the major item of the set is the oval tumbler engraved with stag and boar hunts, the figures and hounds separated by palm trees, and with festoons and flowers above. This is protected by a shagreen case, its lid lining arranged to receive such items as the knife blades, while the remainder fit comfortably inside the tumbler.

The most elaborate version of the silver tumbler was the stirrup cup. Everything associated with fox-hunting in past centuries is now collectors' treasure and especially those silver cups modelled by silversmiths into lifelike renderings of fox masks. Huntsmen delighted in producing silver stirrup cups when pausing for refreshment outside village inns or wayside taverns. These cups seldom held more liquor than could be consumed in a single brief quaff, and varied in size from a 3-inch drammer for spirits, to the 6-inch half-pint for punch.

The fox-mask stirrup cup dates from the early 1750s onward. At first it was a costly luxury hand-raised from a single disc of thick silver plate, of a diameter approximating the combined width and depth of the proposed cup. This was shaped into the basic hollow vessel by repeated hammering, a process occupying days (*158*).

Sterling silver is not sufficiently malleable for deep-raising to be accomplished without prolonged and repeated fluting or crimping to prevent splitting. After each of the six or seven flutings the silver was smoothed, annealed by bringing it to a dull red heat on a bed of fiery court charcoals, and cooled by plunging into cold water. The fox mask was then shaped in high relief by the process known as repoussé or chased embossing.

The thinly pointed ears, smooth inside and haired without, were made separately and soldered into an alert position. The mouth was shown slightly open, displaying vicious-looking teeth (*159*). The short hairs of the muzzle, extending into longer hairs at the neck, were excellently delineated, and the eyes tooled with a wary expression. The rim of such a stirrup cup might be encircled with a smooth narrow band of silver or a flat collar broad enough to take an engraved inscription (*158*) or the name of the hunt with the owner's crest. The neck, in a few instances, was drawn in and the long ears laid back and extended beyond the rim. These now rare fox-mask cups were invoiced by silversmiths as "foxes' heads for drinking cups."

A second group of fox masks dating from about 1760 onward were less costly to produce, being shaped from the plate in right- and left-hand halves extending from muzzle to neck. The slight ridge or faint depression marking the upper seam was utilised by chaser and engraver as a line of parting in the hair. The mouth was usually closed, the lips only being delineated by chasing. An encircling collar of applied moulding strengthened the rim and also served to trim off the line of the hair. By 1765 it was fashionable to engrave the collar in script with a slogan such as "Prosperity to the Melton Hunt" or "Success to Fox Hunting and the Joys of a Tally." These hand-made fox masks appear to have been entirely the work of the better-known London silversmiths.

The cream-coloured earthenware developed by Wedgwood and other potters from this time had become standard equipment by 1790 in coaching houses, inns, and so on. It was no longer necessary to carry a silver drinking vessel, and fox masks like other tumblers virtually ceased to be made. But the sporting fever encouraged by the Prince of Wales, later George IV, prompted the master-silversmiths to

162, 163 TUMBLERS: in Britannia standard silver (162), by John Langwith, York, 1708; height 2 inches; (163) one of a pair, by Thomas Whippam and Charles Wright, 1767
In the collection of Mrs. William B. Munro

164, 165 TUMBLERS: engraved with coat of arms (164), London, 1681. *Courtesy of Messrs. Birch and Gaydon Ltd.* (165) With chinoiserie decoration, maker R.S., 1685; weight 2 ounces
In the collection of Mrs. William B. Munro

166, 167, 168 BEAKERS: with chased decoration (166), maker's mark T.C. with a fish above, London, 1672. *Courtesy of Messrs. Harvey and Gore.* (167) Repoussé and chased, London, 1691. *Courtesy of Messrs. Garrard and Co. Ltd.* (168) Chased with scrollwork, 5¾ inches high, London, 1608
Courtesy of Messrs. E. T. Biggs and Sons Ltd.

169, 170, 171 (*above*)
CUP by Thomas Holland (169), 1801; (170)
BARREL-SHAPED HALF-PINT MUG, by Crespin Fuller, 1810; (171)
HALF-PINT MUG by Richard Richardson, Chester, 1775. *In the collection of Mrs. William B. Munro*

172, 173 (*above*) HALF-PINT TANKARD MUGS: (172) with handle of ridged moulding, by John Cole, 1701; (173) with embossed ornament and hollow scroll handle, by Isaac Dighton, 1693. *In the collection of Mrs. William B. Munro*

174, 175   DEEP CAN, hammered from the plate (174), with cast handle, by Ambrose Stevenson, 1720; (175) BALUSTER PINT MUG by Joseph Smith, 1729; (176) (*right*) SATYR-HEAD JUG, cast, with crabstock handle, height 4 inches, by William Day, London, 1774
In the collection of Mrs. William B. Munro

devise a third group of fox-mask cups. These, cast in heavy silver, tooled, chased, and burnished, were intended for use as prizes in connection with social events associated with the hunt, or as gifts for display purposes, and might be gilded (154).

It was less costly to carve a pattern in soft wood and cast a hollow cup than to raise and shape a fox mask from the plate, even though considerably more metal was needed. Cast fox masks seldom display the individuality that could be achieved by the worker in plate. The long hair towards the rim is shown in deeper relief, the mouth is tooled with an air of unvarying content, and eyes lack the lifelike expression. The cast ears are usually found in the alert position: in some late examples one is alert, the other flat. The collar band was often highly convex and with a flat edge wide enough for the mask to stand upright in a display cabinet. Although sometimes engraved with simple ornament such as anthemion and florette motifs, more usually it was inscribed.

A Regency fox mask might be accompanied by a special display stand recessed at the top to receive the cup, muzzle upward: both were gilded (156). The stand was usually spool-shaped, the expansive lower rim supported on four scroll feet linked by narrow aprons. The collar of the cup was made deeper to accommodate lengthy inscriptions, engraved to be read whilst displayed on the stand, instead of when inverted for use. Inscriptions provide glimpses of otherwise forgotten sporting events such as: "This cup, the gift of Sir Thomas Mostyn, Bart., to the Gentlemen Yeomen of Oxfordshire, Buckinghamshire, Warwickshire, and Northamptonshire, Friends of Fox Hunting, was won by Mr. Edward Deakin's Bay Horse Narbocklush on the 5th April 1820." Few fox-mask stirrup cups were made after the 1820s.

A favourite hound in a pack might be commemorated with a hound-mask stirrup cup, the double-gilt collar engraved with its name and that of the hunt (157). These were not portraits as has been conjectured, but formed part of the fashionable Regency silversmith's current stock: an example noted bearing the London hallmark for 1814 was not inscribed until 1818.

Greyhound masks with ears falling flat and cast in a piece with the head date from about 1810. They were prizes won at coursing meetings and commemorate many a once-celebrated racer who otherwise would be forgotten.

Paul Storr catered for the early nineteenth-century stag hunter by making silver rhytons in the form of a stag head, the rim expanded into trumpet form and edged with beaded moulding. The horns, curving outward and upward, extend from the skull to the long slender neck to form a handle. Each horn was hollow and so designed that one end opened into the cup a short distance below the rim, the other end, concealed, continuing to the stag's mouth. When the drinker held up a partly filled rhyton by the handle and tilted it at the correct angle, the wine poured in a thin stream from the mouth of the stag into his own.

Stirrup cups in the form of race-horse heads were an early Victorian vogue. These were cast and chased with the mouth open and their rims engraved with commemorative inscriptions.

II HALF-PINT MUGS

SILVER mugs have always been peculiarly personal, informal pieces of plate. From infancy every member of a prosperous family would possess at least one of these "half pint cans": many owned a matching pair. The arrival of tea, coffee, and chocolate on the domestic scene created a demand for exquisite cups of Chinese porcelain, but these were brought out only on formal occasions. It has been too easily assumed, perhaps, that delft ware served as an adequate substitute, but a broadsheet of 1672 records that "the smell and taste of Mock China [delft ware] bowls" gave an unpleasant tang to hot dishes. Instead, for more than a century, the handled half-pint mug in silver was the favoured vessel for hot drinks served informally. This vessel should not be confused with the heavier style of beer mug, containing a pint or more.

At first the plain little mugs, with cylindrical bodies and flat S-shaped handles, were inventoried as "long and short canns," a term still used by potters for coffee-cups and half-pint mugs. The long cans were tall and narrow: in short cans the width and depth were about equal. Pint vessels of this shape had long been sold in coarse, rough-glazed earthenware by a class of hawker known as a mugger but the term mug was long retained exclusively for the larger vessel. In the *London Gazette*, 1686, differentiation was made between a silver mug and a silver can, and the assay office price lists of the eighteenth century distinguished between the half-pint can which was assayed for a halfpenny, and the mug assayed for a penny. The price charged by early Georgian silversmiths for supplying the sterling silver and making a half-pint mug was 7s. 8d. oz.; chasing 3s. od. oz. extra; double gilding 4s. od. oz. extra; and about 10s. od. extra for engraving a baroque cartouche with a coat of arms.

This was the vessel the Georgian schoolboy was required to take to his boarding school, the other necessaries being a silver spoon and a pair of sheets. The Verney letters refer to this custom at Rugby early in the eighteenth century, and Timmins' extracts from the *Birmingham Gazette* note a school advertisement of 1789 where this is mentioned. The Fitzwalter account books in the Mildmay archives (Essex Records Office) contain a reminder of another informal use for clean, pleasant silver vessels in an entry dated 11th January 1747 for "a half-pint silver mug for my Lady Fitzwalter to drink her asses milk in £1.13.0." Asses' milk was highly regarded as a health-giving beverage throughout the Georgian period. The Fitzwalter accounts contain numerous payments such as "Asses milk for Lady Caroline £5.18.0" on 31st January 1726.

Half-pint mugs in silver found a place, too, among the equipment of coaching houses where side-tables of silver plate were kept for the well-to-do. Such mugs are recognised by the presence of a standard measure mark struck beneath the rim. Even when English porcelain cups and saucers were made in considerable numbers from 1750 by Bow, Worcester, and elsewhere for everyday use in wealthy homes, the half-pint silver mug continued in some demand.

Few of these silver cans remain that may be dated to Charles II's reign. The earliest in the extensive Munro collection of these half-pint mugs bears the London hall-mark for 1678 (*177*). This has a short, wide cylindrical body raised from the plate, measuring only 2 inches in height and weighing 4 ounces. The D-shaped handle is made from flat plate, its crest rising above the brim. The surface of the metal is noticeably pitted. Its shape closely resembles that of the tiny contemporary silver saucepans used, among other purposes, over a burning charcoal brazier for preparing the hot brandy wine then popular in home and coffee-house.

Drinking glasses were not to be relied upon to withstand the hot liquor without cracking; a silver tumbler became uncomfortable to hold and might slip; the silver half-pint can, therefore, was brought into use. This combination of matching can and saucepan continued into the Georgian period. A similar can $2\frac{3}{4}$ inches deep, its hollow scroll handle crested by a flat thumbpiece, by Ambrose Stevenson, London, 1720, is in the Munro collection (*174*).

An attractive style of half-pint mug was made with a globular body and vertical neck (*181*), repeating a tankard form made from the 1560s. The body might be raised from a single piece of metal, or the mug less expensively constructed from three sections of silver: a saucer-shaped base; a convex body shaped by hammering and joining vertically; and a vertical neck. Joints made with a Roman joint, hard-soldered and vigorously burnished, were virtually invisible. The S-handle was made from a strip of moulding, flat beneath, ridged on the upper surface for strengthening and to enable finger and thumb to take a firmer grip. The body might be plain or decorated with an outline design of chased lines, such as flowers and foliage, birds, and animals. In the Munro collection is an example of 1684 chased with a design of water birds and reeds (*181*): the hammer marks on the plate have successfully concealed any pitting of the metal. The neck is encircled with closely spaced chased rings. Another, dated 1696, is of thicker plate pounced all over to conceal pitting in the metal (*182*). Some of the finer half-pint mugs were double-gilded within and without.

The half-pint mug in the form of a lidless tankard appears to date no earlier than the late 1670s. This was cylindrical of body, tapering from a moulded rim foot to the brim, strengthened by narrow moulding and measuring from $2\frac{1}{2}$ inches to 4 inches deep. This was shaped from flat plate and seamed vertically, a silver disc being inserted as a base. The invisible body seam was the point at which the handle was attached. At first S-handles were of ridged moulding, the crest rising above the brim (*172*). From the mid-1690s the handle might be of the hollow scroll type, gracefully tapering towards the tail, semicircular in section with a flat thumbpiece extending from body to crest. It was usually sliced obliquely across the other end and soldered to the body immediately below the moulding encircling the brim. The lower curve was soldered directly to the body and might end in a heel-shaped slice or curl. A small perforation, known to silversmiths as a blow-hole, was drilled beneath the upper curve of the handle, its purpose being to allow the escape of hot air expanded within the hollow by the heat of the soldering iron, thus preventing a burst. Hollow handles were usual throughout the eighteenth century, the double scroll being frequent from the 1720s.

The majority of tankard mugs—Dean Swift referred to them as tankard cups— were undecorated: others were ornamented with a combination of chasing and pouncing with narrow bands of punched decoration above and below (*179*). Chasing might extend over the entire field from the deep foot rim to the brim. In others the chasing was sandwiched between broad bands of closely spaced lines: the chased design was broken at the front of the body by an escutcheon intended for an engraved coat of arms, crest, or cypher and, rarely, a date.

These tiny mugs from the late 1690s to about 1720 might be elaborated by the addition of simple cut-card work (*178*) encircling the base immediately above the foot-rim and extending about halfway up the body. This ornament consisted of a series of narrow flat or pierced leaf-shaped motifs cut from the plate and soldered to the mug. Two or three cut-card plates in diminishing sizes might be applied one over the other, or the centre of each leaf might be enriched with a plain drop or a mid-rib of diminishing beads. A narrow band of cut-card scalloping might encircle the base. In some otherwise plain mugs a simple cut-card strengthening plate radiated from one or both handle junctions and a row of beads decorated the handle, descending in diminishing sizes. Such work strengthened the Britannia standard silver.

The rim of the tankard mug might now be slightly everted and the body, made of thinner plate than formerly, encircled with an applied rib, usually nearer to the brim than the base.

Simple embossed ornament appeared on half-pint tankard mugs during the 1690s. A frequent pattern was composed of a central band of vertical concave fluting with rounded ends (*173*) bordered with narrow punch-work ornament. The moulded rim foot was deeper and more boldly convex than usual. Spiral or vertical gadroons might encircle the lower part of a mug, alternatively concave and convex, with a band of punched ornament above and chased lines below the rim.

At this period, too, appeared the rare mug with a flat-based lower section, comprising about one-third of the whole and raised from the plate, being joined to a cylindrical upper section with a widely everted mouth. The two parts were soldered together, the seam being concealed and strengthened by an encircling moulded rib (*180*).

The tankard-shaped mug continued to be made until early Victorian times, usually plain and with a deep, moulded rim foot and a scroll handle, the double scroll dating from the late 1720s onward. The handle might be hollow or cast and crested with an acanthus-leaf thumb-rest shaped to the upper curve of the handle. So that the vessel could be inverted on a cupboard shelf the thumb-rest might now be level with the brim, after the style of a lidded tankard.

The requirements of the softer metal compulsory between 1697 and 1720, and continuing as a permissible alternative to sterling and struck with the Britannia hallmark, suggested a new form of mug to silversmiths. This was the baluster or tulip shape (*175*) tapering from base to slightly everted brim in a graceful curve. The rounded base was lifted above the table-top by a concave moulded foot-ring, its extreme diameter approximating that of the widest curve of the body, less frequently by a concave skirt of hammered plate. Such a mug is almost invariably found with a double-scroll handle after the late 1720s. From the third quarter of the eighteenth century the handle–body junctions had substantial strengthening plates with short struts, the upper plate oval, the lower diamond-shaped. These lessened the pull of the handle against the plate, from which it was inclined to become detached.

Most early Georgian half-pint mugs in this form were raised from the plate; in others the lower part was hand-raised, the upper section shaped from flat plate and seamed, the horizontal joint being concealed by a narrow rib of moulding; others were cast and turned. They remained undecorated apart from engraved coats of arms, crests, and cyphers. The weight of such a tulip-shaped mug in plate was greater than a tankard mug of equal height. Both styles continued to be made contemporaneously and from about 1750 until the 1770s were accompanied by the now rare ogee type.

The barrel-shaped mug (*170*) made its appearance in about 1760 and was fashionable for a century to come. In this design the plate was rolled and its basic shape was a factory production seamed and finished by master silversmiths. It was usually encircled with two, three, or four closely spaced chased lines representing hoops and from about 1790 was given a flat-topped handle, square in section. An example 3 inches deep might weigh $4\frac{1}{2}$ ounces.

Half-pint mugs in all the eighteenth-century forms continued into the Victorian era. By about 1830 the thistle-shaped mug had been evolved, its lower part chased with palm leaves. By 1850 half-pint mugs were being termed tankards in silver-smiths' catalogues. A half-pint mug mechanically embossed and gilded inside cost about 4½ guineas in 1850. The thistle and tankard shapes with long, substantial D-handles were the Victorian favourites.

In the majority of half-pint mugs the hall-marks are scattered singly beneath the base: from the 1690s they might be struck in a line to the right of the handle immediately below the rim, but the base remained the more frequent position.

Chapter Seven

I BOTTLE AND DECANTER WINE-COASTERS
AND WINE WAGONS

IN stage-coach days the homes of the gentry were made ready for an evening of hospitality with fragrant dried lavender tossed on the blazing pine logs in the living chambers, and wax candles flaming in wall sconces and candelabra. Bottles of wine were set to cool in the cistern of iced water beneath the side-table or stood darkly upon the rich mahogany of the table-top. Until about the mid-eighteenth century wine was served informally from the bottle, unsealed in the presence of the drinkers by servants who offered the goblets two-thirds filled, carrying them on silver waiters or stemmed glass salvers.

The attendance of servants made private conversation difficult, however. It was well known that waiters would sell overheard secrets or hints of indiscretions to clearing-houses where such information was sought by blackmailers. Letitia Pilkington in her *Diary*, 1758, tells of personal servants whose real profession was blackmail, their positions in private service obtained solely for this purpose.

The eventual result was, naturally, that all but trusted servants were banned from the informal drawing-room and the personal service of wine became fashionable. Wine bottles at this time were of a dark, coarse, heavy glass, comparatively soft and with a high kick in the base, leaving a surrounding rim that quickly became roughened in the cellar. It was found that pushing such bottles from one to another over the mahogany table-tops marred the fine finish of the wood. This defect was overcome by the introduction of silver bottle-stands. Today these are known to most collectors as wine-coasters, but in the past nomenclature has varied. In the *Directory of Sheffield*, 1774, and in the assay office price list of 1777, the term bottle-stand appears. *The Lounger*, 1785, noted that "bottle-sliders are used at the table," and in 1815 Sir Walter Scott employed the same phrase. Wine-slider was an alternative name. Sheffield plate pattern books of the late eighteenth and early nineteenth centuries invariably used the name bottle-stand. Such stands were obviously intended for the reception of bottles of wine labelled with silver or plated wine tickets. Their diameters varied throughout the collectors' period in accordance with changes in wine-bottle design.

Decanter-stands are first noted in Gale and Martin's *Sheffield Directory*, 1787. These were larger in diameter than bottle-stands, which now fitted the new style of bottle measuring about 4 inches in diameter and taller than formerly. Ten years later decanter-stands were further distinguished from bottle-stands by having everted rims.

The term coaster, which the *Oxford English Dictionary* states was derived from "coasting or making the circuit of the table after dinner," dates from the late eighteenth century when double decanter-stands came into use. The earliest literary reference noticed there is in Maria Edgworth's *Belinda*, 1801, where she writes: "Their father pushed them on together, like two decanters in a bottle coaster."

At first the bottle-stand was made entirely of silver, raised from a single piece of plate, with a low gallery and slightly everted rim strengthened by encircling reeded or beaded moulding. This fitted snugly around the base of the wine bottle, at that time measuring 5 inches in diameter. Its under-surface was a trifle convex and highly burnished so that, with a slight push, it would glide smoothly over the mahogany table-top. When the bottle was lifted the stand remained on the table, its silver surface revealing an expansive engraved cartouche enclosing the owner's coat of arms, or merely a crest. By 1760 the bottle-stand was made from two units: the silver base raised with a $\frac{1}{4}$-inch vertical rim and soldered to this a hand-pierced gallery measuring less than 2 inches in height (*190*). Some of these galleries were delightfully worked in low relief repoussé with the background cut away leaving widely open-cut ornament in silhouette such as figures, flowers, foliage, scrollwork, vine-leaves, and grapes. In some instances the decoration formed a panoramic scene, or was composed of four panels divided by moulded ornamental strengthening uprights. The outer surface of the rim was encircled by a narrow strip of moulded beadwork.

An alternative and less expensive method of piercing bottle-stands consisted of building the gallery from several panels (*194*). These were pierced by the saw in geometrical motifs, such as small crosses, diapers, and scrollwork, and five or six in varying designs were soldered together to make a complete gallery: in some instances panels of two designs alternated. The gallery was soldered to the silver base and the join concealed by encircling moulding, often gadrooned or reeded. The rim was strengthened with matching moulding or gadroon and shellwork.

The high kick of the bottle made a rim which pressed flat against the silver plate. This sometimes tended to create a vacuum so that when the bottle was lifted the all-silver stand was liable to accompany it for an instant, then fall with a clatter to the table. This was overcome by replacing the silver base with one of heavy hardwood, such as lignum vitae, boxwood, or mahogany. This was lathe-turned and the surface ornamented with a central boss encircled by three or four concentric rings and polished in its natural colour. The heavy wood gave stability and the turned rings enabled air to reach the kick, so that the bottle was easily lifted from the stand. The centre of the wood base might be inlaid with a silver boss engraved with a crest.

177, 178   HALF-PINT MUGS : (177) cylindrical, raised from the plate, by Thomas Mangy, York, 1678; height 2 inches; (178) encircled with cut-card work, by John Sympsone, Edinburgh, 1693
In the collection of Mrs. William B. Munro

179, 180   HALF-PINT MUGS: (179) tankard mug chased and pounced, maker I.R., 1691; (180) two-piece plain mug, by George Garthorne, 1699. *In the collection of Mrs. William B. Munro*

181, 182   HALF-PINT MUGS with globular bodies and vertical necks: (181) chased; maker's mark I.C., 1684; height 3¼ inches; (182) pounced and gilded, by Benjamin Pyne, 1696; height 3½ inches. *In the collection of Mrs. William B. Munro*

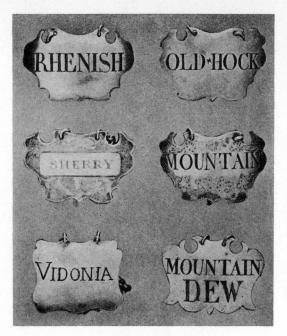

183 BOTTLE TICKETS, popular throughout the
second half of the eighteenth century
In the Victoria and Albert Museum

184 RECTANGULAR BOTTLE TICKETS with
gadrooned, reeded, and knurled borders,
1770–1800
In the Victoria and Albert Museum

185 CRESTED BOTTLE TICKETS hand-worked
from the plate, late eighteenth century
In the Victoria and Albert Museum

186 COCKLESHELL WINE LABELS of the
early nineteenth century
In the Victoria and Albert Museum

Although hand-piercing continued until the end of the century and beyond, it was virtually superseded from the late 1770s by a technique evolved by the manufacturing silversmiths. The gallery, known to the trade as a bar, was made from a single strip of silver about 1½ inches wide and shaped into a ring and invisibly joined by a butt joint, hard-soldered and burnished. The bar, whilst flat, was pierced by fly-press into geometrical motifs such as quatrefoils, diamonds, crosses, circles, diapers, ellipses, and so on. These tools punched silver with extreme delicacy, but patterns were perforce less ambitious than saw-cut piercing (*193*).

Patterns were elaborated in the 1780s, a favourite being two or three rows of short vertical pales supporting applied swags and ornamental medallions cast solid. Vine-leaf piercing was cleverly executed by this method, as were encircling bands of rosettes. The pattern most widely used, because less costly, consisted of four rows of horizontal pales, alternating with circular holes, an unpierced space being left for engraving a crest or monogram. Fashionable designs of the 1780s and 1790s included groups of ten vertical pales spaced by solid rectangles engraved with classic motifs, and bands of piercing encircling upper and lower edges and bordering a wide band of bright-cut engraving. Press-pierced bottle-stands were encircled at base and rim by moulding, the rim usually beaded or corded (*193*).

Bottle-stands with undulating rims date from the early 1780s (*191*). Beneath each crest might be an engraved oval medallion, urn, or other classic motif saw-cut in silhouette. A double row of horizontal piercing might be press-cut immediately below the undulating outline, and the remainder of the gallery press-cut with sparsely placed geometric motifs. Octagonal bottle-stands were made from the 1790s intended for gin bottles.

Silver bottle-stands between 1780 and 1815, particularly during the 1790s, might be enriched with bright-cut engraving, recognised by its delicate faceted effect. The tools employed for this style of engraving were gouges of various sizes, sharpened chisel-wise, bevelled from corner to adjacent corner, and having two cutting points. Edge and point produced what was really a kind of chip carving, outlining patterns of flowers, ribbons, and so on by cutting narrow channels with variously slanting sides.

At this point bottle-stands began to be distinguished from decanter-stands owing to the change in wine-bottle design, the diameter being reduced to about 3½ inches and the height increased proportionately so that capacity remained unaltered. Flint-glass decanters remained 5 inches or more in diameter. By 1800 the bottle-stand was made almost twice the depth of the decanter-stand, measuring about 3 inches in height. The gallery of a fine-quality example was cast and chased in a single ring, elaborately designed surfaces often being worked with a continuous panoramic scene.

The majority, however, were plainly decorated until about 1815, when florid ornament became widely fashionable. Meanwhile engraved and pierced designs continued, the dark glass of the bottle enhancing the pattern in the deep gallery of burnished silver. By about 1830 bottle-stands were made on spreading feet with high insteps, from which rose containers of a height equalling the bottles' diameter. These were used for hock bottles, by then of transparent glass, and were richly pierced either in all-over designs worked by hand, or in geometrical machine-pressed patterns.

Sets of coasters from about 1780 might be accompanied by tumbler-stands with matching, but shallower, galleries. In these the base was of silver and mounted on three low feet in a scroll design. A Sheffield plate catalogue of 1792 illustrates and names these.

Decanter-stands must be considered apart from bottle-stands. The earliest were, of course, identical with those which accompanied bottles. When they broke away into a class of their own they continued the early bottle-stand diameter, were made rather deeper, and with everted rims displaying solid silver moulding. Flamboyant design was required to harmonise with the new-fashioned flint-glass decanters which they carried. These were ornamented with diamond patterns in deep relief cut so that each facet scintillated in the flickering candlelight and was reflected in the highly burnished horizontal rims of the stands. Like bottle-stands and decanters themselves they were sold in matching sets of two, four, or more.

Decanter-stands of the 1790s were often of the half-fluted type, that is, with a band of embossed convex flutes or reeding encircling the centre of the bar, the wide horizontal rim matching with gadrooned moulding. In others the upper part of the gallery might be fluted and rimmed with gadrooning, the lower part pierced. Early in the nineteenth century the positions of fluting and piercing were reversed. Rim mouldings were available in a wide variety and included festoon and bead, leaf and scroll, laurel leaf, egg and dart, escallop shell and scroll. A little-known series comprise those decanter-stands in which the everted rim was extended at four diametrically opposing points and shaped into scroll ornament. The sides of a decanter-stand from about 1810 might take on a slight outward curve, the rim extending horizontally, its surface enriched with a wide ornamental mount. The bar was generally smooth. During the 1820s the rim increased in width and might have a scalloped edge bearing florid applied cast and chased mounts.

Decanter-stands from the beginning of the nineteenth century might have the ring cast in a single piece. In this was soldered a variety of motifs, cast in relief, chased, and burnished. When rims were expansive both upper and lower surfaces were ornamented in this way, a method continued until the 1850s.

The claret jug brought with it a coaster of different design. This was shaped so that the rounded base of the jug fitted snugly into a deep saucer-like receptacle of silver plate rising from a slider of hard wood. From the edge curved outward and downward a wide ornamental rim which might be pierced or cast and chased.

Double-coasters date from the 1790s (*185*). At first a pair of decanter-stands were fitted to a hard-wood slider, usually of mahogany, with baize beneath. The surface and edges were covered with silver plate and a reeded D-handle attached to each end. These were superseded by the double-coaster consisting of a pair of decanter-stands connected by two pairs of rigid couplings in silver, one pair on each side and so shaped as to form loops for the reception of the decanter stoppers while the coaster was journeying around the table. A vertical loop handle was attached to each end.

These were followed by wine wagons, known contemporaneously as bottle- or decanter-carriages (*192*). They were evolved to enable a gentleman at the dining-table to pass the decanters beyond the lady on his left whose glass he had filled, without the necessity of rising from his seat. The early wagon—and according to Sir Edward Thomason, the late Georgian silversmith, they date no earlier than about 1822—was a small silver vehicle with four axle-mounted wheels supporting a pair of silver decanter-stands, and pushed along the table by a long decorative handle hinged beneath the wagon. These were quickly superseded by pairs of decanter-stands, each mounted on a pair of wheels, the upper rims of their galleries being coupled to each other by a pair of rigid couplings. To one end was attached a hinged shaft by which they were pushed along.

In the year following Trafalgar, John Anderson, a silversmith of St. James's, London, introduced a ship model for the table capable of being used for three purposes: first as a soup tureen, then as a trifle dish, and finally as a bottle-wagon. From this evolved the wine-coaster in the form of a "jolly boat," the deck containing two depressions for a pair of decanters, and two smaller ones for their stoppers (*196*). These coasters measured about a foot long with a beam of $5\frac{3}{4}$ inches. By the mid-1820s similar boats were raised on four wheels. At about the same time appeared the boat-shaped bottle-wagon in which the bottle lay on its side. Wine wagons were made in pairs: lots 33 and 34 in the catalogue of the Stowe sale of 1848 were each "a pair of double wine-wagons."

II WINE LABELS

WHEN noble decanters of cut-glass gave a rainbow glitter to the wines of fashion the final elegance consisted of labels hung around their shoulders, exquisitely wrought in gleaming silver. Even among collectors, wine labels today tend to be associated exclusively with such usage in the late eighteenth and early nineteenth centuries, when ever-increasing wealth was paraded with grandiose but gracious feasting. It is not generally realised that such labels were made as early as the 1720s and that their primary purpose for more than half a century was to designate the contents, not of splendid decanters, but of plain, murky bottles.

It was nearly eighty years before the silver bottle ticket was augmented—even then not superseded—by the specifically named "decanter label." Even then, if the earliest certain date for such a silver ticket is about 1720, this essentially Georgian trifle was but handsomely replacing the ticket of parchment, hand-written with the name of the wine, that had long served the same purpose. Such a ticket lacked the silver label's chain but was attached to the pack thread that held down the bottle's sealed cork. The caricaturist, James Gillray (1757–1815), often illustrated this detail and in the same drawing would depict silver wine labels hanging around the necks of carafes.

When London silversmiths of the 1720s began making silver bottle tickets the design was a narrow rectangle shaped to the curve of the wine bottle and suspended from a hand-drawn chain slung around its shoulders. The brilliant sheen of the white metal contrasted effectively with the dark green of the glass bottle.

Sack, shrub, arrack, vidonia, frontignac, constantia, nig, were among the strange liquors recorded upon such tickets, to name but a few of the many listed by Dean Swift in 1740 when he referred to the "silver plates to distinguish bottles and wine by." The name bottle tickets, current in Swift's day, was long continued. In 1759 it appeared in the *London Gazette*; in 1773 the newly-established Birmingham assay office entered such trifles as "labels for bottles," but in 1777 the London assay office was still using the old name. Not until the end of the century did the term decanter label come into use.

By about 1720, when silver wine labels were introduced, silver had become more plentiful in England and coin clipping had been made virtually profitless. The period of superfine, high-standard silver was over and silversmiths were permitted to work in sterling silver once more. The records of the Worshipful Company of Goldsmiths establish that in 1723 John Harvey, of Gutter Lane, submitted silver bottle tickets to the assay office for hall-marking. No example by this silversmith has yet come to light.

A series of bottle tickets struck with a maker's mark composed of the script letters SD superimposed by a crown are believed to be the earliest remaining examples. This work was entered at Goldsmiths' Hall in 1731 by Sandilands Drinkwater of Gutter Lane and he continued in business until 1772. When his mark is found unaccompanied by a complete hall-mark the ticket may be dated later than 1738.

Silver bottle tickets, as distinct from decanter labels, were usually decidedly plain in appearance until 1820 and may be divided into four main groups: narrow oblongs (183), crescents (185), ovals, and escutcheon shapes (184). Piercing dates from about 1770 and embossed work from the 1790s: rare earlier examples are known of each.

In its original form the silver bottle ticket was a narrow silver oblong cut from the plate, smooth edged and plain surface except for the engraved name. Crescents with closely spaced horns, and shaped escutcheons, date from the late 1730s. By about 1740 ornament in the form of threaded borders might be added, and examples are known with feather edging. The escutcheon might be engraved with a narrow border of tiny vine leaves and grapes, sometimes against a matt ground, the space for the name of the wine remaining smooth.

Escutcheon-shaped bottle tickets, containing more silver than oblongs or crescents, were the fashionable type for about twenty-five years from the late 1740s. The majority displayed no more than the name of the wine in letters either saw-cut or engraved. They might be bordered with flat chased vine-leaf and grape motifs (184).

A burgundy label of this type now in Mr. Patrick W. Sandeman's collection, made in 1760 by Samuel Dell, is unusual in having engraved below the name of the wine the words "Hob or Nob." This referred to a style of drinking between friends customary during the second half of the eighteenth century: they wordlessly toasted each other alternately with the clinking of glasses. This was also termed "hob and nob," eventually becoming the well-known hob-nob.

More imagination was put into bottle ticket design from about 1770, but the continued use of the word ticket implied merely a plain label. Gadrooned, beaded, knurled, and bright-cut borders came into use (183). The scroll shape is first noted during the early 1770s with a feather edge and later with a bright-cut edge or chased with a foliated scroll border. Crescents became more frequent at this time and the shallow crescent with wide-spread horns is first noted. Bright-cut borders are found on crescents from about 1775, when an example by John Perry was cut with a pendant motif extending downward from the horn tips.

Tickets made with crestings date as a rule from the early 1770s onwards, although an example made by John Robinson is attributed to 1750. This is a narrow oblong ticket with a threaded and knurled border and a low pierced cresting. Cresting and ticket are hand-worked from a single piece of plate (185).

Space upon which a crest or cypher might be engraved was demanded at this period and this might be in the form of a shield-shaped cresting to the ticket. At first such a ticket was worked from a single piece of plate, but later the cresting might be soldered into position. This shield might rise centrally from the top of a scroll or rectangle and be strengthened by supporters, or the horns of a deep crescent might be elongated and rounded more sharply to support a tiny ornamental shield. In some instances the owner's crest was engraved upon a plain ticket immediately above the name of the wine.

The French mood found fragmentary expression in little perforated designs beautifully wreathed and beribboned. Typical, but now rare, was an urn-shaped label supporting a laurel knot with a label swag beneath (*185*).

The factory silversmiths were pressing blank ticket plates and making slender chains in bulk by 1770, the leading firm being Matthew Boulton and Plate Company, Birmingham. This work was finished by individual silversmiths. In 1773, when the Birmingham assay office was opened, among the first articles to be assayed was a quantity of "labels for bottles" from Boulton's Soho Works. These were distributed by Matthew Boulton as souvenirs of what was to him an occasion, for the establishment of this assay office was in large measure due to his powerful efforts. These labels displayed on the front the full Birmingham hall-mark including the date letter. Silver ticket blanks bordered with piercing were a Boulton product and these, identical in size and piercing, are now to be noted bearing the marks of other makers.

The Boulton firm continued making silver bottle tickets and decanter labels throughout its existence. In the Sandeman collection is a large example of the latter made in 1826. This consists of a shaped plate to which is soldered a cast and chased border of shell, grape, and vine-leaf motifs.

Wine labels struck with the Sheffield hall-mark are not so common as eighteenth-century trade catalogues might lead one to expect. The first Sheffield directory, published in 1774, noted bottle labels among the articles made by the manufacturing silversmiths.

The oval bottle ticket had appeared by the late 1770s and might be surmounted by a shield soldered into position. The pointed oval was in use by 1780, often edged with bright-cutting. An interesting series was bordered with pierced work such as a row of short pales or with a design producing the effect of a zig-zag border. The borders of oblong tickets were now usually clipped; the upper line of the rectangle might be arched, sometimes with a matching curve on the lower edge; and its surface might be domed.

From 1784 wine labels were fully hall-marked, including date letter and duty mark. The presence of date letters permits chronological arrangement. This shows that plain rectangular bottle tickets, often with clipped corners, still predominated numerically, with ovals second and deep crescents third, all with thread, bead, knurled, or bright-cut edges. Oblongs with rounded ends appeared during this period. Crestings for engraved cyphers and crests tended to become larger. The names of wines were now saw-cut into the silver more frequently than before, the original use of this feature being to display the letters by revealing the dark bottle glass against the white of the silver.

A simple hoop might replace the silver bottle ticket and chain from the mid-1780s. Its surface was set at an angle to fit snugly against the sloping neck of either a wine bottle or a taper decanter. It would have been unsuitable for the deeply shouldered bottles customary before about 1770. Such a neck ring was twice engraved with the name of the wine so that it could be read from both sides. In the mid-1790s a plain ticket might be hinged or looped to an equally plain neck ring which was slipped over the neck of the bottle.

Bottle tickets continued to be made in the nineteenth century, exhibiting only minor differences from earlier examples, such as a greater use of rounded ends to plain rectangular tickets; there was a long series with beaded edges. Catalogues illustrated eighteenth-century patterns as late as the 1870s. Neck rings were still made, often with hinged oblong tickets, and cresting still continued, often in association with bright-cut borders.

Bottle-stopper labels date from about 1825 to 1860. In these specially graduated corks of excellent quality were fitted with deep-rimmed flat-topped silver caps. Such a cap might be topped by an upright finger loop with lettering engraved on both sides of an otherwise plain cresting, or it might be flat-topped, with the name of the wine inscribed around its rim. The most notable were elaborations of the latter designs, the inscribed cap being surmounted by a cast and chased figure or animal, such as a lion rampant holding aloft a shield displaying the owner's crest or cypher.

The tickets, though intended primarily for hanging on bottles of the so-called black glass, were so obviously useful that by about the mid-eighteenth century they began to be hung on decanters too. They remained, of course, utilitarian in design. Strangely enough, the first suggestion of highly ornamental design appeared not in silver but in pictorial representations of wine labels engraved, gilded, or enamelled, on the clear flint-glass of what were known as label decanters. These decanters were the shouldered type, the best of them blown from an exceptionally clear glass. They were first advertised in the *Norwich Mercury* dated 26th December 1755, as "new-fashioned decanters with inscriptions engraven on them, viz, port, claret, mountain etc., etc., decorated with vine leaves, grapes etc." Ten years later they were being advertised as "label decanters." The lettering was enclosed in a reserve with mantlings above, vine leaves and bunches of grapes below, the illusion of a suspended bottle ticket being completed by encircling the decanter shoulder with an engraved chain. In the mid-1760s the slimly elegant taper decanter made its appearance, bringing with it the refinement of a silver bottle ticket hanging from its gracefully sloping shoulders. By the 1770s silver wine labels were made rather more ornate when intended to grace shallow-cut flint-glass decanters.

The fashion for ornamenting heavy wide-bodied decanters with elaborate cutting was responsible for more expansive labels. Inconspicuous bottle tickets were no longer suitable for interchange between the new-fashioned cut decanters of glittering flint-glass, and the slender, smooth-surfaced wine bottles in the coarse dark-green or amber metal of the period. Wine labels were now made in two different types for two distinct purposes: the small plain bottle tickets, and the larger, more flamboyant decanter labels, and they were so differentiated (*187* and *188*).

Silver decanter labels displaying designs raised by hand from the plate and chased had become highly fashionable by the turn of the century and their use was frequently noted in contemporary literature. Decoration became progessively more ornate until the 1820s, but hand-raised examples are seldom found bearing date letters struck later than about 1810. These ordinarily lack the profusion of fine detail that marked the arrival of the die-struck label. This only became a practical proposition with the development of hard steel capable of withstanding long runs at the stamp without disfigurement to the die.

Matthew Linwood, of Birmingham, was the first silversmith to specialise in the use of such dies. This was in 1793 and the intricacy of design and superlative craftsmanship were never surpassed. The effects of this mechanism were far-reaching. Silversmiths in their workshops continued the hand-raising of decanter labels from the plate, but it was impossible for them to compete with the stamped and cast work of Birmingham and London. Die-stamped labels of the 1790s and the first years of the nineteenth century are among the most exquisite ever made. Some unwelcome competition came from certain silversmiths who used fine hand-made originals as patterns for taking charcoal casts. These labels, much heavier than the originals, were hand-finished.

The silver decanter label from about 1810 generally consisted of a rectangular or oval name plate to which was soldered an ornamental border cast in high relief and chased: in some instances borders were cast in sections. Flowers, scrolls, shells, and fruiting vine motifs were usual. Reeded scrolls in association with shells or grapes are often noted, as well as the gadroon or thread and shell border. By about 1815 borders might be wider and thicker than formerly (*187*).

The earliest of the celebrated bacchante series in the Sandeman collection bears the mark of Matthew Linwood and the date letter for 1813. This type of decanter label usually displays a scroll label engraved with the name of the wine, surrounded by hand-raised or cast ornament such as a bacchante with a wine jug and a boy among festoons of grapes and vine leaves. Another design illustrates a boy offering wine to a reclining satyr, with grape and vine ornament (*187*).

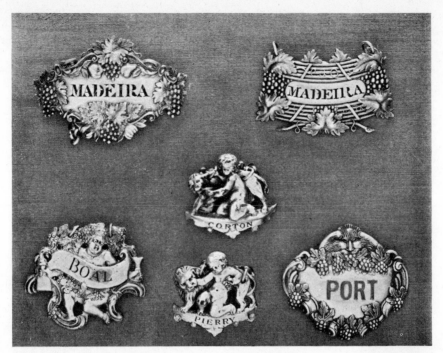

187 WINE LABELS displaying grapes and vine-leaves, 1820s; (*lower left*) Bacchante with wine bottle and drinking vessel. *In the Victoria and Albert Museum*

188 WINE LABELS cast and chased, including the vine-leaf type introduced by Charles Rawlins, 1824
In the Victoria and Albert Museum

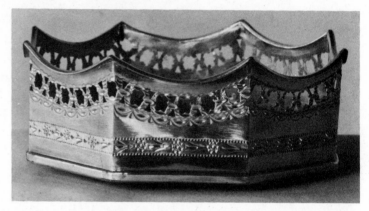

189 DOUBLE DECANTER STANDS with bases of turned wood—the silver by John Emes, 1798, *Courtesy of Messrs. Arthur Ackerman and Son, Inc.*

190, 191 Top and side views of silver-based COASTER (190). By Peter Devese, 1774. *Courtesy of Messrs. N. Bloom and Son Ltd.* (191) COASTER with bright-cut engraving, c. 1780s. *In the Victoria and Albert Museum*

192, 193 ONE OF A PAIR OF WINE WAGONS (192), by T. and J. Settle, Sheffield, 1820. *Courtesy of Mr. John Bell.* (193) COASTER with pierced gallery, by R. Hennell, 1783

194 SET OF SIX COASTERS with hand-pierced galleries, by Frederick Kandler, 1770

195 SILVER-GILT COASTER, part of the Duke of Wellington's ambassador's service. Made by Paul Storr, 1814, to the order of Rundell, Bridge, and Rundell. *In the Wellington Museum*

196 DOUBLE COASTER in the form of a boat, by John Emes, 1800. *Courtesy of Messrs. E. T. Biggs and Sons Ltd.*

197 COASTER struck with Sheffield hall-mark, 1815. *In the Victoria and Albert Museum*

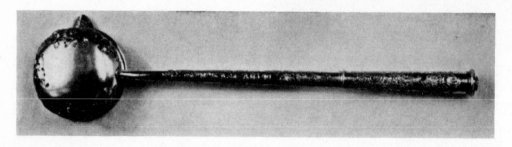

198   PUNCH LADLE WITH LIP: chased ornament on bowl and hollow stem; George I period
In the Victoria and Albert Museum

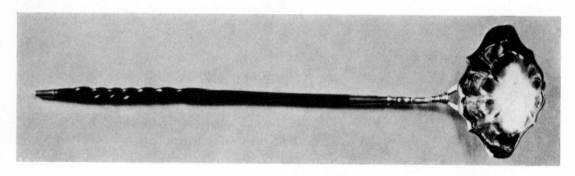

199   DOUBLE-LIPPED TODDY LADLE with whalebone handle; early George III period
In the Victoria and Albert Museum

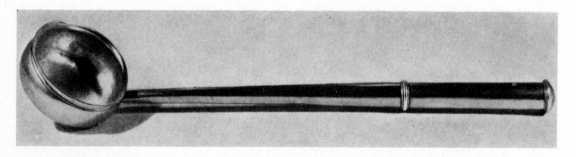

200   PUNCH LADLE with hemispherical bowl and hollow tapering handle, by William Darker, 1729
Courtesy of Messrs. Christie, Manson, and Woods Ltd.

During this decade decanter labels tended to increase in size and become heavier. Typical of the heavy motifs which made their appearance at this time were the lion's mask or boar's mask device set in the centre of the top edge, with thickly entwining vine leaves and grapes; masses of vines trained over trellis-work; and caryatides. This was but the beginning of the great period of elaborate casting by silversmiths and for the next half-century little hand-raised silver was made (*187*).

Borders tended to widen even more from about 1820 leaving but little un-decorated space around the name, which might be engraved in a scroll-shaped reserve. With very few exceptions these floridly designed labels were cast through-out and chased, though the motifs were, in general, similar to those of the preceding period. Many display evidence of adaptation from hand-raised work (*187*).

Decanter labels in the shape of vine leaves upon which the letters were given the clarity of perforation were introduced by Charles Rawlins in 1824. The cast and chased leaf was attached to a stem and tendril. More than thirty varieties have been listed and some are hall-marked on the front.

Bottle tickets in the form of a tall, flat rectangle edged with moulding and con-taining a single saw-cut letter had been introduced by 1805. These were intended to mark wine bottles in individual use, such as by members of a family or in hotel dining-rooms. The letter was intended to indicate the person concerned rather than the name of the wine. In the mid-1820s began a series of decanter labels in the form of silhouette initials. These measured between 1 and 2 inches in height and were separately cast, often in ornamental type, with the surface elaborately engraved or chased. The decanter label composed of the name of the wine in openwork block letters dates from the mid-1830s onwards. In some examples the letters were enclosed within a light frame, often of fret design: in others they were moulded on a bar.

Another device introduced in the course of the wine label's history was the boar's tusk, silver-mounted at each end, with the name of the wine either engraved upon a small silver plate banded around the centre of the tooth, or burnt upon it. The silver mountings, elaborately chased, are seldom found with hall-marks. Tiger claws were similarly mounted.

Despite all their makers' ingenuity decanter labels fell out of fashion when decanters gave place to claret jugs. Bottle tickets were killed by the Licensing Act of 1860. This permitted stores to sell single bottles of wines and spirits for home consumption and made it a legal obligation to label such bottles. A dark bottle pasted with a paper label was a poor substitute for the flint-glass decanter hung with a silver label, but the innovation-loving Victorians discovered that the wine tasted none the worse.

Dr. N. M. Penzer has recorded more than three hundred names of liquors.

inscribed on wine labels, the majority designating hot and rebellious liquors unknown today. The wines most frequently named on silver wine labels in the Sandeman collection are in the following order: madeira, half as many again as port; then sherry; then claret.

Hall-marking is an important consideration to the collector of silver wine labels. No examples have come to light struck with the mark designating the Britannia standard silver that was compulsory between 1697 and 1720 (a seated figure of Britannia and a lion's head erased). Between 1739 and 1784 silver wine labels weighing less than ten pennyweights were exempt from hall-marking. It was still a legal requirement, however, for the maker to strike them with his registered mark, the design incorporating his initials, and submit them to Goldsmiths' Hall, where they were assayed. The charge for assaying a bottle ticket during this period was one halfpenny. At the request of the silversmith they might be struck with the lion passant gardant.

As date letters were never struck on the labels between 1739 and 1784, it is only possible to approximate the dates of examples belonging to this period. Changes in the shape of the shield enclosing the lion passant gardant are helpful in this. From 1720 to 1725 and again between 1729 and 1738 the shield was rectangular with clipped corners: from 1726 to 1729 the shield had a square base and a rounded top. The shield between 1739 and 1755 was indented, following the outline of the lion; after 1756 and until an excise duty was placed on silver in 1784, it was shaped with clipped shoulders and a cyma base.

The name of the silversmith can be discovered from his mark: this will lead to the date of his admission into the Goldsmiths' Company and possibly also the date when he ceased business. The presence of features introduced during this period must also be considered. After 1784 the full hall-marking of silver labels again became compulsory, no matter what their weight, and in addition the monarch's head mark was struck as proof that the excise tax had been paid, an imposition continued until 1890. Many fakes—the word reproduction is inappropriate here—have been issued of wine labels purporting to belong to this period and struck only with a maker's mark. The design of such work is frequently more florid than might be expected before 1784.

III PUNCH- AND TODDY-LADLES AND TODDY-LIFTERS

OUR modern fireside offers no substitute for that symbol of the eighteenth and nineteenth centuries' boisterous bonhomie, the enormous, flamboyantly convivial bowl of punch. Yet the punch of the eighteenth-century coffee-house sophistication had not always been acceptable. It was descended from the rip-roaring seafarer's drink which reached London in the 1620s and only became fashionable when favoured by William III in the last decade of the seventeenth century. Contemporary records are typified by Thomas Aldworth's scornful appreciation when he wrote to a friend, "your company, which we have often remembered in a bowl of the cleerest punch, having noe better liquor." Although Evelyn sampled the drink in 1662 it was yet merely "a drinke very usual among those that frequent the Sea, where a Bowl of Punch is an usual beverage," as Thomas Worlidge wrote in 1675 in his work on *Cider*. He noted punch as a well-known drink: "pale puntz, vulgarly known by the name of punch, is a drink compounded of water, brandy or aqua-vitae, juice of lemons and oranges, and refined loaf sugar." Aqua-vitae was usually arrack, a spirit distilled from the coco-palm and used in fine punch throughout the eighteenth century, but the less expensive rum might also be used.

Punch drinking so captured the imagination and palate of early Georgians that puncheries were established in well-to-do-homes, forerunners of the modern cocktail bar. Here were displayed punch bowls in silver, in blue-painted delft earthenware, or, later, in colourful porcelain, flint-glass goblets, silver spice dredgers, sugar bowls, and nutmeg graters, bottles hung with enamelled or silver labels naming the liquors from which modish punches were made, and long-handled punch-ladles. These ladles were no doubt also used for wassail during the Christmas festivities. Special ladles were reserved for the wassail bowl, however. This is confirmed by the existence of early Georgian examples in which the end of the wooden handle is carved with a wassail bowl in relief.

A punch bowl in silver until the 1730s was usually matched by a ladle of solid silver bearing the same hall-mark. The cylindrical bowl of the Williamite punch-ladle was of thick-gauge metal raised from the plate and provided with a long, flat stem terminating in a broad finial such as were used on spoons of the period.

The Queen Anne punch-ladle was rather less weighty. The ladle still remained cylindrical, with a flat base, vertical sides, its depth approximating two-thirds its diameter, and an applied moulded angular lip extending almost the full depth of the ladle. Instead, in some instances, a small lip for pouring was expanded directly from the ladle. A hollow tapered and collared cylindrical handle measuring at least a foot in length, and terminating either in a turned vase-shaped knop or in a domed cap, was attached at right angles to the lip by means of a flanged collar of foliate outline. The handle was either screwed or soldered into this. A coat of arms might be engraved beneath the base. From the early 1720s the handle might be elaborately worked with engraved and chased all-over ornament (*198*). A few George II examples are known with the vertical sides embossed and chased, including a cartouche framing an engraved crest. A series of cylindrical ladles dating from about

145

1710 were made by a less costly manner. In this design a shaped strip was vertically seamed and a flat disc base of plate was soldered into it.

A punch-ladle that became fashionable from the mid-1720s had a hemispherical bowl, its incurved rim strengthened with a narrow band of outcurving moulding (*198*). This was raised from the plate, but examples have been noted in which the lower half of the ladle was raised from the plate, the upper part curved from strip plate and soldered into position with a seam rendered invisible beneath hammer marks. The weight of all-silver punch-ladles progessively decreased, 10 ounces being common in the 1690s and 6 ounces or even less forty years later.

A less expensive type of punch-ladle was evolved during the 1720s: the silver handle was replaced by one of turned hard wood (*199*). The silver ladle, at first of the hemispherical type, was necessarily heavy to ensure that it sank to the bottom of a full punch bowl, for the wooden handle tended to make it float. A tavern scene by Thomas Patch painted in about the 1740s depicts a full punch bowl with a ladle entirely of wood, its shallow bowl floating on the surface of the liquor.

Lord Braintree's collection of 164 punch-ladles included fifty bearing hall-marks pre-dating 1750. Of these all but five were fitted with handles of turned hard-wood: three were of ivory dating to the 1740s, and two of silver, 1712 and 1715. The remaining 114 were made between 1750 and 1820, 94 having handles of whale-bone, 16 of turned hard-wood, and 4 of ivory dating early in the period.

Silver punch-ladles with turned wood handles may be divided into six main groups according to shape: hemispherical from the early 1720s; oval from 1725; goose-egg from the late 1720s; oval with lips at both ends from the early 1730s; lobed and fluted from the late 1730s; the escallop shell, often miscalled nautilus, from about 1740. These were all raised from the plate, the majority remaining plain, a small proportion being enriched with embossed and chased ornament. The hemispherical type might be encircled around the curve with gadrooning, a band of punched bead ornament above, the base left smooth for the reception of an engraved crest often in a cartouche. Others were embossed with flower and scroll patterns in the fashionable rococo manner. The rim might be expanded into a single pouring lip at right angles to the handle which was fitted in such a way that a full ladle could be lifted to the drinking glass without mishap.

The so-called goose-egg ladle was rather more capacious, the pointed end of the ovoid bowl providing an excellent pouring lip.

The punch-ladle handle was at first inserted into a tapering socket of silver, terminating in an expanded circular, triangular, or foliated flange curved to fit snugly against the ladle. The surface of the flange usually remained plain, but in the case of a decorated ladle its surface might be chased or engraved to form part of the design. By the 1730s the goose-egg, double-lipped oval, and other wide-mouthed ladles were given needed extra support by shortening the socket and extending it with a moulded V-shaped attachment, each arm terminating in a flange by which it was soldered to the curve of the ladle.

In addition to hall-marks, contemporary paintings and engravings illustrate punch-ladles. Trade cards reproduced in *The English Goldsmiths*, 1935, by Sir Ambrose Heal, show nine punch-ladles of the type fashionable between 1734 and 1760. The earliest depicts two examples by John Jackson, "at ye Crown and Pearl, George Street, by Goldsmiths' Hall." One is a plain goose-egg ladle, the other is hemispherical with an everted rim: both have short sockets fitted with plain baluster handles. Richard Boult, who traded at the Blue Anchor and Star, Cheapside, between 1744 and 1753, issued two trade cards during the period, both illustrating goose-egg ladles. The early example is plain with a short socket and double baluster handle; the other has a forked attachment joining ladle and socket and a single baluster handle with a substantial mushroom knop finial. Four other silversmiths at this period show plain goose-egg ladles with sockets and plain baluster stems. Chalmers and Robinson in 1760 illustrated a swash-turned handle tapering towards a solid curved extension soldered to an eight-lobed ladle.

The efficient method of manipulating the ladle to ensure stability is well illustrated in George Knapton's portrait of Sir Bouchier Wray, about 1760. The hardwood handle turned in baluster form is grasped in the centre by three fingers and the thumb of the right hand, the handle passing under the palm so that its knopped finial rests against the wrist; the forefinger presses on the upper surface of the handle-socket joint.

A new English drink called toddy became fashionable in the early years of George III's reign. This was described in the *Sporting Magazine* at that time as "hot grog with the addition of sugar." Usually, however, the grog—a mixture of rum and water—was enriched with lemon juice, sweetened with sugar, and flavoured with grated nutmeg—hot rum punch, in fact.

The hot toddy adversely affected the hard-wood handles of the punch-ladles which were taken into use for dispensing toddy. Constant expansion and contraction of the silver and wood at different rates caused the handle to become loose in the socket, liquor seeping into the joint. This was overcome first by shortening the silver socket and inserting between it and the ladle an extension of solid silver rod, rectangular in section and long enough to ensure that the joint between the wood handle and the rim of the silver socket was raised above the surface of the hot toddy.

This extension became unnecessary, although not entirely dispensed with, when whalebone handles were introduced. These handles were of square or round section near to the socket, with twist- or swash-turning above to provide a safer grip on the smooth surface and prevent slipping in the hand whilst transferring the toddy to its glass. Such a handle usually terminated in a silver ferrule to prevent splitting, its flat end engraved with a crest or cypher.

The whalebone handle was usually fitted to a hemispherical ladle with sides incurving towards an everted rim, spoutless but having a slight outward curve to facilitate pouring. This was shaped from thinly rolled plate by spinning in the lathe. Ornament became more ambitious, ladles being enriched with closely patterned all-over embossed work, or vertical fluting produced by factory processes in Birmingham and Sheffield. The whalebone handle was sufficiently heavy to sink the light-weight ladle to the bottom of the filled bowl of toddy, which had an immense vogue for more than half a century. In the *Butlers' Compendium*, 1823, a toddy-ladle is defined as "a small deep ladle used for conveying whiskey toddy from a rummer or punch-bowl to a wine-glass." Punch-ladles are no longer mentioned.

Master silversmiths of London and elsewhere continued raising ladles from the plate, usually with lips. They also bought partly finished factory-made ladles and completed them to their own designs.

Shapes of the earlier periods were hand-raised, the lobed and fluted type being frequent. The early nineteenth-century ladle was generally hemispherical with a wide lip extending upward above the rim. A favourite embossed and chased decoration consisted of an all-over design of vine-leaves and grapes, with flowers and foliage.

The factory-made ladle of excessively thin silver was given a strengthening rib sufficient to prevent distortion in use. The handle socket was continued in a long slender taper of flat metal, shaped to the curve of the bowl to which it was soldered.

A silver coin of an earlier period might be set into the base of a ladle. Queen Anne shillings are not uncommon in hand-raised ladles bearing George III hall-marks. Silver-gilt ladles might be inset with golden guineas. Crown pieces were found convenient discs of metal to raise into hemispherical ladles from $2\frac{1}{2}$ to 3 inches in diameter. This was done in such a way that the marginal inscription encircled the thickness of the rim. Punch-ladles until the 1770s were usually struck with the London hall-mark, the assay office price list of 1777 showing the charge to have been one penny each. From about 1780 the majority were of factory origin and struck with Birmingham and Sheffield hall-marks. A duty mark, the monarch's head, was also struck from 1784. Hall-marks were usually struck within the bowl. Under the Silversmiths' Act of 1739 punch-ladles were exempt from being disfigured with hall-marks if they were "so richly engraved, carved or chased . . . as not to admit of an assay to be taken of, or a mark to be struck thereon, without damaging, prejudic-ing, or defacing the same, or such other things as by reason of the smallness or thinness thereof are not capable of receiving the marks . . . and not weighing ten pennyweights of gold or silver each.'' Many a hemispherical ladle of substantial gauge bearing a fine set of hall-marks struck during the early Georgian period has been deprived of handle and socket, appropriately embossed and fitted with moulded and chased mask and claw legs, and thus converted into a salt-cellar of far greater antique value. Punch- and toddy-ladles were also made in Sheffield plate: these are listed in a catalogue of 1790.

Instead of a toddy-ladle it was customary to use a toddy-lifter when serving from a rummer. The toddy-lifter, particularly popular in the North and in Scotland, was a long slender tube or neck terminating in a bulbous container with a hole in its flat base. The two forms most frequently found resemble either high-shouldered minia-ture decanters or shoulderless pear-shaped clubs and are rather more capacious than a toddy-ladle. The neck is usually encircled with a single flat collar below the mouth: collarless examples are rare. The body is usually left smoothly plain.

The toddy-lifter would be held by the neck, between the first and second fingers upon which the collar rested. The container was then plunged into the toddy, which entered through the lower hole. When full, the thumb was pressed upon the hole in the neck, thus creating a vacuum. The toddy-lifter was then raised from the toddy and held above the wine glass. Removal of the thumb released the toddy, which flowed into the glass.

Chapter Eight

INKSTANDS

WHEN the Georgian of two centuries ago set out to write a letter he was faced with an arduous undertaking that required a formidable array of accessories. These included a quill pen which he cut from a goose feather with the aid of a razor-edged penknife, ink ground with gum tragacanth, a pounce-dredger containing finely powdered gum sandarac, a dog's tooth or agate for polishing erasures scraped out with the penknife, a quill-cleaner full of small lead shot, wafers or sealing wax and taper. These were arranged on a shallow oblong dish or tray raised on four feet. Rulers and black-lead pens would also find a place here, the latter being pencils with points of lead.

Until the early 1760s the matching containers of ink, pounce, and pen-cleaning shot were of silver and stood loose upon the dish, which was sunk back and front with deep, round-ended channels for the penknife, rulers, sealing-wax, pencil, and so on. It was then found that the crystal clarity of flint-glass provided attractive containers to be fitted with plain silver mounts. These were more convenient to clean and less costly to buy than those of solid silver, and might be either cylindrical or square with cut shoulders.

They were fitted into square or circular sockets or guard-rings soldered to a rectangular platform slightly raised above the rococo-shaped stand, its rims strengthened with wide gadroon and shell moulding. The earliest were hand-made by master silversmiths. The guard-rings were pierced in geometrical designs resembling the current so-called Chinese style of fret-cut furniture decoration. The stand had paw or claw-and-ball feet, or cast and chased openwork corner feet.

At the same time appeared the box-shaped inkstand with pierced sides, solid base, and paw feet, divided lengthwise into two sections by a pierced partition. The rear section was further divided to take inkpot and pounce-dredger in the right- and left-hand corners. The piercing might be in the Chinese geometrical style, or in arabesque scrollwork, flowers and foliage, or other curving design, or in a combination of both. The top edges of the vertical sides were strengthened with wide gadrooned moulding. By 1770 such a stand might be built from sixteen square units, arranged in alternating patterns of geometrical and scroll piercing. Sizes varied from about $12\frac{1}{2}$ inches by $7\frac{1}{2}$ inches to $5\frac{1}{2}$ inches by $2\frac{3}{4}$ inches.

The correct order for placing the glass containers upon the stand has perplexed some collectors. Thomas Gainsborough's portrait of William Pitt, painted in the

201   A SET OF THREE WINE LABELS, cast and chased, with pounced backgrounds to the lettering, by H.S., London, 1835

202   A SET OF EIGHT WINE LABELS, each with a mask of Pan, stamped and chased, by Matthew Linwood, Birmingham, 1818

203 INKSTAND with cut-glass ink-pot and quill cleaner, with wafer box supporting taperstick and extinguisher, by John Angell, 1827. *Courtesy of Messrs. Christie, Manson, and Woods Ltd.*

204 INKSTAND hand-raised from the plate, with four low, hand-pierced galleries fitted with square containers for two ink-pots, pounce-pot, and quill cleaner; by John Longford and John Seville, 1767. *Courtesy of Messrs. Spink and Son Ltd.*

205 INKSTAND with plain tray rimmed with reeded moulding, the solid galleries fitted with silver-mounted cut-glass pounce-pot and ink-pots, by Henry Chawner, 1790. *Courtesy of Messrs. Bracher and Sydenham*

early 1780s, shows a pierced inkstand with the quill standing upright in the central glass container which is the quill-cleaner; ink to the right; pounce to the left. Other portraits record a similar and most obviously convenient arrangement.

"Inkstand," the term used to distinguish the set with glass containers from those completely in silver (204), was first used in 1772 by Matthew Boulton, the celebrated silversmith of Birmingham. As has been indicated in other chapters the development of large-scale price-cutting factory production in silverware from this time introduced such items as inkstands into homes which hitherto had never dreamed of possessing such luxury, a contributory reason being the improvement in plate-rolling technique and the introduction of a tool steel, hard throughout its texture. Factory-made inkstands were produced by the gross in countless designs developed from a few basic forms. Such men as Matthew Boulton and John Fothergill made such plate into partly finished units which were sold to master silversmiths in London and elsewhere, and struck with their marks when sent for assay. Boulton told a Parliamentary Committee in 1773 that he was stamping silverware in his own works and casting his own tool steel.

So fine and lovely were silver inkstands made of thinly rolled silver plate that they became recognised gifts of appreciation. In 1794 the artist John Farrington recorded that members of the Royal Family customarily made presents of silver inkstands engraved with their coronets and cyphers.

An inkstand of the 1770s might be bordered with a pierced and beaded gallery (204), the three or four square guard-rings being made to match. Soon the conventional rectangle gave way to ovals and boat-shapes, occasionally fitted with swing handles. In some of these the pierced edging was low, with guard-rings as much as four times their height. Narrow moulding around the outside of the guard-ring bases was used to solder them to the platform. The sides of the cylindrical bottles were cut with twelve flat vertical facets, and the pronounced shoulders were enriched with diamond facets. The ends of an oval stand might be ornamented with rams' masks, and foliage feet were frequent. In late examples the guard-ring moulding spread further across the platform than formerly.

The canoe-shape had become fashionable by 1780 with highly upcurved ends (208). The gallery was pierced with motifs such as the most frequent vertical and horizontal pales, vases, stars, and circles. The guard-rings were high and sparsely pierced, the remaining silver being ornamented with bright-cut engraving. The twelve-sided glasses continued with deeply cut diamonds encircling their shoulders. The ends of the stand might be fitted with loop handles, turned over and carved beneath the stand. Joins were so perfect that handles and stand appear to have been cut from a single piece of metal. The canoe stand usually contained two glasses, for ink and for pounce, often in facet-cut Bristol blue with deep silver mountings (*208*).

From about 1790 such a stand might be almost flat with triangular ends and low, unpierced guard-rings enriched with bright-cut engraving. The guard-ring rims were threaded to match the moulding strengthening the edge of the stand itself. Strengthening moulding was essential on inkstands to prevent distortion under vigorous cleaning, particularly on factory-made specimens. Glass containers were taller than formerly, vertically fluted to the shoulder, which was cut with deep diamonds. In some instances an oval wafer box in bright-cut silver was placed between the two containers, its lid flat or domed. Moulded and chased scroll feet were usual. Sometimes the wafer box was in cut-glass, matching inkpot and pounce dredger (*206*).

Plain oblong inkstands with raised platforms and sunk pen channels date from the 1780s, the stand and the solid galleries bordered with thread-work (*205*). Such an inkstand might be built from three pieces of shaped plate: corner feet might also be cut from the plate, with applied moulded edges. The glasses might have flat hexagonal faces, and shoulders either notched or encircled with deeply cut diamonds. The inkpot lid might be hinged, with a small knop finial, preventing evaporation of the ink. From about 1790 an oval wafer box, usually half the height of its companion containers, might be substituted for the pounce box. This followed the introduction of mechanically callendered writing paper into which the ink did not sink.

Competition from the Sheffield platers making similar inkstands at less than half the cost of silver, urged the master silversmiths to produce elaborate inkstands of high craftsmanship in a bewildering array of fanciful patterns and raised above the desk on lion paw feet. From the early 1790s silversmiths made some weighty and magnificent specimens. The plateau was encircled with deep aprons, often containing a drawer at the front, and supported three triangular pedestals for urns of finest quality cut-glass. These, however, were more ornamental than useful. Early in the nineteenth century a silver inkstand might be supported on four sphinx figure legs. Panels of engine-turning on the sides of the stand were embellished with lion mask and drop ring handles, and there was a drawer at one end. The vase-shaped containers bore cast and chased ornament and carried silver-mounted cut-glass bottles with a tripod vase in the centre.

Small inkstands were also made in designs it was hoped would not be copied by the factory silversmiths and Sheffield platers. These included the globe inkstand, often gilded, on four outspreading scroll legs with claw and ball feet. The spherical body was held in a framework usually chased with shells and flower festoons, less frequently with festoons and lions' or other masks. The fall-down covers were opened by lifting a tiny ball finial on the decorative cone, pineapple, or acorn knop on top of the framework. The open cover revealed two or three silver-mounted glass bottles, often in Bristol blue. In some cases they enclosed also ivory tablet and pencils. Another popular small inkstand consisted of an oval tray with a horizontal loop handle at the front, and two pierced guard-rings and containers. There was a small wafer box at the front, and a narrow cylindrical quill cleaner at the back.

Early in the nineteenth century the plain oblong inkstand was given a wide gadrooned or ovolo rim (203). Feet became more ornamental and a chased D-handle might be attached to each end. The wafer box became more frequent as callendered writing paper became customary. This rendered pounce unnecessary, and it disappeared entirely from the inkstand after the invention of highly glazed writing paper in the 1820s. The wafer box might now be covered with a miniature chamber candlestick, complete with extinguisher and handle. The tiny socket supported a taper for sealing letters. Wafers had never been proof against the inquisitive. Important communications had to be guarded against unauthorised opening by sealing with wax impressed with the sender's personal seal. Smokeless tapers were sold specially for sealing purposes.

The inkstand was enriched with wider borders from about 1810 and the ends might be cyma-shaped with a large central cast and chased motif. The guard-rings might be made from gadrooned moulding, shaped into three conjoined rings and supported at the ends and centre by matching moulding. The glasses were for the most part cylindrical, deeply diamond-cut at the shoulders, with plain vertical flutes below.

Factory-made inkstands of the 1820s were more flamboyant than ever, with heavy castings. Wider mouldings edged the rims of such a stand, which might have a deep apron front and back, shell motifs on the ends, and expansive corner feet rounded at the angles. The raised platform was higher than formerly with a deeply curved and gadrooned bouge. The guard-rims, two low and one high, contained urn-shaped or spherical glasses, the central larger one intended for wafers and topped by a taper-stick. Paw, or paw and foliage, feet were usual. Many silver-gilt examples belong to this decade. The small, flat, oblong or circular casket inkstand of shaped outline and with four ball-foliage feet dates from the early 1830s. The cover was surmounted by a recumbent lion or other figure.

The Victorian inkstand was floridly ornamental with stampings, castings, and piercings. Two inkpots, one for black ink and one for red, were now provided; inexpensive machine-made envelopes had outmoded the wafer, although it might still be used until the 1860s; the introduction of the steel pen and smoothly-running inks had made the quill cleaner no longer necessary. The variety of designs could be listed in hundreds. One catalogue names beaded border, scroll border, pierced, and Grecian as the most popular in the 1850s. In the Grecian type the sealing-wax box was topped by a pair of undraped figures in solid silver. The glasses —melon-shaped, cylindrical, vase-shaped—were boldly cut in panels with narrow base rings fitting into plain guard-rings of the same height. There were four foliage-spray feet; or, in the case of pierced work, substantial pierced feet.

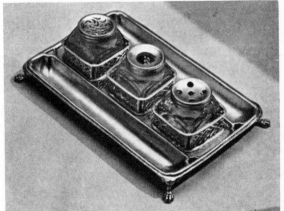

206 CANOE-SHAPED INKSTAND, hand-piercing on tray, galleries and pounce-pot top. Fitted with taperstick, pair of cylindrical quill cleaners, pounce- and ink-pots, and wafer trays, by Richard Cook, 1790. *Courtesy of Messrs. Harvey and Gore*

207 THREE-BOTTLE INKSTAND with hand-pierced galleries, by John Stamper and Edward Aldridge, 1755. *Courtesy of Messrs. Holmes (Jewellers) Ltd.*

208 CANOE-SHAPED INK-STAND on ball feet, with pierced gallery and silver-mounted facet-cut glass pots for pounce and ink, by R. and D. Hennell, 1781. *Courtesy of Mr. John Bell*

209, 210 SILVER-GILT INKSTAND with pounce dredger, ink-pot, quill cleaner, and wafer box (209), by J.T., 1795; (210) BOX TYPE OF INKSTAND with hinged cover to glass ink-pot, four quill holders, and drawer, by G.E., 1807; 2½ inches square. *Courtesy of Messrs. Asprey and Co. Ltd.*

211, 212 TAPERSTICKS: with hexagonal foot (211), Dublin, 1772; height 4½ inches. *Courtesy of Mr. John Bell.* (212) With octagonal base, knopped stem, cylindrical socket, by Thomas Ash, 1700; height 4 inches. *Courtesy of Messrs. William Bruford and Son Ltd.*

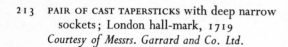

213   PAIR OF CAST TAPERSTICKS with deep narrow sockets; London hall-mark, 1719
Courtesy of Messrs. Garrard and Co. Ltd.

214   PAIR OF TEA-CANDLESTICKS with stems in the form of Harlequins, by William Gould, 1758
Courtesy of Messrs. E. T. Biggs and Sons Ltd.

215, 216   TAPERSTICKS: hexagonal base (215), by Edward Turner, 1725; height 4¼ inches. *Courtesy of Mr. John Bell.* (216) Octagonal base, by James Seabrook, 1716
Courtesy of Messrs. E. T. Biggs and Sons Ltd.

Chapter Nine

I CHAMBER CANDLESTICKS

THE splendid productions of the early Restoration silversmiths in no way distracted them from devising plainly useful domestic ware, such as the chamber candlestick, consisting essentially of a candle socket rising directly from the centre of an expansive saucer tray. Some authorities refer to these as bedroom candlesticks, others as hand candlesticks, but the name chamber candlestick dates from the late seventeenth century. Bedroom is a term of comparatively recent general usage, for the seventeenth- and eighteenth-century chamber was of necessity much more than a bedroom. It was often a place of handsome furnishings and considerable comfort, where desk work could be done and guests and tradesmen received. The nineteenth century had its masculine studies and feminine boudoirs; the present generation has tended to return to the unappetising term bed-sitting-room. Illustrated catalogues of 1790, 1832, 1860, and 1890 all use the term chamber candlestick.

It is a sorry reflection on men's regard for their home furnishings that only in the later seventeenth century did clothing and furniture receive such protection from the melted wax or tallow scattered by the candles carried from room to room. As carpets began to be used on the floors of rich houses, the dainty whim became a necessity: when more and more homes gradually acquired similar gracious furnishings, chamber candlesticks made their appearance in silver, pewter, copper, brass.

Chamber candlesticks were designed for carrying from room to room, for lighting the way upstairs, for use in private apartments, and on most occasions when individual or temporary illumination was required. It became customary in the well-ordered home to set out a side-table in the hall with a number of chamber candlesticks. Each person carried one to his room, lighting it with a spill from a master taper kept burning for the purpose. A supply of candles for replenishment was kept in a horizontal wooden candlebox hanging near at hand or placed at the back of the table.

Ordinary, unpleasant-smelling tallow candles were seldom carried in chamber candlesticks. These measured about a foot in length and were usually inclined to bend, as they were never entirely hard. It was difficult, therefore, to carry one without the hazard of scattering tallow-spots beyond the orbit of the candlestick pan. Furthermore they could not be handled without soiling the hands. The much more costly wax candles were used by those who could afford the luxury. Candles of

English beeswax were preferred on account of their brighter burning and fragrant scent. More frequently, however, imported beeswax was used. Even though bleached to remove impurities which might clog the wick of twisted Turkish cotton, the colour remained a drab yellow, not white as popularly supposed. The melting wax emitted a faintly repellent odour.

Prior to the advent of the chamber candlestick, special candles had been made for carrying by hand around the house. These were tallow candles dipped into virgin wax, so coating them that they could be carried without soiling the fingers, and, according to Sir Hugh Plat in 1602, "the sent of the tallow will not break through to give offence to the fingers: if you would have them resemble yellow waxe candles, then first let the tallow be coloured with Turmericke boyled therein."

The silver chamber candlestick was composed of a shallow saucer with a central convexity supporting a candle-socket, accompanied by a conical extinguisher (223). Early examples were light in weight, made from thin-gauge metal and virtually without ornament. The shallow saucer with a central boss had the edge of its spreading rim strengthened with moulding; the vertically seamed socket with an inserted base was soldered to the central boss and its rim encircled with narrow moulding. The slightly curved lateral handle was shaped from flat silver strip. Handle and socket were pierced with simple motifs such as hearts, diamonds, and crescents. By 1680 the moulding around the rim was broader, and a flat horizontal pear-shaped handle was fitted, sometimes ornamented with beading matching that which might also encircle the rim (226). Stud feet date from about 1700 onwards and the moulding might be gadrooned or fluted, the socket rim decorated to match.

From early in the reign of George II the socket might be fitted with a detachable nozzle with spreading sconce (227). The handle was scroll-shaped, extending from beneath the base to which it was soldered, curving outward and upward, its terminal about 2 inches above the rim. The upper curve was shaped into a substantial thumb-piece. To the terminal was fixed a small socket which accommodated a hook attached to a cone-shaped extinguisher with a turned ball, vase, acorn, or knop finial. The top of the extinguisher finial was usually aligned with the rim of the loose nozzle. The nozzle rim, extinguisher rim, and base rim were ornamented with matching moulding, corded, knurled, gadrooned, or plain. This type of chamber candlestick continued to be made until the 1750s and, with loose nozzle and extinguisher, its weight was about twice that of early forms. Size approximated 6 inches in diameter and $3\frac{1}{2}$ inches in height.

Silver chamber candlesticks from the 1730s might be elaborated and gilded. Some were raised upon hoof feet with shell- and scroll-moulding encircling their pans: other mouldings might now be shaped on the inner edge. Sockets throughout this period were cast in the forms that were fashionable on table candlesticks. The cast socket was enriched at first with one or two centrally placed ribs, the base being in the form of a flattened dome rising into concave or straight sides. By 1760 the socket was vase-shaped with a loose, wide-spreading nozzle. Reeded moulding was used in the last quarter of the century.

Throughout the century chamber candlesticks were made in matching pairs, fours, sixes—seldom more, although a set of twelve has been noted. They were engraved with coat of arms, crest, cypher, or other mark of identification. A set sometimes also bore an inventory mark. These marks appeared on pan, nozzle, and extinguisher, and on the silver snuffers which might accompany silver chamber candlesticks.

The chamber candlestick incorporating a pair of snuffers in its design was made from early in the eighteenth century, with its socket raised upon a slotted support (223). Socket and support were cast as a single entity, the base being expanded to avoid pull upon the flat centre of the tray to which it was soldered. Into the vertical slot, placed at right angles to the candlestick handle, fitted the box of the snuffer, while the loops extended beyond the tray rim to facilitate removal for use.

Chamber candlesticks with rectangular trays raised on four ball feet date from the 1780s. Their rims were broader than formerly and ornamented with gadrooned or reeded moulding, matching that on nozzle rim and thumbpiece. These and many later trays were factory productions, often mechanically raised and shaped.

Early in the nineteenth century the nozzle might be dispensed with and the socket rim considerably extended. The extinguisher might hook to an attachment on the socket placed immediately opposite the handle. By 1820 the tray might be octagonal and borders fluted and scalloped: from the early 1830s square outlines were frequent.

The master silversmiths made elaborate, heavy examples constructed chiefly of castings and containing twice the amount of silver found in factory-made examples. Robert Garrard, for instance, made a chamber candlestick in 1830 with an oval tray enriched by a wide border of moulded foliage: this had a vase-shaped socket chased with foliage and supported by a seated lioness, her tail forming the handle. The weight was more than 16 ounces.

In the 1840s hard stearic candles came into use and, like wax candles, measured about 6 inches in length. Stearic candles were among the earliest to contain plaited and twisted wicks, thus rendering snuffers superfluous, so that they rarely accompanied later chamber candlesticks. Candle replacements in the hall could now be stored in an upright box of wood or japanned iron without risk of their bending, and each candlestick contained a box of matches in its tray.

The Victorian chamber candlestick usually possessed a circular tray, often with a shaped outline, its rising centre directly supporting the socket as in early Stuart examples. The handle consisted of a single chased casting, no longer forming lodgment for the extinguisher, which rested vertically upon a stem rising from the tray. It might now be ogee in form, although the conical form was always more frequent. A popular type took the form of a cast lotus-leaf tray, its stem entwined to serve as a handle, with a central socket shaped as a lotus flower in full bloom. Convolvulus, nasturtium, and other flowers were similarly treated. These possessed neither nozzles nor extinguishers.

Silversmiths continued making simple undecorated chamber candlesticks until the end of the century, the extinguisher becoming a short, decapitated cone suitable for a paraffin candle.

An occasional double chamber candlestick with two sockets is found. This usually bears early Georgian hall-marks and has a shaped tray with a flat pear-shaped handle extending from the centre. Similar candlesticks were made early in the nineteenth century with heavier and more lavishly designed moulding.

Chamber candlesticks from the 1740s might be designed so that candles were protected from the draughts and the billowing curtains responsible for many a disastrous fire. The socket was enclosed within an outer cylinder of silver encircled with a double row of pierced air vents, crosses and circles being frequent. Into this fitted a candleshade of flint-glass, plain or engraved. The cone-shaped extinguisher was provided with a rod rising from its tip, long enough to reach down the shade to the candle flame and put it out without touching the hot glass. With slight variations such candlesticks were made for a century or more.

These were superseded by a less costly type in which a simple wire frame composed of four uprights and two rings was soldered to the tray, enclosing the socket. This formed a holder for a tubular glass chimney which was lifted slightly above tray level by four knops, thus permitting a free flow of air.

Bedroom illumination provided in Georgian coaching houses and inns consisted merely of rush-lights, for which a charge of twopence a night was imposed. John Byng in the *Torrington Diaries* describing his travels in England between 1781 and 1784, frequently mentions this impost and illustrates some of the bills. Those who could afford the luxury carried a pair of chamber candlesticks designed to fit together and much lighter in weight than their domestic counterparts. The deep, handleless, circular trays were plain, a candlesocket being screwed into the centre of each. Nozzles, extinguishers, and snuffers might be included and the complete set carried in a small shagreen case.

II TAPER-STICKS

SLENDER wax tapers burning in miniature candlesticks of silver were for long used as accessible sources of flame in the homes of nobles and gentry. They were particularly in demand during the summer months when fireplaces were screened. They were never intended for illumination purposes and gave considerably less light than the more costly candles, but they were non-odorous, and, being made from spermaceti wax, seldom required snuffing and could therefore be left unattended without fear of guttering. The fumes of spermaceti candles contained arsenic and their use for domestic purposes was therefore discouraged: the single small flame of a taper was not considered harmful. The wax was prepared from a white, brittle, fatty substance found in solution in heads of sperm whale.

These tapers burned in silver taper-sticks measuring about 4 inches in height in the late seventeenth century, with deep, narrow sockets. For more than a hundred years they were used by smokers for lighting the tobacco in their clay pipes, and as such were known as tobacco candlesticks. Complete with burning taper the stick was lifted to the pipe bowl, hence the necessity for a deep socket to prevent the taper from falling out whilst lighting the tobacco. The taper end was wrapped in paper to facilitate removal of the stub from the narrow socket.

Tobacco candlesticks were plain, smooth-surfaced solid silver, never fitted with loose nozzles or burdened with extraneous grease-catching ornament (*213*). Patterns followed those of candlesticks and they might be made *en suite*. They continued in use until superseded towards the end ot the century by "instantaneous light contrivances," and eventually in the 1830s by friction matches.

More decorative taper-sticks following early Georgian rococo design came into use from the early 1740s and continued fashionable for thirty years or so. They were required on the tea-table, for a ceremony which might take place three times in a day between main meals, but was associated particularly with the evening. These taper-sticks, known at the time as tea-candlesticks, held tapers burned for their sweetness rather than for more practical purposes, made from costly English beeswax, pure enough to burn without being bleached, and in consequence emitting a delightful fragrance. They were also brighter-burning than tapers made from imported beeswax. Georgian taper-sticks under that name, as distinct from tobacco candlesticks and tea-candlesticks, were those used with standishes and inkstands. These burned smokeless tapers specially designed for melting sealing wax.

The earliest taper-sticks so far noted bear hall-marks struck in the early 1690s. They were cast in solid silver, foot, stem, and socket being made separately. These were finished by turning in the lathe, then soldered together and polished, the joins becoming invisible. Typical was a stem with a dominant central motif in acorn shape supporting an almost plain cylindrical socket: this was placed directly upon a short instep rising from a shallow circular depression in a spreading octagonal base which might have a stepped rim.

Changes in casting technique at this time made it possible for stem and socket to be cast hollow in separate halves and joined, the seams being highly burnished after soldering and so made invisible. Between 1697 and 1720 taper-sticks were made in Britannia standard silver containing less alloy than sterling. In consequence their hall-marks included Britannia and the lion's head erased.

During the late 1690s stems having central knopped motifs tended to be super-seded by the slender-waisted inverted baluster with a well-developed knop beneath. At first these balusters were circular on plan; then, by the accession of Queen Anne, appeared the first of a long series with baluster stems of octagonal section—foot, stem, and socket displaying this outline and with the socket waisted. The rim of the socket sloped gradually upward and inward until only a thin edge of metal sur-rounded the taper. These taper-sticks were perfectly plain except that a narrow collar might encircle the join between stem and foot, and a coat of arms might be engraved across two facets of the foot. Such a taper-stick with a faceted octagonal base measured from 4 to $4\frac{1}{2}$ inches in height and weighed about $2\frac{1}{2}$ ounces: in the 1730s a similar taper-stick weighed about $3\frac{1}{2}$ ounces.

This was the standard tobacco candlestick throughout the eighteenth century, the smooth flat surfaces assisting the removal of taper drips. In some early eighteenth-century examples the upper surface of the foot might be encircled with sixteen counter-arranged triangular facets which might be repeated around a vertical-sided socket. By the 1730s the base might be hexagonal or square with incurved corners and the stem an octagonal baluster. Ten years later the base corners might be ornamented with chased shells. They were sold commonly in pairs.

Tea-candlesticks, dating from about 1740, were more ornate, reflecting the rococo style of early Georgian silversmiths. Foot and shoulder were square and moulded in relief with masks, shells, or other naturalistic motifs at the corners, skilfully chased and burnished. A detachable nozzle with spreading, upcurving rim was now essential to catch drips of hot grease which would be difficult to remove from moulded ornament. This was of similar outline to the base and reflected similar ornament. Height might be as much as $5\frac{1}{2}$ inches, and some examples were gilt.

The tea-candlestick in the form of a human figure or a demi-figure supported a taper socket above the head, two hands being raised to steady the load of a socket rising from the centre of a circular fluted and scalloped wax-pan, and fitted with a loose nozzle (214). The moulded and chased stem was usually supported by an ornate uprising foot. During the 1750s an interesting series was issued with figures adapted from the Dresden porcelain Italian Comedy figures, Harlequin being the most frequent. There was a fashion revival for figure taper-sticks early in the nineteenth century. At the same time there was a vogue for taper-sticks resembling chamber candlesticks with suitably small sockets, detachable nozzles, and extinguishers. These might be gilt with shell and foliage rims and handles.

Early Victorian taper-sticks—they were catalogued merely as "tapers"—were fashionably made, like chamber candlesticks, in leaf shapes with the stalk curving over to the centre of the leaf to form a handle terminating in a socket shaped as the corresponding flower, such as lotus, convolvulus, or nasturtium. A spray of oak leaves might terminate in an acorn cup to receive the taper, and an ivy leaf in a bunch of ivy berries from which emerged a taper socket.

III   TAPER WINDERS AND HOLDERS

SEALING wax and the equipment required for its use was essential for any seventeenth- or eighteenth-century writer who wanted any privacy for his correspondence. Hence the elaboration—and delightful craftsmanship—of the tools required. The taper holder, whether winder or box, was primarily intended to provide a small flame for melting the wax. A candle was obviously unsuitable as it dripped hot grease when tilted. From the 1790s, however, the small flame of the coiled taper was found convenient, too, for lighting one's way about the house, being lit from a fire or candle by means of a spill. The hazard of sprinkling grease spots was negligible, and if placed down momentarily and forgotten the flame quickly burnt itself out. Flapping curtains would merely extinguish the tiny flame, whereas when candles were neglected they were a frequent cause of devastating fire.

The coil of flexible wax taper was made by winding a wick on a drum and leading it beneath a guide roller revolving in a trough of melted wax. From this it was twisted through a series of progessively smaller holes until a closely knit, solid taper was secured, wound upon another drum. The process bore some resemblance to that of wire drawing. A little turpentine added to the wax made it pliable enough to wind without cracking or flaking. From the 1790s coiled tapers might be coloured blue, green, yellow, red, or pink.

The earliest holders for these coiled tapers were those open-frame stands known to present-day collectors as "wax jacks," and to the silversmiths who made them as wax taper winders and taper holders. The earliest example so far noted dates to about 1680—the date letter of the hall-mark was carelessly struck (218). This held a large coil of flexible taper horizontally between elaborate vertical supports rising from spreading paw-footed scrolls. These supports, terminating in flame finials, bore a likeness to contemporaneous fire dogs and held the circular disc guards, embossed with flower sprays, at the ends of the horizontal-taper reel.

Surmounting this framework was a swivel-action spring-clip, an expansive horizontal disc divided centrally to hold the taper end. This clip was opened for
inserting the taper end by pressure upon a pair of finely embossed and chased
bird handles. The taper winder measured $9\frac{1}{2}$ inches high, $8\frac{3}{4}$ inches long,
$5\frac{3}{4}$ inches wide, and its coil of taper was of thicker gauge than was customary a
century later.

The vertical winder dates from about the same period. This held the coil of taper
on a vertical spindle rising from a circular base mounted on three feet and lifted
by an upward scrolling handle (222). As in the horizontal winder described above,
the end of the taper was held in the centre of an expansive, slightly concave sconce,
gripped by a horizontal swivel-action spring-clip. The smooth flat surface of the
sconce would protect both the letter and the coil of taper from any hot drops of
either grease or sealing wax and would be cleaned easily.

Wax winders are rarely found today belonging to the period preceding the 1780s.
The vertical spindle type continued (222), often accompanied by a conical extinguisher attached to a slender, hand-made chain. This pattern was superseded by a
more compact and much less flamboyant version of the horizontal wax winder holding the coil horizontally in an oval or rectangular frame constructed of silver wire,
either round-sectioned or shaped by passing through a swage block (219). A bar
across the middle of this frame held the coil of wax taper. This frame was supported on a round or oblong stemmed foot encircled with swaged reeding or
moulded gadrooning. The stem was usually in the form of a high dome made by
spinning. A scroll or ring handle might be fitted for lifting the holder, while a handle
extension from the taper bar served for winding and unwinding. At the opposite end
of the bar on a soldered bracket was hooked a cone-shaped extinguisher with a ball-
knop finial.

The top of the frame was designed to hold a flat plate of similar outline to the foot,
with a central aperture for a substantial collar. The end of the taper was pushed
through the collar, no spring grips being required.

Cylindrical box containers for holding the coiled wax taper date from the late
seventeenth century, but few today bear hall-marks of a date earlier than 1780 (217).
There were obvious advantages in keeping the taper protected from damage by heat
or by mice. These taper holders, known to some collectors as bougie boxes,
measured about 3 inches in diameter. The flat-topped slip-on cover was fitted with a
central collar through which the end of the taper could be drawn by hand. The rims
of lid and base were encircled with reeded ribbon or gadrooned moulding, and to
the side of the box was attached a loop or S-shaped handle made from stout flat
ribbon. In a catalogue printed in about 1790 they are listed as wax taper holders.

The majority of these boxes were undecorated, but examples of the late eighteenth

217 CYLINDRICAL TAPER HOLDER with slip-on cover and cone extinguisher, London, 1820 *Courtesy of Messrs. Asprey and Co. Ltd.*

218, 219, 220 TAPER HOLDERS: (218) *c.* 1680. *Courtesy of Messrs. Sotheby and Co. Ltd.* (219) *c.* 1800 *Courtesy of Mrs. Josephine Grahame-Ballin.* (220) By R. and S. Hennell, 1805 *In the collection of Mrs. William B. Munro*

221, 222 TRAVELLER'S TAPER BOX, hinged lid, folding handle, small cover for the taper hole turning on a pin (221). Maker A.L.; diameter 2½ inches. *In the collection of Mrs. William B. Munro.* (222) TAPER HOLDER, *c.* 1780. *Courtesy of Messrs. Asprey and Co. Ltd.*

223, 224   CHAMBER CANDLESTICKS with snuffers and extinguisher: (223) by Abraham Jackson, 1795, snuffers by William Bennett, 1801. *In the collection of Mrs. William B. Munro.* (224) One of a pair, bearing London hall-mark, *c. 1750*

225, 226   CHAMBER CANDLESTICKS: silver-gilt, extinguisher hooked to terminal of scroll handle, three scroll feet (225); by Paul de Lamerie, 1748; (226) with lateral pear-shaped handle, by James Bird, 1716
Both in the Victoria and Albert Museum

227   FOUR CHAMBER CANDLESTICKS with extinguishers, on shallow dishes; slotted sockets for snuffers; late eighteenth century. *Courtesy of Messrs Hicklenton and Phillips*

century might be ornamented with bright-cut engraving, usually bands of flowers and foliage encircling top and bottom.

Between 1790 and the 1820s they might be pierced, at first with a single band of ornament encircling the centre of the body, and later also with vertical pales above and below. By 1815 the cover too might be pierced.

Rising from the centre of the cover was a fixed collar containing a tightly fitting nozzle through which the taper passed. The nozzle was rimmed with thin strengthening ribbon, and few are now found intact with the covers. Vase-shaped nozzles date from about 1820. A cone-shaped extinguisher might be pegged into a loop soldered to the side of the body opposite to the handle, and attached to a guard chain extending to a small eye fixed below the rim. In other instances the chain was dispensed with and a vertical rod rising from the peak of the cone provided a handle for manipulating the extinguisher.

There were pocket taper boxes too, shaped like a one-inch slice cut from a cylinder, of $2\frac{1}{2}$ inches diameter (221). There was a sliding cover over the taper aperture in the centre of the hinged lid, and a folding handle. These were included in the baggage of letter-writing travellers.

Chapter Ten

I BUTTONS

UNTIL the time of Elizabeth I English costume buttons were purely ornamental: garments were fastened by aiglets or hooks and eyes, or by big pins or by girdles. As early as 1300 an English writer recorded a man's robe decorated with "botones from his elboth to his hand." Tudor portraits display dresses with buttons sewn in rows and so close together as almost to touch: a single costume worn by Henry VIII was encrusted with nearly 15,000 buttons.

Ornamental buttons were usually of silk, costing in the late sixteenth century about one shilling and eightpence a gross. More costly were buttons enriched with pearls taken from British rivers or gems dug from the hills of Northumbria, Derbyshire, and Cornwall. Gold, silver, and ivory buttons wrought by jewellers and set with diamonds, sapphires, rubies, and other precious stones were worn by the wealthy from about 1580. The collection of jewellery known as the Cheapside Hoard, dating to about 1600, including twenty-nine matching buttons of gold enamelled in white, blue, and green, and set with table-cut diamonds and rubies. Silver and silver-gilt buttons were also made, the faces of early examples usually patterned in relief with conventional motifs such as dragons, flowers, and cupids' heads. Silver-gilt buttons modelled in the form of death's heads were fashionable sixteenth-century costume decoration, as many as eighteen dozen enriching a single garment.

Silver buttons of the seventeenth century are comparatively rare, however, few being produced while the law required them to be disfigured by conspicuous hall-marking on the face. Not until about 1720 was this mark concealed at the back. From 1739 raised buttons and all sleeve buttons were exempt from hall-marking. Until the 1690s a silver button most usually consisted of a thin plate of metal shaped to fit snugly over a bone or wood mould. This mould was drilled with four vertical holes through which cat-gut was passed to form crossed loops. The silver cover might be plain or ornamented with a simple hand-punched motif. This was fitted over the top of the mould, and the edges folded down to keep it tightly in place. Thus the cat-gut knots were hidden and the loops served as shanks. Suitably punched or engraved such silver buttons were sewn with more cat-gut to naval and military uniforms and to servants' liveries.

Such silver buttons as were made at that period with patterns cast in relief required individual casting. Only in the 1690s was a method developed which made it possible to cast as many as a gross of medium-sized buttons at one time. But sets of cast buttons were too heavy for fashionable wear, as clothing tended to become distorted under their weight, and throughout the first half of the eighteenth century fashion preferred buttons covered with cloth, silk, mohair, velvet, and other textile materials.

Occasionally the use of silver buttons during this period finds mention in contemporary records, however, such as in the description of a lost child advertised in *The Daily Courant* 1707: "a slim little boy, between eleven and twelve years of age, with a kersey coat trimmed with flat new gilded brass buttons, with whitish calimanco waistcoat with round, plate silver buttons and with plate silver buttons on his sad coloured breeches."

Gilded metal buttons on other clothing became a popular fashion in about 1750, and this restored the demand for silver buttons, both plate and cast. The vast majority of raised buttons were made by the old cap-fitting method. A number of silversmiths in London and Birmingham set themselves up as specialist button makers, and they concentrated mainly on raised buttons. As the law did not require these to be hall-marked at the assay office, the temptation to alloy the metal was great. These buttons were made from small silver ingots hammered into very thin plate. Suitable discs were cut from this by means of a punch on a wooden block covered by a thick plate of lead. Each blank was shaped into button form by beating it successively in a series of increasingly concave dies, using a convex punch of steel, until the blank was of the required shape. The silver was annealed from time to time during this process to make it more ductile. This produced the button cap into which ornament in relief was struck by means of dies.

The manufacture of bone and wood moulds was an associated craft carried out on the same premises. A log of hard wood was cut into slices of suitable thickness. From these the moulds were cut by a piercer operating a bow-saw. Very small moulds were turned from a wooden rod in a small lathe. As in earlier days the moulds were drilled and threaded with cat-gut loops.

The space between the relief-patterned silver and the mould was filled with a hard composition, preventing accidental flattening of the *relievo* and making the button firm and solid. The cap was then placed face downward in a shallow dish of sand over a chafing dish of burning charcoal. When the cement in the cap liquefied, the mould was slipped into position. After cooling, the edge of the cap was folded around the upper edge of the mould. The button was then burnished in the lathe.

In buttons made after about 1770 the collector may find the wooden mould replaced by a silver-gilt underplate. The lower part of such a button was formed from another silver blank in the same manner as the cap, but was left much flatter and without any relief impression: the shank was soldered to this underplate. Cap and underplate were then joined by soldering, the junction being cleaned in a lathe.

A traveller's sample case of the 1770s still remains containing four cards set out with a display of seventy-two buttons. All but thirteen have wooden moulds, the remainder bone. A few have plain flat faces upon which local engravers could inscribe crests, cyphers, or inscriptions to order: the remainder are decorated in relief with formal motifs.

Factory silversmiths in Birmingham and Sheffield applied Richard Ford's invention of die-stamping, patented in 1769, to the production of buttons, and evidence of its use is a guide in dating specimens. The silver was rolled in strips of suitable width from which blanks were cut with small fly-presses. The die-stamp then shaped the blank and at the same time impressed it with an intricate pattern in high relief. This was one of the factory silversmith's processes made possible by the invention of cast tool steel, hard throughout. In this case the steel was softened to enable the dies to be sunk, then tempered to hardness.

Shanking was an important operation for the button's life depended upon the efficiency of this process. The improvements in the methods are easy to observe and to date. A loop of silver wire was soldered to the back of the hand-made button, individually applied to each button with blow-pipe and solder. The two ends of the loop were merely brought together, and since the point of contact with the button was small, there was always danger of a breakaway in use. The next step, dating from about 1780, was to continue the ends of the wire into two short, flat extensions, thus giving a greater attachment area with consequent increase in safety. These early wire loops were made from hand-drawn silver wire, which may be recognised by not being perfectly round. It was of finer gauge than was used later. Shanks tended to be oval rather than circular.

The button was then ready for gilding. Early gilding was thick. The buttons were laid out flat by placing their shanks in a row of small holes. They were then brushed with an amalgam of mercury and gold, the mercury volatilised by heat. This method of gilding was always used for fine buttons. But from about 1790 there was also a less costly method. Single, double, and triple gilding was done, the latter being sold under a seven-year guarantee. Newly gilded buttons were brownish in colour. A chemical process corrected this and heightened the colour of the gold, which was then burnished in the lathe with a tool carved from a hard, smooth block agate quarried in Derbyshire.

Few silver buttons of any importance were made in the nineteenth century. The vogue for raised buttons in gilded silver virtually ceased owing to competition from cheap gilded brass, but the demand for ungilded plate buttons increased. These are sometimes discovered still in their original sets for coat, waistcoat, sleeves, and tails.

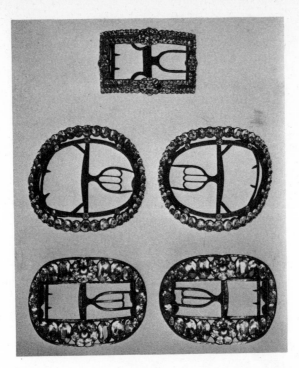

228   SILVER SHOE BUCKLES set with paste diamonds; mid-eighteenth century
In the London Museum

229   SILVER AND PASTE SHOE BUCKLES. *Courtesy of Messrs. Harvey and Gore*

230, 231 SILVER-GILT TABLE SNUFF-BOX, lid with dead game subject in high relief, finely chased (230). Maker T. E., London, 1819. Size 3¾ inches by 2⅝ inches. *Courtesy of Messrs. Asprey and Co. Ltd.* (231) SILVER-GILT SNUFF-BOX, lid embossed with greyhound, by John Lamb, 1820
Courtesy of Messrs. William Bruford and Son Ltd.

232 Two oval SNUFF-BOXES, *c.* 1700, two late eighteenth-century VINAIGRETTES, two early nineteenth-century SNUFF-BOXES. *Courtesy of Messrs. Asprey and Co. Ltd.*

233 A COLLECTION OF SILVER-GILT VINAIGRETTES, including two embossed with country houses, by Nathaniel Mills, Birmingham, early nineteenth century. *Courtesy of Messrs. Harvey and Gore*

Engraved motifs are innumerable, ranging from designs of personal interest to the portraits of George IV, William IV, and Queen Victoria, naval, military, and political characters, and celebrities as diverse as Jenny Lind the singer and James Rush the Potash Farm murderer.

Collectors will find little difficulty in placing raised buttons into chronological groups based on recognition of manufacturing processes. Silver buttons are also classed according to the type of ornament displayed. Crests and cyphers will be found in wide variety from finely engraved plate buttons to the flimsiest of silver-gilt in high relief. Fairbairn's *Book of Crests* is an invaluable aid in the identification of armorial buttons, but it must be emphasised that the sketch does not always agree with the blazoning. Many livery buttons were engraved with complete coats of arms and were then necessarily large, approximating the size of a five-shilling piece: the majority display crests only. Even the three rows of little globes that decorated the page's jacket might be engraved with them. Coachmen and footmen wore convex plate buttons: other servants wore flat plate buttons. A wide range of crested buttons was made in Sheffield plate and date from 1760 to about 1840. They usually show some sign of "bleeding" and are therefore easily distinguished from silver. Eighteenth-century plate buttons were ornamented with a network of curved lines forming roses, stars, overlapping circles, interlacing zig-zags, and hundreds of other geometric patterns all produced by the rose machine.

Hunting and other sporting buttons date from early in the eighteenth century onwards. These might be of gold or silver plate, or of silver cast in a single piece with a wedge or cone-shaped shank. The face of the button displayed a fox mask or some other appropriate trophy in relief: the motif might be engraved after about 1750. The earliest recorded hunting buttons bear the 1738 hall-mark, the set consisting of six large, twelve medium, and six small buttons. On coursing buttons the portrait of the hound and its name were engraved on the flat surface, and sets of racing buttons might each be engraved with the named portrait of a different horse. The silversmiths Thomas Wallis, the spoon-maker of Red Lion Street, Clerkenwell, and John Sanders of White Horse Court were well-known makers of Georgian sporting buttons between 1780 and 1812: some fine-quality pheasant-shooting and cock-fighting sets bear their hall-marks. The factory silversmiths produced raised buttons with relief designs devised for followers of almost every sport, even including pig-sticking. Some of these are rimmed with emblems of the sport concerned.

The demand for silver sporting buttons continued to early Victorian days. Charles Dickens wrote a magazine article on the subject of sporting buttons: "There is a series of buttons which one may see as one would so many pictures in that sort of badge called 'sporting buttons.' Members of a hunt or fancy sporting association distinguished themselves by wearing these miniature pictures: here a covey of partridges with almost every feather indicated in the highest finish; there a hound clearing a hedge; now a group of huntsman and pack; and again, a fishing net meshing the prey; or the listening stag or bounding fawn.''

II BUCKLES

SILVER buckles graced the shoes of English men and women in the fifteenth and sixteenth centuries, but marble effigies and church brasses suggest that they were serviceable rather than handsome. Not until the 1650s were they introduced as an elegant whim of fashion, but once established they were not really ousted for 150 years. Samuel Pepys recorded the acquisition of his first buckles on 22nd January 1659: ''This day I began to put buckles on my shoes.'' At about the same time John Evelyn wrote that he preferred the new buckles to immense roses on his shoes. The *London Gazette* soon commented on the new fashion: ''Certain foolish young men have begun to fasten their shoes and knee bands with buckles instead of ribbons . . . which surely every man will own were more decent than these new-fangled, unseemly clasps or buckles.''

The fashion for buckles, once launched, continued to the point of extravagance and during the next century and a half millions were made in a variety of material ranging from precious metals to porcelain. Buckles became costly pieces of jewellery encrusted with precious stones and valuable enough to be detailed in wills. Augustus Hervey, son of the Earl of Bristol, for instance, in 1781 bequeathed to Mrs. Jane Sheppy ''all my wearing apparel, silver shoe- and knee-buckles and one pair of silver gilt shoe-buckles, and one pair of stone-set knee buckles.''

At this time it was estimated that more than five thousand people were employed in buckle-making at Birmingham, including forty licensed silversmiths. Only five years later, however, the buckle trade was doomed by the new fashion for shoe strings and by the end of the century the buckle was ''out.''

Buckle-making had been a lucrative branch of the silversmith's craft, many establishing themselves as specialists in this work. Anthony Elliner, who had a work-shop under St. Dunstan's Church during the 1740s and 1750s, announced on his trade card that he made ''silver buckles, black tin buckles that keep their colour as well as silver, paste buckles, stay buckles, steel and metal buckles,'' whilst at the same time Joseph Lowe of Holborn informed customers that he made ''all sorts of Hat, Stock, Stay, Girdle, Knee and Shoe Buckles in wrought silver and set with stone.'' Silversmiths specialising in buckle-making might term themselves buckle-smiths, such as George Taylor of Blue Anchor Alley, Bunhill Road; George Baker, Northampton Court; Thomas Clarke, Strand; Richard Boult and John Buhl, both of St. Martin's Lane; Robert Elliott, Gutter Lane; and many others.* The buckle was important enough to form a motif sometimes on a painted shop sign, such as the board hung by M. Bille, of the Hand and Buckle, St. Martin's Court.

A silver buckle (*228*) was composed of four units: the chape or backpiece attaching it to the strap, curved to fit snugly against the surface it was intended to decorate, and containing the other units; the tongue, at first a single sharp spike, but seldom found other than forked, for gripping the material; the roll, for holding one end of the object to be buckled; the middle bridge or pin upon which the tongue swung on a central lug and the roll upon two outer lugs. Careful craftsmanship and hammering were required to obtain the necessary thickness on the bridge and taper towards the buckle ends. Such a buckle, of course, was completely removable from the shoe or garment it fastened.

The finest silver buckles were hand-made throughout, the chape cut and shaped from the solid plate. Others were built from short lengths of silver moulding, drawn wire, or swaged ribbon. In a third group the chape was cast and chased, the pin, tongue, and roll being hand-made. The Birmingham factory silversmiths from about 1770 issued drop-stamped silver chapes and smaller ones from the hand-press.

The tongue, swinging from the bridge and following the curve of the chape, might be single-spiked, or double-spiked, often in the form of a miniature pitch-fork, but more usually was a decorative rectangle prolonged into two spikes. The single- and double-spike and pitch-fork tongues were hand-wrought, the rectangular types sawn from the plate, the ornament within the rectangle supplying additional strength essential with large buckles. The tips of the prongs rested on the surface of the chape, extending about halfway to its edge. In some instances solid lugs were made and drilled to take the bridge-pin; in others the plate was merely curled over and soldered.

The roll, occupying the other half of the chape and hinging to the bridge with a pair of lugs, was at first shaped from the plate. A little wider than the inner line of the chape, it extended a considerable distance beyond. The surface within the chape was decorated with chasing or engraving and its terminal with a border of embossed ornament. Buckles possessing such a roll tended to ride out of position, looking untidy and falling off. This fault was lessened early in the eighteenth century by the introduction of a skeleton roll, at first concealed beneath the framework of the chape, with two short inward-facing spikes on the cross bar, giving considerably greater security if properly fixed and adjusted. This invention was responsible for the wide popularity of the buckle. The early plate roll continued to be made, however, for examples are known struck with hall-marks of the 1730s.

* Sir Ambrose Heal, *The English Goldsmiths*

Jewels had already been set upon buckles when the 1690s witnessed the introduction of fine-quality paste made to resemble rose-cut diamonds. This at once suggested the development of buckles for shoes, waist, and knee as effective day-time jewellery. These buckles might be basically square, oblong, or oval, and small sizes were preferred. The roll was all-over saw-cut, chased or engraved, the chape of an unjewelled buckle receiving matching ornament. For ordinary purposes the chape was usually smoothly plain, but for formal occasions jewelled ornament was always essential.

The whims of Parisian fashion and the designs evolved by one or another celebrated shoemaker or tailor ensured an ever-changing pattern of size, shape, and ornament. Fashionable buckles of the early eighteenth century were rectangular, tending to be longer than wide, and set with square jewels. A typical jewelled buckle of the period combined amethyst or amethyst paste with diamond paste, and table-cut amethysts with faceted corners alternated with smaller rose-cut diamond pastes. *The Spectator* No. 16, 1711, recorded as a new mode "a pair of silver garter buckles below the knee lately seen at the Rainbow Coffee-house." Knee buckles, barely an inch long, were chased and burnished castings, the popular shape somewhat resembling a figure 8 with a rounded surface which might be corded.

Silver buckles solid-set with paste had become the rage by the 1730s. Fashionable shapes were now irregular, the thistle being frequent. Backs were often flat and engraved. It was at this time that the vogue began for filling the chape with woven hair and protecting it with flint-glass. Tiny cast motifs might be applied to the surface of plate chapes. Even necklaces conformed to the fashion. At this time a necklace did not entirely encircle the neck, but ended in loops threaded with black velvet ribbon fastened with a tiny jewelled buckle: bracelets were made to match.

Conversation pieces and portraits of the eighteenth century illustrate many examples of fashionable silver and jewelled shoe buckles. The celebrated portraits of the Lords Baltimore, proprietors of Maryland, sold at Sothebys in 1933 by Sir Timothy Eden, illustrated a chronological series of buckles. Gerard Soest's portrait of the second Lord Baltimore, painted in the 1660s, shows him wearing expansive roses of red ribbons on his shoes and at the kneebands. The third Lord Baltimore, painted by Sir Godfrey Kneller in the 1690s, illustrates silver buckles with narrow-framed chapes, width exceeding depth, and set directly on the instep. The fourth baron, painted in about 1715, wears broad-framed rectangular buckles set high on the instep, almost vertically, with the lower rim curved to rest upon the instep, and drawn to a deep point at each corner. In about 1740 the fifth baron was painted wearing large oval buckles of irregular outline, low on the instep; the portrait of the sixth baron painted in the 1750s shows wide, rectangular jewelled buckles, twice the size of those worn by the third Lord Baltimore.

Several of Hogarth's conversation pieces record shoe and knee buckles of the mid-eighteenth century. His painting of the Strode family, 1750, details three pairs of shoe buckles: one jewelled pair of irregular outline, the others almost square in chased silver. The small knee-buckles are plain. The portrait of Sueton Heatly by Johann Zoffany, R.A., in the 1780s, illustrates buckles with wide-framed chapes extending over the insteps almost to the soles of his shoes, and elaborately hand-pierced. The knee buckles are of the tall rectangular type set with jewels. Children also wore buckles. Hogarth's "Graham Children" in the National Portrait Gallery display an excellent pair of cast and burnished buckles of the mid-eighteenth century.

Jewelled buckles until about 1750 were solid set: that is, the stones were set in the solid silver and were not visible from the back of the buckle, which might be elaborately engraved and include a crest in the design. Open setting then became fashionable for precious stones, thus distinguishing them at a glance from paste. Their introduction prompted the author of *Monsieur à la Mode* to write in 1753:

"His buckles, like diamonds, must glitter and shine
Should they cost fifty pounds they would not be too fine."

Paste and coloured gems were still set solid, usually backed with Indian ink or lamp black rather than coloured foil as formerly.

In 1763 a greatly improved paste was on sale in London. This had been invented in Paris during the previous year by Joseph Strass and more closely resembled the diamond than any earlier production. These stones were cut larger and squarer than earlier paste, resembling rock crystals rather than diamonds. Stones were set close together, an effect of grace and lightness being achieved by combining pastes of various sizes and colours, such as emerald, sapphire, and topaz, in a single buckle. Thus the inner row might consist of tiny stones very finely faceted and another row of larger stones interspersed with small and medium sized rosettes. Large pastes were generally cut with twelve facets, the smallest with six. One outstanding charm of these buckles is the way in which the metal was hammered by hand in convex facets following the contour of the setting. This painstaking finish, together with perfection in welding, involved an astonishing amount of skilful labour. Although other tints are found, blue was the colour of the period. Of a magnificent sapphire blue, finer than many actual sapphires, a blue paste loses much of its loveliness by artificial light, and was used predominantly on daytime buckles.

The coronation of George III in 1761 set the fashion for exceptionally wide rectangular shoe buckles reaching almost to the ground on either side of the instep. At first they might measure 5 inches wide and 1 inch broad, with narrow frames. Gradually, during the following decade, they became almost square, with wide frames which might be jewelled, hand-pierced, chased, engraved, or smoothly burnished. Such a pair, with knee-buckles to match, was worn by Sir Richard Arkwright and appear in his portrait painted at this time.

James Boswell recorded, in 1778, Dr. Johnson's dislike of these giant silver buckles during a visit they made to Wirgman's, the well-known toy-shop in St. James's Street: " . . . after he had been some time in the shop he sent for me to come out of the coach and help him to choose a pair of silver buckles, as those he had were too small. This choosing of silver buckles was a negation. 'Sir,' said he, 'I will not have the ridiculous large ones now in fashion; and I will give no more than a guinea a pair.' Such were the principles of the business; and after some examination he was fitted."

A patent buckle was evolved in 1784 by William Eley, a silver bucklesmith of Aylesbury Street, Clerkenwell. Two years later he moved to larger premises at No. 14 Clerkenwell Green. In Eley's patent the buckle bridge was enclosed in a spring box having just enough elasticity to hold tongue and roll firmly in position. The trade in buckles had so much declined by 1796, however, that by then Eley had become a plate worker.

Eley's buckle was followed by other patent buckles in which the bridge, tongue, and roll were replaced by a spring clip occupying the entire space within the chape, holding firmly and unruckled the fabric or leather latchet. Some will be noted stamped with the name "Boulton and Smith's Patent" or "Dadley's Patent Fastener." Before either patent has expired the vogue for the buckle had disappeared.

Silver buckles of all sizes were required to be hall-marked until 1739, the cost of assay being fourpence a dozen. Because of disfigurement through careless hall-marking the backs of buckles were made flat and small sizes were comparatively rare. From 1739 exemption from hall-marking was given to buckles set with jewels or stones, and highly wrought buckles weighing less than 10 pennyweights. This brought about greatly increased demand from a public unwilling to buy silver buckles whose appearance had been impaired by hall-marking, and supported the silversmiths who formerly had been unwilling to take the risk of their work being made virtually unsaleable at the assay office. Shirt buckles, whatever their weight, were made exempt from hall-marking in 1790.

There was a late Georgian and early Victorian vogue for belt buckles as feminine dress accessories. In these there was merely a chape and tongue. The variety in pattern was enormous, but except for reproductions of heavy ancient buckles made by the electrotype process during the 1850s and 1880s, they are not yet collected.

Chapter Eleven

I SNUFF-BOXES

WHEN Beau Nash dazzled Williamite London with his elegant handling of jewelled snuff-boxes, he transformed snuff-taking into a fashionable social accomplishment. Exquisite snuff-boxes, like the manners required for their graceful display, had been delighting the Court of France for more than thirty years, but now the English goldsmith began to make his own brilliant contribution to this work, styled to suit the foppish airs and graces now expected of the accomplished snuff-taker. Snuff-boxes were created in every lovely and precious material, but in silver particularly the English craftsman was in his element, creating unostentatious but finely proportioned, delicately ornamented and superbly finished boxes that are the joy of the modern collector.

In Nash's day the box was engagingly slender, carried in the left-hand waistcoat pocket; upon withdrawing it the well-schooled snuff-taker gave the cover three smart taps near the hinge, lifted the lid, placed a pinch of snuff on the back of the hand or the thumb-nail, and inhaled. The snuff-box was tapped to dispel the powdered tobacco leaf from the mouth of the box, lest opening it might produce a cloud of dust: a jerky, pull-off lid was never used on a pocket snuff-box. Less formally the snuff-taker carried a snuff-grater fitted into a carved ivory or hardwood case, and a plug of tobacco to be rasped, thus producing snuff powder when needed.

Accompanying the snuff-box in the ceremonial of snuff-taking was a handkerchief for dusting the hands and upper lip: this was of lawn and measured 18 to 24 inches square with a 3-inch border of lace. The popularity of snuff-taking brought into use more serviceable cambric or cotton handkerchiefs, however, known as snuff-napkins, used also to protect the neck-cloth from falling snuff. By about 1700 they were usually termed snuff-handkerchiefs, the more costly variety merely handkerchiefs.

For more than a century and a half the snuff-box occupied the position in national life held by the cigarette case today, and appeared in materials ranging from jewelled rock crystal to painted pewter. Goldsmiths, jewellers, and enamellers combined to create magnificent specimens set with gem-encircled portraits framed in richly worked gold. Less flamboyantly, many more snuff-takers turned to the silversmith for satisfying designs based on traditional good craftsmanship. These might be embossed, chased, or engraved and enriched with double gilding. Occasional examples were set with colourful gem stones or pastes. Sizes varied from the miniature which milady carried in pocket or bag, to large table and mantelshelf boxes. Mrs. Verney Lloyd in October 1714 gave her sister-in-law "a silver snuff box, I guess about 20 shill."

No chronological classification of silver snuff-boxes by form alone is possible. Hall-marks of course serve the purpose of dating, but in most early Georgian examples, and many later ones, the slight but continual friction of a chamois-lined pocket has made them indecipherable. Dating such pieces must depend upon methods of craftsmanship and associated ornament. Always, the craftsmanship had to be of a high order. The lid of a snuff-box was required to fit closely yet to open without a jerk which might smother its owner with snuff. *Pandora's Box*, 1719, noted this feature of the silver snuff-box:

> "Charming in shape, with polish't rays of light,
> A joint so fine that it shuns the sharpest sight."

The hinge too was joined invisibly with watch-maker's precision, extending the full width of the rectangular lid. In the oval shape, opening lengthways, the hinge was placed across the lid about one-fifth of the way from the end, and here too the joint was originally almost imperceptible. Constant working of an ill-made hinge soon wore the lugs, causing the lid to fit loosely and let snuff leak into the pocket. Even the slight projection and thumb-lifter on the lower front of the lid was a hazard seldom introduced, since the projection might catch against the clothing when being lifted from the pocket and spill the snuff.

The majority of early Georgian silver snuff-boxes were constructed from sections of hand-beaten plate; in others the box was raised in a single piece, with a lid of plate; in some instances a shallow circular snuff-box was turned from a solid cast disc about $\frac{3}{4}$ inch thick, and was fitted with a hinged lid; other specimens, of plate, were given cast lids. The late Georgian silversmiths continued to use hand-beaten plate, but soon the factory silversmiths superseded this with rolled plate; round snuff-boxes began to be spun; others were built from rolled plate virtually concealed beneath heavy ornamental castings.

Oval snuff-boxes outnumbered other shapes in silver during the early Georgian period (232). Trade cards illustrated in *The English Goldsmiths* by Sir Ambrose Heal depict ovals, mostly with curved sides, from about 1725 to 1760, the single exception being rectangular and about 1760. Rectangular snuff-boxes were made with rounded corners; they were very shallow, some but $\frac{3}{8}$ inch deep. In such a design the lid and base corners were encircled with plain strengthening moulding and ornament was restricted to the top. This might be engraved on the outside with a coat of arms in an expansive ornamental cartouche, or the outside might be entirely plain and a picture engraved within the lid. Irregular shapes were numerous too, some designed on the escallop shell outline, with straight hinges. Among the other lid treatments of the period was casting in all-over high relief in intricate figure scenes, usually adapted from well-known paintings and enclosed within borders (*230*). These were finished by hand-carving. Alternatively, cast ornament, chased and burnished, might be applied to a lid (*231*), or a raised effect might be achieved with embossing and chasing, in an intricate all-over pattern, in contrast to the flat formality of others patterned in rose engine-turning. A gilded snuff-box with heavy repoussé work on the sides might have its lid set with a portrait or other picture painted in enamels, or with a miniature portrait painted on ivory protected by glass. An enamelled central motif might be accompanied by colourful gem stones set at the corners and ground flat.

Double boxes containing two qualities of snuff were made. Sometimes the base as well as the top was a hinged lid and there was a horizontal partition between. When an oval design was so treated the sides were of sturdy hammered plate, or else were encircled centrally by strengthening moulding around the thinly rolled metal. Another design of double box was a deep rectangle, divided centrally and with both lids hinging on the vertical partition. Yet another design had an enamelled medallion set in the centre of the lid forming the cover of a tiny compartment for patches. In the *tabetière à secret* the central plaque concealed a second portrait or other painting, revealed only by touching a secret spring. These are not frequent in silver.

The interior of the silver snuff-box was gilded to prevent discoloration of the metal by the snuff and its added flavouring ingredients such as mustard, ginger, jasmine, orange flowers, ambergris, and green tea. Gold remained brilliantly radiant, a perfect ground against which to offer a pinch of snuff. Embossed sides and lids were lined with gilded plate to prevent accumulations of snuff in the interior recesses created by such ornament. There was a late eighteenth-century vogue for lining snuff-box interiors with a thin veneer of highly polished tortoise-shell.

Late Georgian snuff-boxes from 1760 until about 1810 were most usually rectangular, and by the end of the century the sides were tending to become rounded rather than vertical, their depth varying from $\frac{3}{4}$ inch to $1\frac{1}{4}$ inches. A favourite style of ornament consisted of a central circular plaque chased with a classical scene in a setting of rosettes on a diaper ground. Or a plaque of chased ornament—often a mythological subject—was set off by such minor ornament as trophies, scrolls, horizontal surface lines, and the like. Most formal, and most widely acceptable, were snuff-boxes ornamented on their six surfaces with engine-turning. Many oval boxes were made too, displaying every kind of eighteenth-century snuff-box ornament. One uncommon series of late eighteenth-century oval snuff-boxes had a quizz glass concealed in a basal recess, from which it swung out with a section of the ornamental side.

Niello work decorated many a silver snuff-box during the final quarter of the century. Lid and sides were ornamented with incised pictorial designs and the lines were filled with a dark metal composition of silver, copper, lead, and sulphur, ground to a fine powder. This was pressed into the incisions and fused to metal-hardness in a muffle. The surface was then ground flat and polished.

The early nineteenth-century tendency to use silver lavishly and replace exquisite, costly hand labour with heavy castings was expressed even in snuff-boxes. There was a marked change of mood, but snuff-boxes escaped the disastrous excesses of some table silver. There was, for example, a vogue for boxes bearing scenes adapted from Dutch oil paintings. Such ornament, cast in high relief and chased, was held in a rim shaped from flat plate which might be engine-turned. In another series the cast framing constituted the major ornament. A plain box made from rolled plate had wide, boldly convex moulding soldered around the lid and entirely covering the sides. The lid centre might be engine-turned or else engraved, with a religious scene, perhaps, or a commemorative motif. At this time the lid decoration might include a tiny central rectangle for the owner's name or initials.

The sporting snuff-box associated with the early nineteenth century was usually of the communal type, with rounded corners and projecting rims, the sides vertical and engine-turned, the lid displaying an applied cast and chased motif in silhouette, such as horse or greyhound, with a ribbon above for the animal's name, and another below for the occasion commemorated and the date. Pocket snuff-boxes were also made, engraved with scenes of prize-fighting and the like.

Small snuff-boxes slightly curved to fit the waistcoat pocket date from about 1815 as a popular type. They were usually engraved.

Silver has always proved a particularly amenable material for use in combination with more colourful wares. Throughout the period under review jewel-encrusted gold snuff-boxes had their less ostentatious counterpart in boxes of silver-mounted shell and variegated stones. The top and base of a box might be of shell or stone and the sides of silver elaborately embossed or cast. Under the Act of 1739 such early Georgian work was exempt from hall-marking, whereas snuff-boxes generally were required to be hall-marked. In the last quarter of the century the snuff-box lid might be of some other material such as carved ivory or mother of pearl bound and clamped in silver and hinging on a silver box, with sides chased and engraved.

By the 1830s the ornate, highly effective silver harnessing technique was being applied to snuff-boxes. The box, of agate or other variegated stone, was harnessed with chased silver openwork in an all-over design of birds, animals, flowers, foliage, and scrollwork, so that colourful stone and lively silverwork immensely enhanced each other. By the late 1840s the birds and other vivid motifs on the lid might be set with innumerable small gem-stones. Such boxes are found in both white and gilded silver.

The vogue for snuff had declined by the time of the Great Exhibition, 1851, where very few silver boxes were shown. Those catalogued were elaborately ornamented in high relief, embossed with classic scenes such as Daphne teaching Chloe to play the flute. Although in continuous use until the end of the century few were of much interest.

For everyday use the most popular size of box at this period was little more than half an inch thick and a couple of inches long. Indeed, a snuff-box is not always to be distinguished immediately from a bonbonnière or a sponge box. These possessed characteristics very similar to those of the smaller snuff-boxes.

As essential to Georgian etiquette as the pocket snuff-box was the large table box, passed round with the wine, and the mantelshelf box found in every well-appointed drawing-room. A tiny scoop was included for replenishing the pocket box. Charles Lamb's sister Mary would carry several snuff-boxes when making afternoon calls. Such calls were normally of scarcely fifteen minutes duration, yet she would return home with her stock of snuff quite replenished. Hence the early nineteenth-century vogue for table and mantelshelf boxes, handsome double-gilded pieces, that had musical boxes set in their bases. Each time the lid was opened a little tune tinkled, automatically announcing the fact if a pilferer was at work.

II SPONGE BOXES AND VINAIGRETTES

AN aromatic orange carried in the hand was for centuries the Englishman's safeguard against disease in days of perfunctory sanitation. The orange pulp was removed and replaced by a sponge soaked in aromatic vinegar. The pungent vinegar seeped through the scented orange skin which gave it a pleasantly zestful aroma. Aromatic vinegar in Tudor days was made with the fresh leaves of garden herbs, selected from among such pungent specimens as wormwood, rosemary, sage, mint, and rue, and with lavender flowers, spiced with cinnamon, cloves, or grated nutmeg, even perhaps a hint of wholesome garlic. These were steeped in vinegar for two weeks. After filtering, camphor mixed in alcohol was added.

Although the aromatic orange continued in popular use until the eighteenth century, Henry VIII banished it from his court in favour of a jewelled pouncet box enclosing a tiny sponge soaked in aromatic vinegar. This was of gold or gilded silver in the shape of a flattened sphere with an elegantly perforated lid. Pouncet boxes, magnificent objects of the goldsmith's craft, were adapted to fit the heads of ebony staves such as Henry VIII displays in one of his portraits by Hans Holbein. The portrait of Jane Heckington, wife of the Master of the Robes to Henry VIII, shows that women, too, carried such staves crowned with richly worked pouncet boxes of gold. More usually, however, the pouncet box hung from the waist by a black cord, until early in the seventeenth century. To Elizabethans the ceremonial of inhaling the piquant odour from the pouncet box was a social grace.

Pouncet boxes were more widely used during the seventeenth century. Every doctor, clergyman, and merchant whose occupation took him into disease-ridden districts carried a plain silver pouncet box for the pocket, or set in a walking stick handle. After the restoration of the monarchy there was an improvement in design, the perforations being covered by a tightly fitting hinged lid, to preserve the volatile oils in the vinegar when not in use. The name was changed to sponge box, the shape resembling a circular snuff-box but taller. The outer lid was chased with designs encircling an engraved coat of arms, and the inner pierced lid, swinging on the same hinge-pin, might be engraved with a monogram repeated and entwined, small holes being drilled in the unengraved spaces. Some boxes were provided with lidded bases for holding musk. In another design the sponge box was in the shape of a tiny silver vase, the body containing sponge and aromatic vinegar, with a tiny recess beneath the foot for musk.

Silversmiths' trade cards of the mid-eighteenth century frequently mention sponge boxes and occasionally illustrate an example. Sponge boxes continued to be made into the early nineteenth century when, under the influence of Sir Walter Scott's novels, they became known once again as pouncet boxes.

Some late eighteenth-century and early nineteenth-century examples were advertised as essence boxes. These were made with handsome openwork lift-off lids without hinges and without inner grids. Such essence boxes contained perfumed pastilles, small rectangular scented tablets consisting of rice starch, magnesium carbonate, and powdered orris root. These were saturated with a favourite perfume or essence.

When Georgian chemists of the 1770s evolved an improved, more powerful aromatic vinegar with a strong acetic acid basis to be enriched with concentrated perfumed oils, silversmiths designed a new container, drastically reduced in size. This was catalogued as an aromatic vinegar box. The Duchess of York in 1801 presented Hannah More with "an elegant gold aromatic box." The name *vinaigrette* appeared at about the same time. Formerly this had been applied to a pungent condiment prepared with vinegar, popular until the introduction of smooth sauces by the Hanoverian royal cooks. Evelyn in *Acetaria*, 1699, refers to "vinaigrets to sharpen the appetite."

Commercial aromatic vinegars were again improved during the 1820s, now consisting of strong acetic acid, alcohol, and oils selected from mint, rosemary, juniper, rue, sage, mace, camphor, cinnamon, lavender, lemon, and cloves. A few drops of this aromatic vinegar might be added to the water used for washing the face, and was sold under the name of *Vinaigre-de-toilette*. Such aromatic vinegar possessed a lasting, penetrating quality, for an occasional vinaigrette is discovered with the original sponge still emitting a faint, delicate scent.

The vinaigrette was usually carried loose in the pocket or bag. In about 1830 the fashion was introduced by Wardell and Simpson for suspending the dainty little article on a fob or chain. Such a vinaigrette was provided with a tiny collared eye soldered to the right-hand end and fitted with a loose ring: or, less frequently, a fine chain was attached to the sides.

The silver vinaigrette appears to have been evolved in about 1780 and became a Birmingham speciality, vast numbers being made between then and the 1850s, mostly by watch-case makers. Indeed, some collections purport to contain examples struck with Birmingham hall-marks of 1768, 1771, and so on before an assay office was established in that city during August 1773. Yet vinaigrettes are not entered on the assay office price list of 1777. Vinaigrettes attributed to 1777 and 1779 have been inspected, but these, lacking the duty mark, could have been made in the present century and the date letter mechanically worn. One collector has an example bearing a hall-mark for 1912.

The earliest vinaigrettes resembled miniature sponge boxes and were round or oval with lid exteriors flat chased or bright-cut engraved. These were supplanted by the now familiar small, shallow, rectangular box with an outer cover hinging lengthways. When opened this reveals a finely pierced and engraved inner grid clipping down tightly over a sponge. Both lid and grid swing from a seven-lugged hinge, three of the lugs attached to the grid.

These vinaigrettes were solid and heavy compared with the later and slimmer feather-weight variety, the cases plain or sparsely engraved or chased, and the grids pierced with circular holes. The light-weight vinaigrette was basically a factory production made from thinly rolled plate by mechanical processes and then decorated by hand or machine. The largest measured no more than $1\frac{1}{2}$ inches by 1 inch with a thickness of about $\frac{3}{8}$ inch.

Vinaigrette cases might be enriched with flat chasing, engraving, engine-turning, applied cast and burnished ornament, and from about 1830 by pressed embossments. The lid design might incorporate a plain-surfaced shield, scroll, or rectangle inscribed with the owner's crest or cypher. Both sides of pendant vinaigrettes were decorated to match.

The inner lids or grids of vinaigrettes from the early 1790s were delicately fretted and enriched with chasing and engraving in intricate, highly ornamental designs. This constituted one of the charms of the vinaigrette, giving its owner infinite pleasure as the aromatic vapours were gratefully inhaled. The grid might be pierced and engraved with an all-over coat of arms or crest. More usually, however, the design included figures, flowers and foliage, birds, leaping fishes, bowls of fruit, and scrollwork enclosed in a frame, usually smoothly plain, sometimes engraved. A popular early nineteenth-century design was a cornucopia with emerging fruits and masses of foliage in bright-cut engraving. In some rare late Georgian vinaigrettes the grid was pierced and embossed, the outer lid being set with a wide border of cast ornament.

Grids in Victorian vinaigrettes were less ornate. There was a reversion to round holes drilled in concentric rectangles, or a bold St. Andrew's cross, all other ornament being dispensed with. Sometimes these plain grids are found as replacements on earlier boxes. The grids and interiors of silver vinaigrettes were gilded to prevent discolouring action by the acetic acid which did not affect the film of gold. Many were also gilded on their outer surface.

Vinaigrette shapes are numerous: they might be round, oval, oblong, square, hexagonal, octagonal, of irregular outline, or representing hearts, purses, escallop shells, travelling chests, and books mostly by Gervase Wheeler. In a series made in the form of a verge watch, the round lid flies open at a touch upon a stud operating a concealed spring. There were flexible fishes measuring about 3 inches long: these are always struck with an early Victorian hall-mark.

The early 1830s saw the beginning of a vogue for decorating vinaigrette lids with press-embossed pictures in high relief, many being the work of Thomas Spice. Sometimes this embossment was so exaggerated that parts of the picture projected as much as a quarter of an inch above the lid. Such pictures included national buildings and well-known country houses, such as St. Paul's Cathedral, Windsor Castle, the Houses of Parliament, York Minster, Warwick Castle, and Newstead Abbey.

Some late Georgian vinaigrettes were so tiny that they may be completely hidden beneath a shilling. An example in the Christie collection is so minute that it is set in a gold finger ring. Its hinged circular lid, measuring $\frac{3}{8}$ inch across, has a flat amethyst centre encircled by pearls and an outer circle of amethysts. This jewelled lid opens to reveal a hinged grid beneath which lies a tiny sponge.

Vinaigrettes might be made from more colourful materials after the mid-1820s. A step-cut panel of agate, cornelian, amethyst, onyx, bloodstone, or sardonyx might be set in the lid, and later the box itself might also be constructed from such stones set in silver mounts and with a silver grid. Uttoxeter paste—a pale blue opalescent gem stone—and aventurine are occasionally noted in this connection. Vinaigrette miniatures of Scottish snuff mulls belong to this period. A tiny silver-mounted horn has a lid set with a cairngorm, over a pierced grid.

By the 1840s the vinaigrette was no longer carried by young ladies: Charlotte

Brontë in *Jane Eyre* refers to the custom of matrons "offering vinaigrettes and wielding fans." At the same time Emily Eden, visiting Chatsworth, was interested to note that "My Lady's Woman" carried her mistress's vinaigrettes to church and placed them in the pew.

Ten years later the vinaigrette was fast declining as a fashionable accessory in favour of silver-mounted double-ended cylindrical glass bottles in various brilliant colours. In one section was carried aromatic smelling salts requiring no sponge, and in the other one of the numerous newly-invented "artificial essences." Yet in 1855 Thackeray wrote in *The Almack's Adieu*: "and at parting I gave my dear Harry a beautiful vinegarette."

Silver vinaigrettes were hall-marked, nine out of ten being struck with the anchor of Birmingham, makers' initials including those of Joseph Taylor, John Shaw, Nathaniel Mills, Samuel Pemberton, Thomas Wilmore, and Cocks and Bettridge. So carefully were the hall-marks struck that, small as they are, they are easy to decipher if unrubbed. A full set of marks was usually struck on the bottom of the vinaigrette or around the lip; the standard mark and the maker's mark on the underside of the lid; the grid was struck with the standard mark or the maker's mark, rarely both. In some instances a full range of marks appears within the lid.

III   POSY HOLDERS

Every early and mid-Victorian lady had her *porte bouquet* or *bouquetier*, for a posy of flowers to carry in her hand as a colourful, scented alternative to the fan. This might be of gold, or later of gilded silver, and most usually consisted of a thin handle – a pear shape, cone or crook – surmounted by a decorative trumpet or funnel cup deep enough to hold flower stalks or shallow to take a nosegay of closely arranged flower heads. This style was followed by the cornucopia and a design with a spring-fitted handle that opened to form a tripod stand (247).

The flower bouquet was usually held in place by a strong pin inserted across the mouth of the cup through perforations drilled in the side. In late examples the thick end of the pin was threaded to screw into the cup perforation. As an alternative the interior of the cup was fitted with four downward projecting spikes so that the flower stalks could be pushed in but not easily withdrawn.

When the cups were of cast silver they were exquisitely chased, double gilt and burnished. Others were fretted. Many were in gold or silver filigree, most usually in cornucopia form, the cup shaped as a flower-bud with each petal filled with filigree flowers and leaves, and the lower part of the body composed of coiled milled wire. The cup might be set with a tiny miniature portrait silhouette, cameo or painted enamel, or with a miniature reducing mirror for viewing the surrounding company. Others displayed Scottish pebbles, translucent or opaque.

Chapter Twelve

I TOYS

WHEN goldsmith John Sotro in about 1750 announced himself on his trade card as a toyman and a maker of children's toys, he was stressing a distinction that has long lost its significance. But the collector of miniature silver quickly becomes aware that such "toys" would be wasted as children's playthings. Exquisite, costly toys in gold and silver were the delight of wealthy Stewart and Georgian sophisticates, but such trinkets were for adult enjoyment, with an adult subtlety about their very childishness. Today they are particularly fascinating for their meticulous record of passing vogues, in furniture, table ware, tea equipages, and innumerable household details from fire-grate to foot-warmer.

Ideally, but rarely, a collection of these delicate miniatures is set in an elaborate, individually designed dolls' house. Until the 1730s these were costly creations designed by architects who supervised their construction by cabinet-makers. Miniature furnishing accessories were often ordered from the craftsmen specialising in the production of such articles in full size: furniture might come from cabinet-makers, tiny kitchen utensils from pewterers, braziers, and coppersmiths; diminutive silverware from silversmiths. Alternatively, they followed the furnishing vogue current in the wealthiest homes of post-Restoration England, and all these miniature replicas of furniture, table ware, and the whole range of domestic household equipment, might be created in silver. Such silver toys had already delighted French and German nobility for two hundred years. The daughter of Henry II of France in 1576 ordered a set of silver toys, including "buffet pots, bowls, plates and other articles such as they make in Paris," to be sent to the children of the Duchess of Bavaria.

In England the vogue for silver toys followed closely on the court fashion for silver furniture in Charles II's reign. The earliest pieces came from Holland, but hall-marks prove their manufacture in London for at least a century from 1665: few examples have been found struck with provincial hall-marks. A wide range of dolls' house furnishings might be accumulated over the years, long after the owner could find excuse to indulge in less sophisticated playthings. Fortunately many were hall-marked so that some chronological sequence can be determined.

A superlative collection of more than fifty silver toys accompanied the West-brooke baby house which for nearly two and a half centuries has been handed down from mother to daughter as a family heirloom. The majority of these are struck with

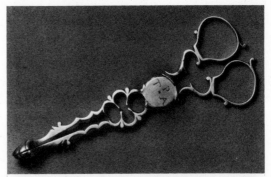

234 (*left*) SILVER-GILT CORDIAL POT on three dolphin-mask feet, *c.* 1690. There is no strainer in the spout. Maker's mark FS with coronet above; height 4⅝ inches. *Courtesy of Messrs. Christie, Manson, and Woods Ltd.*

235, 236 (*right*) SUGAR TONGS; London, 1750. *Courtesy of Messrs. Asprey and Co. Ltd.* (236) STRAINER FOR USE WITH PUNCH BOWL, with flat rest each side, by Matthew Walker, Dublin, 1729. *Courtesy of Messrs. Sotheby and Co. Ltd.*

237 DISH CROSS WITH LAMP, by William Plummer, 1774. *Courtesy of Mr. John Bell*

238, 239 HONEY HIVE with bee finial, on dish with reed-and-tie rim (238), by John Emes, 1802; (239) TABLE BELL with baluster handle, London, 1774. *Both by courtesy of Messrs. Harvey and Gore*

240 OVAL SPOON TRAY with fluted border by
Simon Pantin, 1713. Length 6¼ inches
In the collection of Mrs. William B. Munro

241 SET OF FOUR SILVER DISHES with original glass lemon holders diamond-cut in high relief; by William
Abdy, London, 1807. *Courtesy of Messrs. E. T. Biggs and Sons Ltd.*

242 GROUP OF LATE EIGHTEENTH-CENTURY SILVER, including mustard pots, salt-cellars, funnel, cream jug,
and muffineer. *Courtesy of Mrs. Josephine Grahame-Ballin*

London hall-marks, a high proportion of them with Britannia and the lion's head erased, showing the metal to be of the high standard quality compulsory between 1697 and 1720.

A grate with a fireback in repoussé work included in this collection is struck with the maker's mark I.D., also found on a mug, six plates, and four chargers. A wall down hearth with firedogs, tongs, shovel, and poker bear the London hall-mark for 1718 and the maker's mark C L showing them to have been made by Jonah Clifton, Foster Lane, London, a well-known specialist toymaker. His mark was registered in Goldsmiths' Hall in 1708 and examples of his silver toys have been noted dating from that year until 1727. There are two chairs in the later seventeenth century style bearing the mark of Matthew Madden registered in 1696, and a three-legged pot made by Thomas Ewesbury in 1713. A rare detail is a foot-stove, such as were used in wealthy homes, in plate silver decorated with ornamental piercing, "to laye under their feete when they write, or studie, in cold weather, or in their co[a]ches to keep their feet warm." A Warwick cruet frame, with three casters and a pair of oil containers, has features which suggest it to have been made in the 1720s.

An essential part of the charm of such tiny pieces was their close adherence to the fashions and customs of the moment. The range of objects included furniture, everything for the tea equipage, candlesticks with snuffer and tray, warming pans, tankards, and innumerable other objects of domestic silver. Silversmiths were notably accurate in reproducing original detail and proportions, and the consistent careful construction and meticulous finish suggest the nimble fingers of women assistants.

Much of this silverware in little was shaped from metal of the thinnest gauge, easy to bend to required forms but requiring careful soldering. Some of the most attractive hollow-ware was hand-raised from the plate. Candlestick stems might be turned from slender cast rod, and applied units such as handles, feet, and so on might be midget castings. Early toys might be enriched with engraved ornament: dainty repoussé work, as a general rule, dates from the late 1720s.

Because of their small size and the thin gauge of the silver used, these toys frequently weighed less than 10 pennyweights: after 1739 this exempted them from the necessity of being hall-marked. Silversmiths, however, continued to strike their own personal marks. Craftsmanship on these flimsy, light-weight toys did not, as a general rule, equal that of the earlier, and fully hall-marked, pieces. Fully hall-marked pieces continued to be issued: these usually weighed more than the scheduled maximum for exemption, and full-sized punches were used by the assay office. Fully hall-marked toys have been noted with the initials of Edward Medleycott, 1748, and Samuel Herbert & Company, 1750–1758. Medleycott's piece was a handsome tea kettle and stand measuring 5½ inches in height and engraved with the arms of Isaac Shard, F.R.S., who died at Peckham in 1766.

Every precaution should be taken when acquiring miniature toys lacking a full series of hall-marks. Modern reproductions struck with makers' marks are far more numerous than originals.

Perhaps the first London silversmith to specialise in the production of delicately wrought silver toys, often engraved, was George Middleton (1660–1745), a descendant of Sir Hugh Middleton (1560–1631), the celebrated goldsmith and court jeweller to James I and Charles I. George Middleton registered his mark GM with three crescents, two above and one below his initials, at Goldsmiths' Hall in 1684. One of his earliest productions, a rack of spoons with trifid ends, dates to that year. From his St. Martin's Lane workshops came some of the most meticulously finished silver toys, including furniture in the style current late in Charles II's reign with ''cane'' seats and backs, the chairs and day-beds being notable.

Middleton's toys were always struck with the full series of London hall-marks, the assay office having small punches designed for this purpose. By 1691 Middleton's personal mark had been altered, at his request, to the initials GM with two mullets above and one below. This change possibly took place at the beginning of a brief period of partnership with John Campbell at the St. Martin's Lane workshops.

In that year Campbell moved to the sign of the Three Crowns near Hungerford Market, now the site of Charing Cross Station. Whether the partnership continued here is unknown. In 1708 Middleton joined Campbell at the Three Crowns, the partners then engaging in the business of banking as well as silversmithing, a development that led eventually to the establishment of Coutts Bank.

At least one of Middleton's apprentices engaged in the manufacture of silver toys. This was Isaac Malyn, a plateworker of Gutter Lane, who registered his mark in 1699 and is associated with toys throughout the period of Britannia standard silver. His productions so closely resemble Middleton's that it is possible he supplied toys to the order of his former master who struck them with his own mark before submitting them to the assay office.

Augustine Courtauld of Church Street, St. Martin's Lane, who registered his mark at Goldsmiths' Hall in 1708, was probably the most prolific maker of silver toys. He was pre-eminent in this branch of his craft, toys and domestic ware alike being notable for exquisite detail. His toys included furniture of all kinds, complete tea equipages, cruet frames with casters of silver; sets of wall-sconces; two-handled covered cups of a type associated with the seventeenth century.

John Sotro, at the Acorn in St. Paul's Church Yard, whose trade card (in the British Museum) was mentioned above, has left his mark on a set of four silver salt-cellars and a pair of sauce-boats, perfect miniatures of fashionable styles of the 1740s, and marked with the date letter for 1743.

Hall-marks show that at least fifty silversmiths made toys between 1665 and 1739. These include RD crowned, 1665; FC, 1669; G crowned, 1670; EM in mono-gram, 1677; CK under a mitre, 1686; WP with mullet below, 1689; and IC over a star, 1691. Later were Edward Jones, 1696; Jonathan Bradley, 1696; Matthew Madden, 1697; John Cole, 1697; William Matthew, 1698; Nathaniel Green, 1698; Matthew Pickering, 1703; Joseph Smith, 1707; Jacob Margas, 1708; Jonah Clifton, 1709; James Godwin, 1710; George Smart, 1715; James Morson, 1720; Edward Coven, 1724; John le Sage, 1725.

A second series of miniature silver ware was made in the early nineteenth century of even smaller dimensions, but confined almost entirely to tea-table ware (246). Whereas the seventeenth and eighteenth century productions measured between $1\frac{3}{4}$ inches and $2\frac{1}{4}$ inches, the later issue might be a third of these measurements. They were made by mechanical methods in forms fashionable during the period and were lavishly engraved and chased. They were seldom heavy enough to require hall-marking and because of the chasing might lack even the maker's mark.

II MISCELLANEOUS SILVERWARE

Cordial Pots

THE rare dispenser of aromatic cordials (234) closely resembles a teapot, but is much smaller, measuring about $4\frac{1}{2}$ inches in height, and has no strainer to the spout entrance. It was used on the tea-table from the 1690s until late in the eighteenth century. The formal dinner of early Georgian days began at four o'clock and after dessert the ladies left the gentlemen to their wine and withdrew to the drawing-room. There, at seven o'clock, they were served with tea, cordials, and bread-and-butter.

Cork-Screws

This tool is of such universal acceptance now that it is difficult to realise how long it was preceded by a straight-shanked rod of steel terminating in a short boring screw such as is found on a gimlet. This dates back to the fifteenth century when it was known as a wimble or augre, fitted with a heavy transverse T-handle. An occasional plate inventory includes an auger. By the mid-seventeenth century the 3-inch helix spiral terminating in a sharp point had been invented: such cork-screws were at first known as worms. The name bottle-screw dates from the 1680s: the name cork-screw is noted first in references of 1720. Both names were then used con-currently until the end of the century.

Dining-room cork-screws with handles of silver—usually large open ovals, double-gilt—came into such widespread use that trade cards illustrate them almost consistently from the 1740s. As an alternative the handle might be T-shaped, or moulded in an ornamental form, chased and burnished. Often a motif of personal significance was included and such handles might be set with gem-stones.

The steel shank until the mid-1780s was either cylindrical or turned in a series of ornamental knops. Thereafter it might be vertically ribbed, ground with hexagonal or octagonal facets and highly burnished. From about 1780 the steel worm was usually fluted at a cost of about 75 per cent extra, easing the passage of the spiral through the cork with less risk of causing it to crack and fall to pieces whilst being withdrawn from the bottle neck.

Perfume bottles, vials of aromatic vinegar and other toilet accessories, tightly corked when received from the shop, were opened with miniature cork-screws, spiralled throughout their length. Such cork-screws were included in the fashionable étuis of mid-Georgian days.

Pocket cork-screws of burnished steel protected by detachable silver sheaths date no earlier than the 1750s. The sheath was of cast silver and at first might be vase-shaped with a small foot used as a tobacco stopper. In this design the handle might be flat, made from heavy plate.

By the 1760s it was customary to use the sheath as a handle. The screw was topped by a ring with a flat inner surface of such a diameter that the tapering sheath when detached slipped exactly halfway through it, forming a T-handle, The sheath, which might taper either towards or away from the point of the spiral, was turned and drilled from a solid cylinder of silver. The mouth interior was threaded to fit matching threads cut into the lower part of the shank immediately above the spiral: the other end was ground flat to serve as a tobacco stopper. The sportsman's pocket cork-screw had a T-shaped handle, and one end in the form of a whistle, the other cut as a seal, with the end of the sheath used as a tobacco-stopper.

There was also a series of pocket cork-screws with silver rings so designed that they would slip on the newly invented split-ring with the keys. In others a flat disc was attached to the upper edge of the ring: this might be cut with the owner's seal or engraved with his crest or cypher.

From the late eighteenth century onwards a pocket cork-screw might consist of a deep, horse-shoe bow, its outer surface facet-cut and its incurved ends shaped into thick lugs with the cork-screw spiral hinged between them. When folded its point fell just short of the inner curve of the bow. Also hinged between the lugs might be an ear-pick, snuff shovel, tweezers, button hook, and bodkin, suggesting that this design was carried in the feminine handbag. The continental cork-screw of the eighteenth century spiralled in the opposite direction from the English where the method was to insert the point in the cork and turn to the right.

Nineteenth-century cork-screws for the most part continued the earlier forms and sizes: few were made in silver after the 1830s.

Dish Crosses

This was a purely utilitarian innovation of the 1750s (237), but produced some designs in which the outline is shapely and the detail pleasing. The intention was to keep food hot upon the table or sideboard. Heat was supplied from a spirit lamp, and the four pivoting arms radiating from it were designed to support any flat-bottomed dish within the current range of sizes. The arms could be adjusted in two ways. With the lamp as its central point, the X could be spread wide for a round dish or made long and narrow for an oval dish. The centre of each pair of arms was a ring encircling the rim of the lamp, one placed above the other so that they revolved independently to permit the arms to be adjusted. A further adjustment ensured that the dish rim was held secure, important for a serving dish.

Each arm, rectangular in section, terminated in a shapely little vertical scroll leg, usually on a shell- or petal-shaped foot, and long enough to raise the lamp slightly above the table-top. To support the dish, each arm was fitted with a pierced sliding socket. From this rose an ornamental bracket or dish rest, vertically for an inch or more to lift the underside of the dish clear of the flame, and then with an outward curve terminating in an expansive motif matching or harmonising with the foot, such as a ram's mask in association with a hoof foot below. These bracket dish rests could be moved to any position along the arms. Small rosettes on their ends prevented them from sliding off.

An attractive dish cross is sometimes found with a separate spirit lamp, its flame warming the dish through a disc perforated in scroll patterns. This forms the axis on which the arms revolve. The circular lamp might be plain with perhaps a gadrooned rim or chased with spiral fluting with a shaped gadrooned rim.

By about 1800 the dish cross began to be superseded by the individual stand consisting of an oval ring into which the covered dish fitted, supported on four feet linked by stretchers that held the spirit lamp.

Honey Hives

There was a thirty-year vogue for these attractive and rare honey pots (238). Examples have been noted bearing hall-marks from 1789 to 1822. Until about 1810 the shape closely followed that of a skep bee-hive, about 5 inches high, the upper third forming a lid with an upright ring handle. The lower part held the honey, and the interior might be gilded or glass-lined. From the late 1790s the skep stood upon a circular dish with a wide reed-and-tie rim. The skep itself was spun in a single piece and chased to represent reeding and tying, with an entrance for the bees. The finial might be in the form of a well-modelled silver bee, an upright reed-and-tie loop or an upright disc which might be engraved with a crest. In this design the skep served wholly as a lid, fitting down over the glass vessel that contained the honey. In the late years of the Regency such a silver honey pot was made with vertical sides and a domed top. This fitted a silver stand of the same diameter, recessed to receive a more convenient vertical-sided glass honey vessel.

Leg-of-Mutton Holders

This carver's accessory of the early nineteenth century was never very popular. It consisted of an ivory or ebony baluster handle with a silver socket for slipping over the end of a leg-of-mutton bone, to which it was fixed by means of a thumb-screw. This device enabled the carver to manipulate the big, heavy joint for slicing more elegantly than if he took the obvious course of steadying the bone with his fingers.

Lemon Strainers

Punch-making in the eighteenth century was a social accomplishment and, according to the best tradition in punch building, the drink was mixed before the eyes of one's guests. Bates in his *Dispensary*, 1694, declared that "a pleasant and grateful Punch is made with the following quantities: Fair water; Brandy A, a quart; choice pure lemon juice, a pint; double refined sugar 1 lb. and if you so please add one grated nutmeg."

This was the recipe used by the directors of the East India Company who regaled themselves with punch at their meetings, spending five shillings on lemons. These were squeezed over a hemispherical strainer of about 4 inches diameter with flat extensions from the rim resting on the edge of the punch bowl. The strainer was raised from the plate and the rim strengthened on the inner surface with plain moulding. It was pierced at the base in a formal design of scrollwork, with six or seven rows of circular piercing above. The flat rests, cut from the plate and enriched with piercing and wavy edges, each measured about 4 inches long and about $1\frac{1}{4}$ inches wide except where they were expanded to join the strainer. A crest was engraved upon the surface of one rest. Open scroll handles date from about 1730 until the end of the century (236).

Silversmiths' trade cards occasionally illustrated lemon strainers. Richard Boult, at the Blue Anchor and Star, opposite Wood Street, Cheapside, and John Fossy, Lombard Street, both offered identical patterns in the mid-eighteenth century, with elaborate openwork rests. Early examples entirely hand-made might weigh more than 5 ounces; factory productions from the 1770s might weigh no more than 2 ounces. Matthew Boulton, in 1773, used the term punch strainers. The assay office four years later marked a change in fashion when it listed them as orange strainers, charging one penny each for the assay. Claret and orange juice was a fashionable drink in the early eighteenth century. On the 9th October 1714, Lord Fermanagh "toasted our friends at Claydon in claret and orange." From the 1750s orange juice was also an essential ingredient of fashionable punch, replacing the zestful lemon. By the 1780s the hemispherical strainer was made by the spinning process, its rim being strengthened by drawn reeded ribbon. A gradual decline of punch drinking followed the introduction of toddy in the 1770s, and by the end of the century silversmiths no longer made lemon and orange strainers.

Marrow-Spoons

"Mary bones of Beefe" delighted Morton in 1638, when describing the table delicacies enjoyed by Englishmen. Pepys recorded the pleasure he derived from marrow bones in 1668 and a century later Tucker wrote that he had supped amply from "a pair of marrow bones in a dish." The soft, fatty substance found in the cavities of bones and known as marrow was believed to be a source of vigour and energy. Marrow continued in great demand until the close of the Victorian era when marrow on toast was a costly dainty.

A spoon for extracting the delicacy at the dining-table was a refinement dating from late in the seventeenth century until early in the twentieth century. The earliest literary reference to such a spoon quoted by the New Oxford Dictionary appeared in the London Gazette, 1693, where it was referred to as a marrow-spoon, a term used consistently until the 1830s when the name marrow-scoop appeared in silversmiths' catalogues. The number of existing examples struck with Queen Anne hall-marks suggests that their use increased at that time: few are known struck with an earlier hall-mark.

The marrow-spoon maker was a specialist silversmith and from about 1750 large numbers appear to have been made in Birmingham although bearing the London hall-mark. Edward Sawyer, 19 Great Charles Street, Birmingham, was a well-known maker of "all kinds of silver marrow spoons and ladles." He registered his mark in Birmingham early in 1774, a few months after the establishment of an assay office in that town: formerly, although working in Birmingham, he was registered with the London assay office. Marrow-spoons bearing Sawyer's mark have been noted dating from 1749 to 1780. Other Birmingham makers were George

Smith, registered in London until 1774; Matthew Boulton, registered at Chester in 1763, and in Birmingham 1773; Robert Fox, registered in London.

The marrow-spoon is double-ended, the two scoops being separated by a short round waist. It has one narrow, elongated bowl with straight parallel sides and rounded ends, and a handle consisting of an even narrower scoop, little more than a deep, concave flute. Either end could be used for extracting marrow, depending upon the size of the bones. Such a spoon was made in a single piece from a rod of silver, the ends being expanded and then shaped on swages. The length and width of the scoops vary slightly, but such variations are only in accordance with individual silversmiths' whims. Both spoon and flute face in the same direction and the hall-mark is struck on the back of the stem.

A marrow-spoon of the eighteenth century generally has a wider, shorter bowl and scoop and a longer dividing stem than was usual from about 1800. In the early nineteenth century the scoop was deeper and tended to be rather longer than formerly, and the flute narrowed slightly towards the stem which might be square or rectangular, though normally round.

A spoon intended for use with spoon-meat, a usual dish in England until the early 1800s, may be found with a bowl of normal proportions and with the long, narrow handle fluted as a marrow-spoon to permit extraction of marrow from any bones included in the serving.

Marrow-spoons continued to be made throughout the nineteenth century under the name of marrow-scoops. The spoon-shaped end was abandoned and the long, narrow scoop had a handle matching those of forks and spoons. A silversmith's cata-logue of the 1860s lists marrow-scoops with handles in French, fiddle, threaded, shell, king, and Victoria and Albert patterns in that order, the latter group being three-fifths more costly than the first. By about 1900 a catalogue by the same silver-smith lists handles as fiddle, French, early English, Georgian, lily, threaded, Queen Anne and Louis Quinze patterns.

Pincushions

Silver frames to hold emery-filled pin and needle cushions were fashionable in the seventeenth century and continued to be made with little basic alteration until Victorian days. Shapes and styles of ornament were merely modified to reflect passing vogues: a William III specimen, for example, is likely to be octagonal, embossed with gadrooning, and mounted on four scroll feet. Such a frame has been noted measuring $6\frac{1}{4}$ inches square and $2\frac{1}{2}$ inches high. But the majority of remaining examples are considerably smaller.

The frame was fitted with a cushion crammed with powdered emery, and

243 (*above*) A PAIR OF TOY TAPERSTICKS cast and turned in Britannia standard silver, by Joseph Daniel, 1716. *Courtesy of Messrs. Garrard and Co. Ltd.*

244 (*right*) MINIATURE COFFEE-POT AND TEA-POT, by Augustine Courtauld, *c.* 1720, and two tankards by Jonah Clifton, 1709. *Courtesy of Messrs. William Bruford and Son Ltd.*

245 (*left*) MINIATURE EARLY GEORGIAN FIRE-PLACE AND CANDLE SCONCES. *In the Victoria and Albert Museum*

246 TINY SILVER-GILT TEA SERVICE, late Georgian, the tray struck with the uncrowned leopard's head *Formerly in the collection of Her late Majesty Queen Mary*

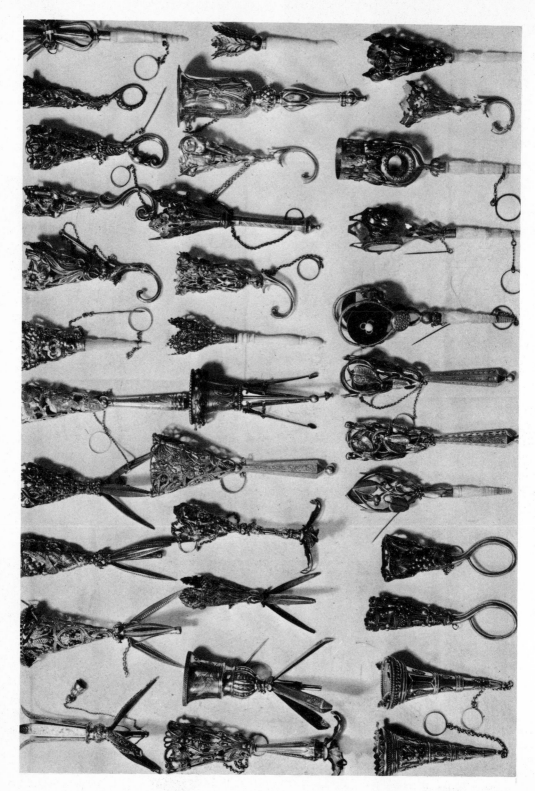

247 SELECTION FROM THE GRAHAM WIGAN COLLECTION OF POSY HOLDERS

extremely heavy for its size. Pins and needles were pushed into it half a dozen times to polish off rust and dirt for the steel used until early Victorian days quickly rusted when exposed to the air.

Shells

Escallop shells (*249*) were part of the table service from the 1730s until mid-Victorian days. They might contain either pickles or pats of butter, the latter moulded with coats of arms or other ornament. At first such a shell was small, measuring about 4 inches across, with a wide, out-curved handle or thumb-piece at the "hinge" or beak. They were found in pairs, fours, eights, and dozens with identical hall-marks. One set of eight examined, bearing the London hall-mark for 1740, weighed 20 ounces.

The escallop shell and thumbpiece were raised from the plate in a single unit and it was customary to engrave a crest on the thumbpiece. Usually three shell feet were soldered beneath, but in the 1740s and 1750s two fumidas shells with clusters of seaweed might form a cast and chased foot. These almost doubled the weight of the piece. By the mid-1750s the thumpiece was made horizontal and might have a shaped rim; the three feet might be snail-shaped but escallop shell feet were more frequent. From about 1760 until the 1770s the shell might have pierced sides and three ball-and-claw feet and be fitted with a blue glass liner.

With the establishment of the factory silversmith the escallop shell could be stamped and the thumbpiece, then known as the mount, applied as a separate unit. From 1770 the rim of the thumbpiece might be strengthened with punched beading. Such a shell weighed about 2 ounces, seldom exceeded in subsequent examples. The rim foot is noted from 1780, sometimes reeded. The surface of the thumb-piece might be chased and later ornamented with bright-cut engraving, often in the form of a border enclosing a crest. From early in the nineteenth century the thumb-piece might be edged with gadrooned shell and foliage moulding. Such shells continued to be made until the 1840s when a design is to be noted with three dolphin feet and a stamped escallop shell handle attached with the curved side upward. The interior might be gilded. The firm of Watson and Bradbury in their pattern book of 1822 illustrate small examples as salt-cellars (*q.v.*) and the large sizes for pickles.

Skewers

Slender wooden skewers were long used to fasten meat to the revolving spit and to keep the joint in shape whilst it roasted on the down hearth. These giant pointed pins were turned from dogwood until the mechanical jack-spit was devised for use with the wall-grate late in the seventeenth century, when beech wood was pre-ferred. Skewers remained in the meat on the silver or pewter dish whilst it was carved at the side table. In early Georgian days, however, it became customary to place the carving dish upon the table for the hostess to carve. The crude beech skewers were therefore removed and replaced by decorative garnishing skewers turned from hard *lignum vitae*. These measured nearly 18 inches long, the design including a 12-inch spike, a 5-inch turned handle, and a carved finial. Examples have been noted with shorter spikes. Such a skewer thrust into the meat on the dish offered a projecting handle to aid the carver. Swift, in his satirical *Advice to Servants*, bade them "send up the meat well stuck with skewers."

These wooden skewers were soon reproduced in silver. As carvers became more efficient, the long handle was dispensed with and by 1750 a new type had been evolved, cut from flat plate. In shape, this design resembled a bodkin, with the faces of the blade flat and terminating in an elongated eye invisibly soldered into position. This aided its withdrawal from the meat when required. Such skewers are very scare. By 1760 the oval loop-terminal might be moulded with a shell decoration or as a corded ring. After about 1765 the blade was chamfered or bevelled and this and the circular loop were stamped in a single entity. From 1770 the skewer might be made with a decorative end in relief, such as the shell and thread pattern matching dining forks and spoons. Some have flat, pierced disc tops: others are shaped as arrows.

Silver skewers were made in sets of varying lengths. The smaller ones, 6 or 7 inches long, were used for game and small joints of meat. Large joints might require skewers 11 to 15 inches long. They might also be sold in pairs: the silver sent by Matthew Boulton to the opening of the Birmingham assay office in August 1773 included a pair of skewers weighing 5 oz. 7 dwt.

A crest or cypher might be engraved on the front of the blade. The hall-mark was usually struck close to the loop where the metal was about $\frac{1}{4}$ inch thick. Fakers have been known to transfer these marks, which were not struck in a vertical line, to other articles of silver, or to incorporate the skewer blade into a more valuable piece of modern plate.

Spoon Trays

The spoon tray (240) was part of the tea equipage from the 1690s to the 1730s. A conversation piece in the collection of the Worshipful Company of Goldsmiths, attributed to Thomas Hudson, illustrates an example containing three spoons and measuring about 7 inches long and nearly 4 inches wide. This oval tray has a flat base, fluted sides, and a flat cyma-edged rim strengthened with moulding. After about 1720 the tray was usually plain with a sloping rim which might be incurved at the corners. The weights of seven examples noted show them to have averaged 2 oz. 5 dwt.

Sugar Crushers

With the introduction of toddy in the 1770s, these were required for crushing the loaf sugar used to sweeten a glass of the hot drink. The earliest type resembled a pestle with a turned stem, often in baluster or double baluster form, and an ornamental finial. These are found engraved with crests and bearing hall-marks as late as the 1890s. More frequently and less expensively, the crusher was made with a twisted wire stem, an oval or circular loop handle, and a plain, sturdy crushing disc. Examples have been noted bearing hall-marks from 1778 to 1902. Late Georgian sugar crushers were cast in a range of patterns seemingly unending: some were given expansive claw-shaped crushers.

Table Bells

For centuries silver bells have been celebrated for their melodious tone, impossible to achieve with base metals. The silver must be virtually pure. It is recorded that Elizabethan bell-founders added a small proportion of silver to their bell-metal in the mistaken belief that the resulting bells emitted a purer note.

Magnificently worked table bells were produced by the goldsmiths of the Italian renaissance in both gold and silver. Horace Walpole possessed "a silver bell enriched with carving by Benvenuto Cellini"; this was bought in for £252 at the Strawberry Hill sale of 1842. Silver table bells in England date from Elizabethan times onwards, although earlier examples are recorded.

The inventory of the domestic plate belonging to the Earl of Northampton, taken at the time of his death in 1614, included a silver table bell weighing 22 ounces—a giant in comparison with a typical 3-ounce Victorian tea-table bell.

A portrait of Margaret, Duchess of Newcastle, painted in the early 1660s, shows her sitting at a table set out with a clock, a silver standish and its equipment, and a silver table bell. The sound-bow of the bell is widely everted, its diameter being double that of the bell-dome proper. The stubby knopped handle, measuring less than half the height of the dome, is soldered directly to the bell.

Silver table bells long remained the usual method of summoning a domestic servant into the room: Queen Elizabeth I rang one at Richmond Palace, and Queen Victoria at Windsor. The distinctive silvery tone could not possibly be mistaken for any other sound.

Bells were cast by a method resembling the *cire perdue* process used by silversmiths for complicated castings. The thick lower rim of the bell is known as the sound-bow; the section above is the waist which, like the shoulder above it, is much thinner than the sound-bow; at the top is the crown to which the handle is attached. Inside is the clapper with a ball which strikes against the sound-bow.

By the 1660s the handle, shaped in the form of a pure baluster, constituted about half the bell's total height. Later in the seventeenth century the handle might be cast in the form of a figure such as a rampant lion, an undraped demi-figure, or the crest of the owner. The spread of the sound-bow was less extensive than formerly and the weight of a table bell varied between 3 and 6 ounces, its height between 3 and 5 inches. The obvious design prompted by the figure handle was the silver table bell cast and chased in the form of a serving woman wearing a wide skirt and apron, her hands clasped before her. An example has been noted bearing the hall-mark of 1692 and a similar bell is illustrated on the trade card of Thomas Clark, silversmith of the Golden Head, Strand, in about 1750, demonstrating that such table bells continued in fashion.

Silver hand bells were included in early eighteenth century standish equipment. The handle might be a substantial baluster with a finial, and the bell base was thickened and gadrooned. The waist or shoulder was encircled with an incised rib until the 1720s: then a raised rib became usual and the handle finial a large ball or mushroom knop. By 1730 the inverted baluster was preferred. This pattern continued throughout the eighteenth century, but from about 1740 the shoulder of the dome might be ornamented with a moulded design. The head and shoulders might be fluted and the sound-bow edged with corded moulding. These bells measured about four-and-a-half inches in height. Ivory or ebony might replace the solid silver handle, shaped in similar baluster form, with a silver finial and ferrule, and from the 1750s the ivory might be stained green (239).

Matthew Boulton sent a table bell to be assayed on the occasion of the opening of Birmingham assay office in August 1773: this weighed almost 9 ounces. During the last quarter of the eighteenth century, however, comparatively few silver table bells were made, possibly because of competition from the Sheffield platers who issued table bells of bell-metal screwed within plated covers: these were fitted with ivory handles. The assay price list of 1777 makes no reference to bells, suggesting that few were submitted for assaying.

In the late 1790s there was a revival of the silver table bell, sometimes with a reeded sound-bow. From about 1810 the bell might be chased in an all-over design of flowers and foliage or grapes and vine leaves on a matted ground, and the solid silver baluster handle returned. These bells weighed about 8 ounces. In the 1820s and 1830s there was a vogue for a low hemispherical table bell edged with heavy moulding, the upper half covered with applied strap-work. The handle was cast and chased in numerous florid forms, demi-figures being frequent. But the hemispherical bell always emitted a poor tone.

By the late 1830s the sound-bow might be expanded to such an extent that it appeared to lie flat upon the table, although only its rim actually came in contact with

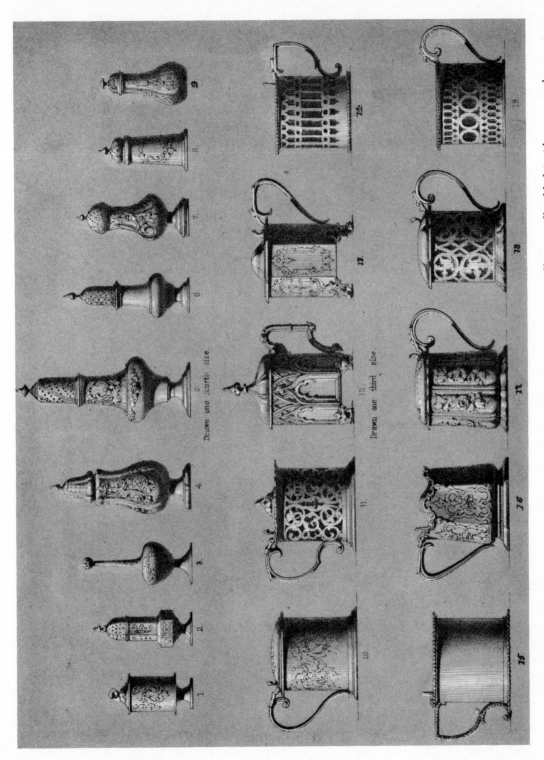

Drawn one fourth size

Drawn one third size

248 PAGE FROM AN EARLY VICTORIAN SILVERSMITH'S LITHOGRAPHED CATALOGUE: muffineers, all gilded inside, engraved 3s. extra, embossed 4s. extra; and mustard pots, plain, pierced, and engraved. *Courtesy of Messrs. Elkington and Co. Ltd.*

249 PAGE FROM AN EARLY VICTORIAN SILVERSMITH'S LITHOGRAPHED CATALOGUE: egg frames with spoons and escallop shells

Courtesy of Messrs. Elkington and Co. Ltd.

the wood. The rim might be edged with plain, simple swaged ribbon, but in many instances it was shaped and decorated with florid moulding. By the 1840s table bells might be cast with all-over patterns in high relief and chased, historical and classical scenes being preferred. Handles were cast and chased, amorini, child bacchanals and the like being fashionable. It was usual for Victorian table bells—they were then catalogued as tea bells—to be gilded at a cost of about eight shillings extra for plain surfaces and about two guineas for high-relief work which required burnishing.

Tea-Cups

When the Governor and Company of Merchants of London Trading in the East Indies, more briefly known as the East India Company, was but a few years old, the directors ordered from a London silversmith "three silver porringers to drink chaw [tea] in." This was in 1615 and for another thirty years tea remained a fashionable curiosity, sipped semi-cold from silver porringers. The earliest reference to a special tea-cup so far noted occurs in Pepys' *Diary*, September 1660, when he observed that he "did send for a cup of tee."

Tea no doubt was served in silver cups, probably tiny tumblers. In the late seventeenth century *Lives of the Norths* it is recorded that tea "was boiled in a coffee-pot and served in cups no larger than thimbles." The earliest examples so far noted consisted of a pair of cups and saucers, convex fluted with scalloped rims, and with narrow, vertical rim feet, made by Mark Paillet in 1700. Sir Charles Jackson, who noted tea-cups bearing the London hall-mark for 1684, describes a silver tea-cup of 1707 as having "an ogee outline with narrow concave flutes radiating from the base and extending upwards to a slightly everted rim, with a narrow applied moulded foot." This measured $2\frac{7}{8}$ inches in diameter and $1\frac{3}{4}$ inches in height. The flutes were intended to strengthen the cup, shaped from strip plate, thinly hammered, and with an inserted base. In some instances the flutes ended about half-an-inch below the rim. The earliest silver tea-cup to be noted with a handle dates to 1727, although some late seventeenth-century two-handled cups are believed to have been intended for tea. The silver tea-cup became outmoded during the early years of George I: Addison in 1714 noting that "the fashion of the tea cup now runs through a wonderful variety of colour, shape and size."

Thimbles

English-made thimbles in silver and silver-gilt date from early in the sixteenth century onwards. The dome was cone-shaped and the rim was often engraved with a short motto or line of verse, a feature repeated early in the eighteenth century and again in early Victorian days. Throughout the sixteenth century the thimble was made in two sections: the domed upper third was hand-raised or cast and covered with hand-punched indentations; the lower portion shaped from the plate and vertically seamed. The joins were virtually invisible. Less expensively the tip might be almost flat and inserted in a slightly tapering cylinder: such a thimble might cost one shilling and eightpence or two shillings, with a plain narrow rim which could be engraved with the name of the owner or giver, or both.

The band of the early Georgian thimble, if not left plain, was flat chased or engraved with scrolls, and with a cartouche enclosing a tiny crest or cypher, or a wreath of flowers and foliage.

Until the mid-eighteenth century all indentations were hand-punched and inevitably displayed irregularities of placement: afterwards they were impressed symmetrically by the rose machine.

By late Georgian days the silver thimble was made in a single piece by spinning. Some late eighteenth century thimbles were banded immediately above their rims with filigree work, made separately from flat wire and soldered edgeways to the ground of silver. The scrolled pattern might include a shield-shaped or oval panel engraved with the owner's crest or cypher. Other thimbles might be bordered with coloured stones or paste.

Rim bands in the early nineteenth century continued to be flat-chased, but the designs became florid and closely spaced; others were engraved in the bright-cut technique. Many early Victorian thimbles were of the souvenir variety, the cylinder being engraved below the indentations with a view of a well-known building such as St. Paul's Cathedral, London Bridge, the Tower, and others of a purely local character, now difficult to identify.

Thimbles made between 1739 and 1790 were exempt from hall-marking. From then until 1890 the monarch's head duty stamp was included in the hall-mark.

Tobacco Stoppers

These were required for tamping down the tobacco leaf throughout the period of the small-bowled clay tobacco pipes used until about 1850. The leaf was not processed in the modern style and in consequence was difficult to keep closely packed in the small bowl. Silver tobacco stoppers are recorded from the 1620s. Examples were submitted to the London assay office for hall-marking in 1631 and six years later the Goldsmiths' Company bought a silver tobacco stopper for the Company's use, and had it engraved with the Company's arms. In 1696 the Coopers' Company was presented with a silver stopper together with a tobacco pipe and tobacco box also of silver.

At first the silver tobacco stopper was cast in a single piece, with a short downward tapering rammer for tamping the tobacco in its bowl. Many were in the form of turned balusters with the rammer resembling a desk seal mount. In others the rammer was surmounted by a chased and burnished crest, head, figure, animal: motifs were endless. Trade cards of the mid-eighteenth century show fashionable tobacco stoppers with T-handles and loop handles. The more ornamental silver castings were in the majority, however, throughout the period of their use. Tobacco stoppers were always hall-marked.

Wine Strainers

Tapering funnels used for decanting wine came into widespread use during the 1760s, following the introduction of shouldered decanters in crystal-clear flint-glass. Examples have been noted struck with hall-marks of the previous century, however. *The Innkeeper's and Butler's Guide*, 1806, describes an additional use for them "to run the wine through when necking the bottles." A pair of wine strainers weighing 3 oz. 18 dwt. were sent by Matthew Boulton to the opening day of the Birmingham assay office in 1773 and these were differentiated from punch strainers.

The body of a wine strainer was urn-shaped or of ogee outline, the close-mesh detachable strainer fitting into the waist. The lower part of the bowl, with two narrow air-vents, fitted into the decanter neck. At first the body was raised from hand-hammered plate; from the 1790s it was spun from rolled metal. The rim of the eighteenth-century wine strainer was strengthened with applied gadrooning, beading or swaged moulding. Early in the nineteenth century the rim was widely everted and decorated with flower and foliage moulding (*242*).

The straight, tapering tube extending below the centre of the body was shaped in a curve at the end so that the opening was at right angles. The clarity of the flowing wine could thus be inspected as it cascaded down the side of the clear flint-glass: this also prevented aeration of the falling wine. In all cases the wine strainer, including the mesh, was gilded within, but the exterior remained severely plain, apart from an engraved crest or cypher.

The Victorian wine strainer had an extremely wide moulded rim. The bowl was ogee-shaped in outline, and might be rounded or octagonal on plan with a reeded or smooth rim. The octagonal shape, which continued down the tube cost nearly half as much again as the spun type.

Until the 1820s the wine strainer rested tube uppermost upon a circular, saucer-like stand with a domed centre, its rim encircled with moulding similar to that on the wine strainer itself.

MARKS

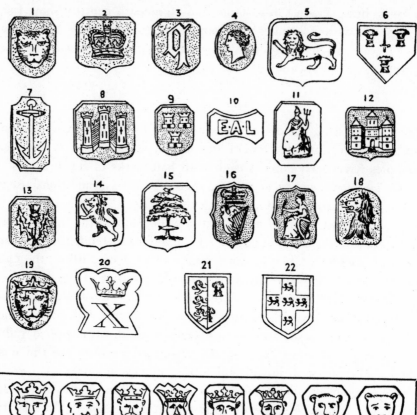

23

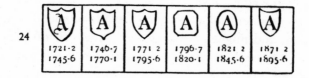

24

Ⓐ	Ⓐ	Ⓐ	Ⓐ	Ⓐ	Ⓐ
1721·2	1746·7	1771·2	1796·7	1821·2	1871·2
1745·6	1770·1	1795·6	1820·1	1845·6	1895·6

25

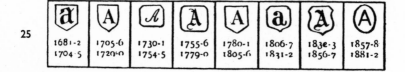

1681·2	1705·6	1730·1	1755·6	1780·1	1806·7	183e·3	1857·8
1704·5	1729·0	1754·5	1779·0	1805·6	1831·2	1856·7	1881·2

1   Leopard's head uncrowned: London hall-mark from 1822.

2   Crown: Sheffield hall-mark introduced in 1773.

3   Date letter: this is changed every year: at the London assay office May 29th; Birmingham and Chester July 1st; Sheffield, a variable date in July; Glasgow, the first Monday in July; Edinburgh, a variable date in October.

4   Duty mark: the monarch's head from December 1st 1784 to April 30th 1890, denoting payment of excise duty.

5   Lion Passant, more exactly lion passant gardant: standard mark for sterling silver in England.

6   Dagger erect between three garbs: hall-mark for Chester, 1784 to 1879.

7   Anchor: hall-mark for Birmingham from 1773.

8   Castle with three towers: hall-mark for Exeter, 1640 to 1876.

9   Three castles: hall-mark for Newcastle-upon-Tyne.

10 Maker's mark: initials, as used since May 28th 1739.

11 Britannia: hall-mark used on the high or Britannia standard silver compulsory from March 1679 to June 1720, and still a legal standard.

12 Castle: hall-mark for Edinburgh from 1681.

13 Thistle: standard mark for sterling silver in Edinburgh.

14 Lion rampant: standard mark for Glasgow from 1819.

15 Bird, tree, fish, and bell: hall-mark for Glasgow from 1819.

16 Harp crowned: standard mark for Dublin from 1637.

17 Hibernia: hall-mark for Dublin from 1807. Between 1784 and 1807 Hibernia was the Irish duty mark.

18 Lion's head erased: standard mark on Britannia standard silver.

19 Leopard's head crowned: hall-mark for London until 1822.

20 Letter X crowned: hall-mark for Exeter, 1570 to 1640.

21 Chester, 1701 to 1784.

22 York, 1812 to 1857.

23 Types of leopard head-marks from 1479 to the present day.

24 Date letters and shields indicating the alphabets used at Dublin, 1721 to 1896.

25 Date letters and shields used at Edinburgh, 1681 to 1882.

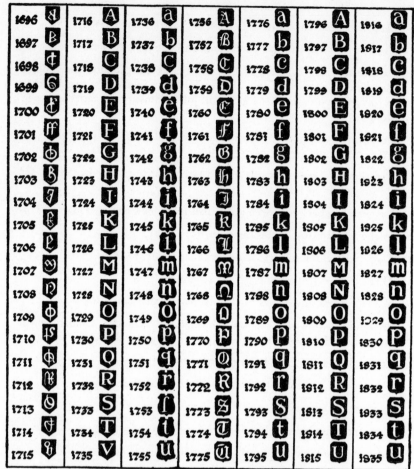

Later cycles — *each of twenty letters as above* — commence thus :—

A 1836   **U** 1856   **A** 1876   **a** 1896   **a** 1916

The date letter is changed on May 29th of each year.

LEADING DATES AND SPECIMEN MARKS.

1697 (Mch.27) to 1720 (June 1) Higher Standard.	1697	
1720 Old Standard restored.	1721	
1784 to 1890 Sovereign's head	1784	
(or duty mark) added.	1786	
1822 Leopard's head without crown.	1822	
	1837	

DATE LETTERS STRUCK AT THE LONDON ASSAY OFFICE FROM 1696 TO 1835
The hall-mark at this office is the leopard's head
By courtesy of Mr. Henry Oliver

1799-0	1800-1	1801-2	1802-3	1803-4	1804-5	1805-6
a	b	c	d	e	f	g
1806-7	1807-8	1808-9	1809-0	1810-1	1811-2	1812-3
h	i	j	k	l	m	n
1813-4	1814-5	1815-6	1816-7	1817-8	1818-9	1819-0
o	p	q	r	s	t	u
1820-1	1821-2	1822-3	1823-4	1824-5	1825-6	1826-7
v	w	x	y	z	𝔄	𝔅
1827-8	1828-9	1829-0	1830-1	1831-2	1832-3	1833-4
ℭ	𝔇	𝔈	𝔉	𝔊	ℌ	𝔍
1834-5	1835-6	1836-7	1837-8	1838-9	1839-0	1840-1
𝔎	𝔏	𝔐	𝔑	𝔒	𝔓	𝔔
1841-2	1842-3	1843-4	1844-5	1845-6	1846-7	1847-8
𝔎	𝔖	𝔗	𝔘	𝔙	𝔚	𝔛
1848-9	1849-0	1850-1	1851-2	1852-3	1853-4	1854-5
𝔜	𝔍	A	B	C	D	E
1855-6	1856-7	1857-8	1858-9	1859-0	1860-1	1861-2
F	G	H	I	K	L	M
1862-3	1863-4	1864-5	1865 6	1866-7	1867-8	1868-9
N	O	P	Q	R	S	T
1869-0	1870-1	1871-2	1872-3	1873-4	1874-5	1875-6
U	V	W	X	Y	Z	𝔞
1876-7	1877-8	1878-9	1879-0	1880-1	1881-2	1882-3
𝔟	𝔠	𝔡	𝔢	𝔣	𝔤	𝔥
1883-4	1884-5	1885-6	1886-7	1887-8	1888-9	1889-0
𝔦	𝔨	𝔩	𝔪	𝔫	𝔬	𝔭
1890-1	1891-2	1892-3	1893-4	1894-5	1895-6	1896-7
𝔮	𝔯	𝔰	𝔱	𝔲	𝔳	𝔴
1897-8	1898-9	1899-0	1900-1	1901-2	1902-3	1903-4
𝔵	𝔶	𝔷				

DATE LETTERS STRUCK AT THE BIRMINGHAM ASSAY OFFICE
FROM 24TH JUNE 1799 TO 1899
The hall-mark at this office is an anchor

DATE LETTERS STRUCK AT THE SHEFFIELD ASSAY OFFICE FROM 24TH JUNE 1773 TO 1915

The hall-mark at this office is a crown

Table 1 — 1773 to 1837

Year	Letter	Year	Letter	Year	Letter	Year	Letter	Year	Letter	Year	Letter	Year	Letter
1773-4	E	1774-5	F	1775-6	D	1776-7	R	1777-8	B	1778-9	S	1779-0	A
1780-1	C	1781-2	M	1782-3	G	1783-4	B	1784-5	J	1785-6	P	1786-7	K
1787-8	L	1788-9	W	1789-0	N	1790-1	L	1791-2	M	1792-3	U	1793-4	O
1794-5	M	1795-6	Q	1796-7	Z	1797-8	E	1798-9	V	1799-0	E	1800-1	N
1801-2	H	1802-3	M	1803-4	F	1804-5	G	1805-6	B	1806-7	A	1807-8	S
1808-9	P	1809-0	K	1810-1	L	1811-2	C	1812-3	D	1813-4	R	1814-5	W
1815-6	O	1816-7	T	1817-8	X	1818-9	I	1819-0	V	1820-1	Q	1821-2	Y
1822-3	Z	1823-4	U										
1824-5	a	1825-6	b	1826-7	c	1827-8	d	1828-9	e	1829-0	f	1830-1	g
1831-2	h	1832-3	k	1833-4	l	1834-5	m	1835-6	p	1836-7	q	1837-8	r

Table 2 — 1838 to 1914

Year	Letter	Year	Letter	Year	Letter	Year	Letter	Year	Letter	Year	Letter	Year	Letter
1838-9	s	1839-0	t	1840-1	u	1841-2	v	1842-3	X	1844-5	A		
1845-6	B	1846-7	C	1847-8	D	1848-9	E	1849-0	F	1850-1	G	1851-2	H
1852-3	I	1853-4	K	1854-5	L	1855-6	M	1856-7	N	1857-8	O	1858-9	P
1859-0	R	1860-1	S	1861-2	T	1862-3	U	1863-4	V	1864-5	W	1865-6	X
1866-7	Y	1867-8	Z	1868-9	A	1869-0	B	1870-1	C	1871-2	D	1872-3	E
1873-4	F	1874-5	G	1875-6	H	1876-7	J	1877-8	K	1878-9	L	1879-0	M
1880-1	N	1881-2	O	1882-3	P	1883-4	Q	1884-5	R	1885-6	S	1886-7	T
1887-8	U	1888-9	V	1889-0	W	1890-1	X	1891-2	Y	1892-3	Z	1893-4	a
1894-5	b	1895-6	c	1896-7	d	1897-8	e	1898-9	f	1899-0	g	1900-1	h
1901-2	i	1902-3	k	1903-4	l	1904-5	m	1905-6	n	1906-7	o	1907-8	p
1908-9	q	1909-0	r	1910-1	s	1911-2	t	1912-3	u	1913-4	b	1914-5	w

Index

The numerals in **heavy type** refer to the *figure numbers* of the illustrations